DBT

3 Books in 1

Borderline Personality Disorder, Borderline Mother and Dialectical Behavior Therapy.

Regulate Your Emotions, Build and Sustain Your Relationships Before They Fall Apart

DAVID LAWSON PHD

© Copyright 2020 by David Lawson PhD
- All rights reserved.

The content contained within this book may not be reproduced, duplicated or transmitted without direct written permission from the author or the publisher.

Under no circumstances will any blame or legal responsibility be held against the publisher, or author, for any damages, reparation, or monetary loss due to the information contained within this book; either directly or indirectly.

Legal Notice:

This book is copyright protected. This book is only for personal use. You cannot amend, distribute, sell, use, quote or paraphrase any part, or the content within this book, without the consent of the author or publisher.

Disclaimer Notice:

Please note the information contained within this document is for educational and entertainment purposes only. All effort has been executed to present accurate, up-to-date, and reliable, complete information. No warranties of any kind are declared or implied. Readers acknowledge that the author is not engaging in the rendering of legal, financial, medical or professional advice.

TABLE OF CONTENTS

BORDERLINE PERSONALITY DISORDER..1

Introduction 2

Part One: Understanding Borderline Personality Disorder? 4

Chapter One: What is Borderline Personality Disorder? 5

Chapter Two: The Traits of Borderline Personality Disorder............................7

Difficulty Regulating Emotions: 7

Intense Emotions: 7

Heightened Sensitivity to Criticism: 7

Identity Disturbance and Distorted sense of Self-image: 7

Manic efforts to avoid abandonment 8

Black and white thinking: 8

Reckless and impulsive behavior: 8

Unstable Personal Relationships: 9

Self-Damaging Behavior: 9

Disassociation: 10

Chapter Three: The Hidden Signs of Borderline Personality Disorder 11

Struggling to maintain relationships: 11

Low self-esteem: 11

Self-harming tendencies and talk of suicide: 12

Having Unhealthy Boundaries: 12

Heightened Emotions: 12

Lack of concentration: 12

Chapter Four: The Different Faces of Borderline Personality Disorder - Types of BPD 14

Discouraged Borderline: 14

Borderline Witch: 16

Borderline Hermit: 16

Chapter Five: What Are the Causes of Borderline Personality Disorder? 17

Genetics: 17

Issues with Brain Development: 17

Environmental Factors: 18

Chapter Six: Diagnosing Borderline Personality Disorder 19

Part Two: How to Cope if you Suffer From BPD 22

Chapter Seven: What to Expect if You Have Been Diagnosed with Borderline Personality Disorder 23

Chapter Eight: Learning to Control the Emotional Storm 27

Chapter Nine: Who can help you? 36

Chapter Ten: Useful tools 41

Chapter Eleven: Specific Therapy skills for Managing BPD 49

Chapter Twelve: Getting Help from Your Loved Ones 54

Part Three: How to Cope When Your Loved One Has Borderline Personality Disorder..... 60

Chapter Thirteen: Managing a Loved One with BPD 61

Chapter Fourteen: How to Speak to Someone With BPD 63

Chapter Fifteen: Being in a Relationship with Someone with BPD 70

Chapter Sixteen: Parenting a Child with BPD 74

Don't take it personally. 74

Chapter Seventeen: Disarm Those Who Are Manipulating You 77

Chapter Eighteen: Breaking Up with Someone who has Borderline Personality Disorder.. 85

Give yourself permission to end the relationship. 85

Conclusion 90

BORDERLINE MOTHER 91

Introduction.. 92

Chapter One: Understanding The Borderline Mother 99

Chapter Two: How It Had To Be.. 106

2.1. What does a healthy family look like?..107

2.2. Home family 110

2.3. A family with a very young child..110

2.4. A family with a preschooler 110

2.5. A family with a school-aged child 111

2.6. A family with an adolescent 111

2.7. The departure of children from their parents 111

2.8. The postpartum family 112

2.9. An old family 112

2.10. A functional family 113

2.11. Normal family as average (normality as mediocrity) 114

2.12. Normal family as optimal (normality as optimal) 114

2.13. Normal family relationships (Normality as a process) 115

2.14. A dysfunctional family 116

2.15. Symptoms of dysfunctional families: 117

Chapter Three: The Main Styles Of A Borderline Mother 121

3.1. The unfortunate truth 121

3.2. Specifics of BPD 121

3.3. The main styles of a borderline mother 122

3.4. Depression and anger 122

3.5. Pure rage 122

3.6. What went wrong? 123

3.7. Please don't do this 123

3.8. Look up and never look back 124

Chapter Four: Types Of Abuse 125

4.1. The six most common forms of child abuse by a borderline mother 126

Chapter Five: Typical Behavior Of A Child With A Borderline Mother....................132

5.1. Children who are abused by their mother with Borderline Personality Disorder vs other abused children. 133

5.2. Your behavior 134

5.3. The consequences of the abuse itself 135

5.4. Aggression 135

5.5. Panic 136

5.6. You don't have a complete personality 136

5.7. Your mother didn't even know what she wanted from you 137

5.8. Feelings of guilt 137

5.9. Consequences of abuse - drugs and alcohol 138

5.10. You have become skeptical about life itself 139

Chapter Six: Which Mask Are You Wearing – The Consequences In Adulthood 141

6.1. Colors are important 141

6.2. How does your face develop and what does it mask? 142

6.3. The endless loophole 142

6.4. A school example 143

6.5. The mask is not real 143

6.6. Let's go back a little 143

6.7. What are you protecting? 144

6.8. Why are you hiding? 144

6.9. Why do we protect our masks? 145

6.10. Masked love – another example 145

6.11. Identity crisis 145

6.12. You don't need to be someone else 146

Chapter Seven: Learn How To Defend Yourself Against Them 147

7.1. About everything 147

7.2. How to approach this problem 148

7.3. Specific examples 148

7.4. Example 148

7.5. Here is another specific example 149

7.6. Another example 149

7.7. Understand the nature of mental illness 150

7.8. The optimal approach for you 150

7.9. Give your mother space, be careful and safe 151

7.10. Basic rules for combating a BPD mother's anger: 151

7.11. You need to follow these four rules: 152

7.12. Things you must never forget 152

7.13. What else do you need to know? 152

7.14. What does all of this mean?..154

Chapter Eight: How To Help A Child Cope With A Borderline Mother...........................155

8.1. How to deal with a mother suffering from Borderline Personality Disorder 155

8.2. What is social anxiety? 156

8.3. They think bad things will happen 156

8.4. Shame or social anxiety...157

8.5. Kids need help 158

8.6. Hard life 159

8.7. What is violence?...159

8.8. Silence is a problem..160

8.9. A no-win situation - what's going on in the victim's head?.................................160

8.10. These are children's jobs 160

8.11. How to deal 161

8.12. Tips for children...161

8.13. How can you help your child withstand the pressures of a mother with Borderline Personality Disorder?..162

Chapter Nine: How To Overcome The Trauma Of The Borderline Mother As An Adult ..164

9.1. What is trauma?...164

9.2. Big and small traumas...165

9.3. How does trauma affect the psyche?...165

9.4. Why does trauma persist and create unpleasant symptoms? 166

9.5. Suppression maintains trauma and its harmful effects..166

9.6. Can we permanently clear the trauma and its symptoms?....................................167

9.7. What does the process of trauma purification look like?......................................167

9.8. How do we know that trauma has been deactivated, purified? 167

9.9. Transferring memories 168

9.10. The cells are complete 168

9.11. How to break that vicious circle? 168

9.12. How to overcome traumatic events..169

9.13. What other methods can help overcome traumatic events? 170

Chapter Ten: Start Your Healing Process 174

10.1. Forgive your mother...174

10.2. Spiritual prerequisites...175

10.3. Forgiveness is a process that takes time...175

10.4. Giving up judgment...175

10.5. Pitfalls in the process of forgiveness...176

10.6. To forgive means to give yourself love...176

10.7. At every moment, each of us does the best we can...176

10.8. Let go of the past...176

10.9. Why is it so difficult sometimes to let go of the past, even when we try?...177

10.10. Avoid bad moods...178

10.11. Start living a new life...178

10.12. Relieve stress...178

10.13. You can't change anything...178

10.14. Learn how to take control and become happy...179

10.15. Release your fear...179

10.16. What steals your inner peace?...179

10.17. Love yourself...179

10.18. Get happier...179

10.19. Make new friends...179

10.20. Yesterday is history...180

10.21. The present is important...180

10.22. The past affects your present abilities...180

10.23. Become successful...180

10.24. Make your days happy...181

10.25. Avoid creating problems...181

10.26. Stop being depressed...181

10.27. Work on confidence...181

10.28. Set a goal...181

10.29. Be a role model...181

10.30. Be positive...182

10.31. More energy...182

10.32. Better health...182

10.33. Start creating a new chapter in life 182

Conclusion 184

DIALECTICAL BEHAVIOR THERAPY 186

Introduction 187

Chapter 1: What is Dialectical Behavior Therapy? 192

    How DBT Works 193

    Is Dialectical Behavior Therapy really effective? 195

Chapter 2: DBT Applications 196

Chapter 3: Why Mindfulness is a superpower 215

    Elements of mindfulness 216

    How Mindfulness Can Reshape Your Brain 217

    Other Benefits of Mindfulness 221

    What Mindfulness Truly Means 223

    Three States of Mind 223

    The Core Mindfulness Skills 224

    Mindfulness Exercises 226

    Mindfulness Is for Anyone 231

Chapter 4: Fundamental DBT Skills 233

    DBT Distress Tolerance Skills 233

    DBT Emotion Regulation Skills 237

    DBT Interpersonal Effectiveness Skills 241

Chapter 5: Learn Not To Be Overwhelmed By Painful Situations 244

    Managing Stress Using DBT 244

    Managing Worry Using DBT 245

    Dealing with Post-Traumatic Stress Symptoms using DBT 249

Chapter 6: Emotional Control 253

Chapter 7: Interpersonal Effectiveness 264

    Interpersonal Effectiveness Exercises 269

Tips for A Better Life 271

Chapter 8: Frequently Asked Questions 275

Conclusion 278

BORDERLINE
PERSONALITY DISORDER

DAVID LAWSON PHD

INTRODUCTION

As with many other mental illnesses, there is plenty of stigma attached to borderline personality disorder, or BPD. Thanks to stereotypical portrayals of mental illnesses in film and television, many people view those suffering from disorders like BPD as being wild, uncontrollable and weak.

If you or a love one has been diagnosed with BPD, it can present a number of challenges. Thanks to these damaging stigmas, people suffering from mental illness often have to contend not only with their disorder, but with the stereotypes and discriminations of others. Common preconceptions surrounding BPD include the belief that sufferers are always overly dramatic, manipulative and attention-seeking.

While these traits can appear in sufferers of BPD, the truth is far more complex. In this book, we will take a look at the realities of borderline personality disorder, analyzing exactly what the illness is and the types of behaviors it can lead to. In part one, we will look closely at both the overt and more subtle symptoms associated with BPD, to assist you in determining whether you or a loved one may be afflicted. We will also examine the underlying causes of the disorder, and the different forms of BPD can take. Methods of diagnosis will also be discussed.

So what if you have been diagnosed with BPD? Does this mean you no longer have the potential to live a normal and fulfilling life? Does it mean you have to conform to the stereotypes of being unstable, angry and helpless? Of course not. With the right tools and treatment, BPD can be managed effectively, allowing you to have a rewarding career, close friendships and meaningful relationships.

In part two, we will look at the many tools you can employ to keep the disorder under control. We'll take a look at effective methods for handling unpredictable emotions, along with specific therapies often used in managing the disorder.

Of course, relating to your loved ones can be a huge challenge when faced with BPD. Thanks to the violent mood swings and unpredictable behavior associated with BPD, it is likely you will fear unintentionally hurting those you care about. In order to manage this, we will take a look at the things it's important for your loved ones to know in order to help you cope with BPD. Our guide will help you explain your illness to your family, friends and partner, helping them to understand and empathize with what you are experiencing. Following these guidelines will assist you in creating a secure and loving support network, making the disorder more manageable.

As we have touched on, borderline personality disorder can be just as difficult for loved ones as it can be the sufferer themselves. Perhaps your family member, child, parent or partner has been diagnosed with BPD and you're struggling to know how to react. Perhaps that's why you picked up this book. In part three, we will take a close look at how to cope when those close to you are suffering from this disorder. We will examine how to speak to those with BPD in order to avoid conflict, and ways to manage being a relationship with a BPD sufferer.

As people with BPD can often be manipulative, or emotionally aggressive, it can be just as important to take care of yourself in such situations. We will look closely at ways to disarm those who are attempting to manipulate you, in order to facilitate a harmonious relationship for both parties. And if you decide that, for whatever reason, the relationship has no future, we will address ways of breaking up with a BPD sufferer in order to produce the minimum amount of conflict and distress.

Living with BPD does not have to be a life sentence. Following the advice provided will help both BPD sufferers and their loved ones have and a happy and fulfilling life.

PART ONE

UNDERSTANDING BORDERLINE PERSONALITY DISORDER?

CHAPTER ONE

WHAT IS BORDERLINE
PERSONALITY DISORDER?

Borderline personality disorder, or BPD, is a pattern of mental behavior that causes sufferers to have difficulty controlling their emotions and impulses. Thanks to their often aggressive and unpredictable behavior, with BPD will often experience many unstable relationships in all aspects of their lives. BPD causes sufferers to feel uncomfortable in themselves and exhibit strong emotional reactions to seemingly routine events and circumstances. They live though a pattern of extreme emotional highs and lows.

Borderline personality is so-named as people suffering from the disorder were originally believed to be on the borderline between psychosis (difficulties determining what is real) and neurosis (a mild mental illness largely characterized by depression, anxiety).

People with BPD often experience high levels of anger and distress and take offence easily. Sufferers struggle with a low sense of self-esteem, having regular painful thoughts about themselves and others. Unsurprisingly, this often leads to ongoing problems in their family and social life. This low sense of self-worth and regular stream of negative thoughts can lead to self-harming and, in severe cases, suicide.

Many people with BPD live their lives with an ongoing pattern of unstable social relationships. They are prone to developing intense, almost obsessive attachments to others, which can change almost without warning to feelings of intense anger and dislike for the same person. This fluctuation from extreme to another is highly indicative of borderline personality disorder.

BPD appears in approximately 2% of the general population, with women three times more likely to suffer from the disorder than men. BPD usually appears during the teen years, with symptoms gradually improving as sufferers go through life.

The causes of BPD are unclear, but can be traced to environmental, social, neurological and genetic factors. BPD can also be sparked by difficult life events such as childhood trauma. Many experts believe the illness is brought about by a combination of factors, such as genetic and environmental.

Drug and alcohol abuse, depression and eating disorders are all commonly associated with borderline personality disorder. Sufferers of BPD often experience other mental illnesses in conjunction with the disorder, such as depression, post-traumatic stress disorder, or bipolar disorder. Thanks to the plethora of other illnesses that can co-exist alongside borderline personality disorder, BPD can often be difficult to identify and diagnose.

While borderline personality disorder has immense destructive power for both sufferers and their loved ones, the good news is, it is treatable. In part two of this book, we will address numerous ways BPD can be treated and managed, allowing sufferers and their loved ones to live their lives to the fullest, with minimal degrees of stress and conflict.

CHAPTER TWO

THE TRAITS OF BORDERLINE PERSONALITY DISORDER

As mentioned in the previous chapter, people with borderline personality disorder often also suffer from other mental illnesses, including issues with anxiety, eating disorders and substance addiction. BPD has many symptoms in common with illnesses such as bipolar disorder, often making it difficult to distinguish and diagnose.

Let's take a look at some of the most common symptoms and traits associated with BPD:

- **Difficulty Regulating Emotions:** Perhaps the most recognizable trait of borderline personality disorder is the sufferers inability to regulate and control their emotions. People with BPD will often "act out" in ways that may seem out of proportion to the situation, or seemingly unprovoked.

- **Intense Emotions:** People with BPD will often react to a situation or event in a way that seems disproportionate to what is happening. They are prone to rapid and violent mood swings and can fluctuate between states of intense happiness to crushing depression in very short spaces of time. Sufferers of BPD describe the disorder as an "emotional roller coaster."

- **Heightened Sensitivity to Criticism:** People suffering from borderline personality disorder are prone to taking criticism very badly, often taking offense and acting out in response to even the smallest piece of disapproval.

- **Identity Disturbance and Distorted sense of Self-image:** People who suffer from BPD often have trouble making sense of their own identity. They often find it difficult to pinpoint their likes and dislikes, passions, beliefs and values. They are often unsure about their long term goals, particularly with regards to employment or relationships.

As a result, people with BPD often feel lost or empty, with little sense of direction. BPD can also cause one's self-image to rapidly fluctuate between healthy and unhealthy.

- **Manic efforts to avoid abandonment**: Perhaps the thing that BPD sufferers fear the most is abandonment. This is often due to the trauma they experienced as a child, which led to the condition. (More on this in Chapter Five.) People with BPD want and need human connection, but they fear their friends and loved ones will leave them the minute they get angry or frustrated. In an attempt to avoid abandonment, BPD sufferers will often go to extremes to avoid being abandoned, such as ending a relationship or friendship at the first sign of trouble. In this way, they avoid abandonment by being the ones to end the relationship.

- **Black and white thinking**: Also known as "splitting" or "all-or-nothing thinking," black and white thinking refers to an inability to reconcile oneself with the both the positive and negative aspects of a situation or person. People who think in such a way will generally see a situation as either all good, or all bad, with no middle ground. In BPD, sufferers have a tendency to focus on the negative side of events; their bad representation dominating the good representation. For example, a person suffering from BPD may see love and sexuality as lude and perverse, rather than acknowledging the tender qualities of such relationships. In the same way that a person with a black and white thinking may see another person or situation as all good or all bad, they will do the same for themselves, seeing themselves as either flawless, or inherently bad. While most people have the ability to acknowledge that two contradictory states can exists at once – i.e. no one is either "all good" or "all bad," people with BPD are unable to accept the ambivalence of this. Instead, they shift rapidly from one extreme to the other, in order to accommodate their fluctuating emotions. If they are in a "bad" state and focusing on a person's negative qualities, they have no awareness of the same person's positive traits.

- **Reckless and impulsive behavior**: Sufferers of BPD are likely to engage in damaging behaviors such as impulse buying, binge eating, unsafe sex, drug and alcohol abuse and reckless driving. While impulsive behavior is not in of itself necessarily a symptom of BPD, it is the difficulties BPD sufferer face in controlling their impulses that lead to impulsive and reckless behavior. Often, sufferers of BPD engage in reckless behavior in an attempt to either calm the emotional storm inside them, or to "wake" them from a sense of emptiness and detachment. But this impulsive behavior may not always take the form of something that appears to be damaging. The impulsiveness of borderline personality disorder can also lead sufferers to engage in behaviors such as:

- oversharing emotions
- quitting their job unexpectedly
- joining and then quitting different groups or hobbies
- clearing out all their belongings in an attempt to "start again."
- Abruptly cancelling or changing plans

- **Unstable Personal Relationships:** Thanks to both their difficulties controlling their emotions and their deep-seated fear of abandonment, BPD sufferers will often find themselves in a string of damaging and chaotic personal relationships. We will explore relationships and borderline personality disorder in details in Parts Two and Three.

- **Self-Damaging Behavior:** Often used a coping mechanism against overwhelm, BPD sufferers are prone to self-harming, both physically and emotionally. Examples of this may be sabotaging their own work at school or in employment, rather than facing the stress associated with meeting deadlines, or engaging in alienating behavior in order to drive others away. Often, sufferers of BPD will engage in these types of behaviors in order to gain a little relief from their emotional pain. Of course, this relief is almost always short-lasting and can result in guilt and shame. This leads to a cycle, in which the sufferer then turns to destructive behavior in an attempt to relieve the guilt. As time progresses, self-damaging behavior can become an instinctive and unconscious response to emotional pain. More obvious forms of self-destructive behavior such as eating disorders, substance abuse, self-injury and sex addiction are also associated with BPD. It is estimated that at least 10% of BPD sufferers will attempt suicide throughout their lives.

- **Disassociation:** Zoning out or feeling as though they are not in the "real world" is a common trait for people suffering from BPD. Disassociation refers to a disconnect between a person's thoughts, emotions, behaviors, memories and identity. Disassociation is a common coping mechanism for people with BPD, along with a number of other mental health disorders such as PTSD and acute stress disorder (both of which can co-exist alongside BDP). Disassociation can be broken down into several facets:

  - *Depersonalization:* A person experiencing disassociation often feels a sense of disconnect between themselves and their body. It is akin to watching yourself within a dream, or from outside your body.
  - *Derealization:* A similar experience to depersonalization, derealization is a sense of being separate from the world around you; including other people and the objects around you. If you are experience derealization, the world around you can feel unfamiliar and strange.
  - *Amnesia:* Disassociation can lead to short periods of amnesia or "lost time," in which the sufferer cannot remember what they were doing at a particular time in the day.
  - *Identity Confusion:* The feeling of being attached from yourself and the world can lead sufferers of disassociation to question who they are.
  - *Identity Alteration:* Identity alteration is the act of behaving differently as brought about by your circumstances, for example, not recognizing the world around you due to disassociation. While all of us experience identity alternation from time to time (behaving differently in unusual circumstances), it is a common trait of suffers of BPD. Some BPD sufferers have reported struggling so much with their identity and knowing who they are they have changed their name multiple times by deed poll.

Knowing these common symptoms can help you if you believe you or a loved one may be experiencing borderline personality disorder. However, there are a number of hidden signs of BPD that are not so overt. In the following chapter we will take a look at some of the more subtle symptoms of borderline personality, and how to spot them.

CHAPTER THREE

THE HIDDEN SIGNS OF BORDERLINE PERSONALITY DISORDER

While many of the symptoms of borderline personality disorder are difficult to miss, there are also traits of the illness that are much more subtle. A person exhibiting these more subtle signs is said to be experiencing "quiet" borderline personality disorder.

Whereas people with BPD often experience violent mood swings which are easy to recognise, those with quiet BPD are more likely to internalize their feelings. While they still experience the same fluctuation of emotions, the disorder can be much more difficult to spot.

To recognize "quiet" BPD in either yourself or a loved one, look out for the following traits and symptoms:

- **Struggling to maintain relationships:** People with quiet BPD may speak about how they find it hard to keep relationships, whether romantic or otherwise. These relationships will often have been ended by the other person, unable to cope with the BPD sufferer's wild mood swings and aggression. However, as mentioned in Chapter One, it is also common for people with BPD to preemptively end a relationship they feel is struggling as they so often fear being abandoned.

- **Low self-esteem:** While quiet sufferers of BPD may be less prone to self-damaging behavior such as reckless driving or violence, they are still likely to suffer from a severely diminished sense of self-worth. Often, this will only be noticeable to others by paying attention to the way they speak about themselves. They may say things like "I can't do anything right," or "Why would you want to spend time with me?"

- **Self-harming tendencies and talk of suicide:** As with the above example, to recognize these traits in quiet sufferers of BPD, it is important to pay attention to the way they speak. Their comments relating to self-harm or suicide might seem on the surface to be flippant, throw-away lines such as "It makes me want to bash my head against a brick wall," or but this seemingly innocuous comments can be a mask for much deeper issues.

- **Having Unhealthy Boundaries:** In the same way that BPD sufferers are prone to black and white thinking, people with quiet BPD will often obsess about a person, seeming to care greatly what this person thinks of them. On the flip side, they may also have times of needing to completely detach from others, pulling away to the point of isolating themselves in order to create what they perceive as a safe space between them and the world.

- **Heightened Emotions:** People suffering from BPD generally experience emotions much more easily and deeply than the general population. This can have both negative and positive effects. People with BPD often exhibit great levels of excitement, enthusiasm, joy and love but, conversely, can often feel overwhelmed by negative emotions such as anxiety, depression, guilt, anger. Everyday emotions are often highlighted, with sadness being transmuted to grief, for example, mild embarrassment being replaced by intense humiliation and panic taking the place of nervousness.

- **Lack of concentration:** Another more subtle trait of BPD is the inability to concentrate. This is often due to the intense emotions building up inside one's head, leaving them with little room to think about anything else. Inability to concentrate is a form of disassociation and can appear as though a person is simply zoning out. A BPD sufferer who has zoned out can be identified by an expressionless face and/or flat vocal delivery. They may also appear distracted.

Familiarizing yourself with these more subtle symptoms of borderline personality disorder can help you identify whether you or a loved one may be suffering from the illness. If you suspect yourself or someone you love is experience borderline personality disorder, it is important to seek professional help. We will be looking at how to get help more closely in Chapter Nine. Parts Two and Three will also offer tools and tips for managing borderline personality disorder, bother for sufferers and their families and friends.

CHAPTER FOUR

THE DIFFERENT FACES OF BORDERLINE PERSONALITY DISORDER - TYPES OF BPD

Just as no two people are the same, so too are no two experiences of borderline personality disorder the same. As we have already seen in Chapters One and Two, there can be a great difference in the behaviors of people suffering from "quiet" borderline personality disorder and more outward manifestations of the illness.

Borderline personality disorder can also be broken down into four different types, as proposed by American psychologist Theodore Million, in his 1995 book *Disorders of Personality DSM-IV and Beyond.*

Million's four categories of BPD are as follows:

- **Discouraged Borderline:** People suffering from discouraged borderline personalities often exhibit avoidant, depressive, dependent tendencies. People with this form of BPD are often submissive and humble, and prone to pliant behavior. They often feel hopeless, powerless and vulnerable. Someone with a discouraged borderline personality can be clingy and tends to go along with the crowd for fear of upsetting the people around them. They can behave in a somber and dejected manner. Below the surface, however, is an anger waiting to erupt. When it does so, it can lead sufferers to self-injury and even suicide.

- **Petulant Borderline:** A petulant borderline personality is characterized by a heightened sense of negativity. Sufferers of this form of BPD are often highly impatient, stubborn and resentful. They are sullen and defiant and feel easily slighted. They are easily disillusion and disappointed in life. People with a petulant borderline personality disorder fluctuate between desperately relying on people and keeping their distance out of fear of being disappointed or let down. Their emotions are prone to swing between feelings of unworthiness and rage.

- **Impulsive borderline:** Sufferers of impulsive borderline personalities are prone to histrionic or antisocial behavior. This form of BPD is characterized by frenetic, flighty behavior. They can often be flirty and charismatic, able to draw people to them. They are highly energetic and are constantly seeking the next thrill. However, when things do not go their way, sufferers are quick to become agitated, gloomy and irritable. They fear any form of loss, leading them to frequent suicidal tendencies.

- **Self-destructive borderline:** Self-destructive borderline personalities are often highly depressive and masochistic. They carry around a constant sense of bitterness, which they regularly turn inwards. People with this form of BPD are often prone to self-harming and self-punishing. They are often angry, highly strung and moody and are prone to suicidal thoughts and behaviors. Their self-hatred is prone to reach extreme levels, leading them to many types of destructive behavior, ranging from reckless driving, to poor healthcare, to performing derogatory sexual acts.

In addition to these four borderline types proposed by Million, psychologist Dr. Christine Lawson also identified four types of borderline personalities in her book *Understanding the Borderline Mother.*

- **Borderline Queen:** Someone with a borderline queen personality is prone to perfectionism. They are prone to take mild criticism very personally and will become aggressive and indignant if anyone suggests they have made a mistake. Thanks to their perfectionism, borderline queens often disassociate from their own negative traits and emotions, believing them a flaw, so is often unable to accept his or her own mistakes. People with this borderline personality regularly feel the need to one-up people around them, particularly their therapists and loved ones.

- **Borderline Waif:** Unlike many other borderline types, the borderline waif does not exhibit a great deal of aggression or outward hostility. Instead, they appear to be fragile and victimized by all life has thrown at them. Waifs are generally depressed and discontented and worry easily. Borderline waifs believe themselves to be helpless victims and often refuse to accept help in order to keep their 'victim' mentality alive.

- **Borderline Witch:** Someone exhibiting a borderline witch personality can be extremely aggressive and controlling. They seek to punish people for the smallest of indiscretions and are prone to "borderline rage" – the destruction of objects that are of value to those they believe have wronged them. Borderline witches are adept at black and white thinking, particularly when it comes to their loved ones. Parents with this personality will often idealize one of their children over the rest or seek to play one family member off against another. (More on this in Chapter Seventeen.) People with a borderline witch personality can be extremely domineering and intrusive, often violating the boundaries of those around them. They are prone to using the thoughts and feelings of those around them a weapon, leading their loved ones to become withdrawn and restrained in their presence. Borderline witches can be extremely paranoid and suspicious, with their hostile behavior masking their own fear of loss of control.

- **Borderline Hermit:** People with a borderline hermit personality view the world as an inherently dangerous place. They have large amounts of paranoia and suspicion and have trouble trusting those around them. Thanks to their belief that everyone is out to get them, borderline hermits will withdraw from the world and isolate themselves. For many sufferers of a borderline hermit personality, the disorder stems from sexual abuse or other equally damaging childhood trauma.

CHAPTER FIVE

WHAT ARE THE CAUSES OF BORDERLINE PERSONALITY DISORDER?

As mentioned in chapter one, the causes of BPD, like many other mental disorders remain unclear. Experts believe BPD is unlikely to be caused by any single factor, but rather a combination of contributing elements.

Some of the factors that are believed to contribute to this disorder include:

- **Genetics:** Having a parent with borderline personality disorder may make you more susceptible to the illness. Studies have shown that, in the case of identical twins, when one twin has the disorder, the other has a 2 in 3 chance of developing it as well. At present, however, there is no definitive proof that a gene exists for BPD, meaning genetics' effect on borderline personality disorder is still under question.

- **Issues with Chemicals in the Brain:** Experts believe many people who suffer from BPD have problems with the neurotransmitters in their brain. Neurotransmitters are chemicals that act as "messengers," transmitting signals between the brain cells. In particular, altered levels of the neurotransmitter serotonin are thought to play a part in the onset of BPD, as serotonin levels have been linked to depression, aggression and destructive urges.

- **Issues with Brain Development:** Thanks to MRI scans conducted on sufferers of BPD, researchers have identified that the condition may be associated with issues in three specific parts of the brain. In many people with BPD these parts of the brain were either undeveloped or showed unusual activity. These parts are:

  - *The orbitofrontal cortex,* responsible for decision-making and planning

- *The hippocampus*, which is responsible for regulating behavior and exhibiting self-control
- *The amygdala*, which plays a substantial role in the control of negative emotions such as aggression, anxiety and fear.

- **Environmental Factors:** Genetic and biological factors such as brain make-up are far from the only elements believed to play a part in the onset of BPD. A number of environmental factors are also common among sufferers of borderline personality disorder. Many of these stem from our experiences as children, as our childhood plays such an enormous part in the shaping of our adult lives. Some of the issues experienced by BPD sufferers include:

  - Parental neglect as a child
  - Being a victim of emotional, physical or sexual abuse, particularly as a child
  - Being exposed to long-term fear or stress, particularly as a child
  - Growing up with a family member who suffered from a serious mental condition, or who had problems with drug and alcohol abuse

Issues of neglect or abuse in childhood can manifest themselves in a number of different ways in our adult life. Childhood trauma can cause us to bury our true feelings and present a "false self" to the world, can drive intense feelings of lack of self-worth and cause a range of attachment issues that present themselves in all kinds of relationships. For sufferers of BPD, the effects of childhood trauma can be seen in traits such as expecting others to be a parent to you, idealizing others, or expecting others to bully you.

CHAPTER SIX

DIAGNOSING BORDERLINE
PERSONALITY DISORDER

As discussed in Chapter Two, if you believe yourself or a loved one is suffering from borderline personality disorder, it is crucial to get professional help as soon as possible. BPD can lead to violence, damaged relationships, any number of dangerous behaviors, and even suicide. It is not something that you should attempt to handle without the help of a trained psychologist, or other mental health professional.

Self Diagnoses:

While you have likely identified several of the traits mentioned in Chapters One and Two, the following questions can help you determine whether you might be affected by BPD:

- Do your emotions change very quickly?

- Do you often experience extreme anger, sadness or distress?

- Do you often feel empty or unfulfilled?

- Are you constantly afraid the people I care about with leave me?

- Are most of your romantic relationships intense and unstable?

- Does the way you feel about the people in your life tend to fluctuate from one extreme to the other?

- Are you ever tempted to engage in self-injury or attempt suicide?

- When you feel insecure in a relationship, do you ever lash out or behave impulsively in a desperate attempt to keep your lover close?

- Do you ever engage in dangerous behavior such as binge drinking, drug use, unsafe sex or reckless driving?

If you or your loved one answered yes to several or all of these statements, it may indicate borderline personality disorder.

Professional Diagnoses:

BPD will be officially diagnosed following a clinical assessment by a mental health professional. The generally accepted method of diagnosis involves presenting the patient with a list of characteristics and asking them whether they feel such characteristics accurately represents them. By actively involving patients in their own diagnosis this way, sufferers are likely to come to terms with the disorder more quickly.

Mental health experts have produced a list of nine symptoms associated with borderline personality disorder. For a person to be diagnosed with BPD, they must exhibit at least five of the following traits:

- Fear of abandonment

- Unclear or changing self-image

- Unstable relationships

- Impulsive and/or self-destructive behaviors

- Tendency towards self-hard or suicide attempts

- Extreme mood swings

- Difficulty controlling rage

- Paranoia or suspicion of others' motives.

- Persistent feelings of emptiness

Such an evaluation will also discuss the severity of these symptoms and when they began, along with determining when they may have begun. Of particular relevance are any suicidal thoughts a patient may have experienced, along with thoughts of self-harm, or doing harm to others.

An assessment may also include physical tests to rule out other triggers of these symptoms, such as thyroid conditions or drug and alcohol abuse.

As previously mentioned, BPD can sometimes be misdiagnosed, thanks to its similarities to other mental health disorders such as depression, bipolar disorder and post-traumatic stress disorder. As a result, mental health professionals might experiment with a range of treatments and therapies in order to identify the most suitable path towards recovery.

So what if you or a loved one has been diagnosed with borderline personality disorder? What does this mean for your relationships, and your life in general? There is no doubt that BPD presents an enormous array of challenges to both the sufferer and those around them. But all is not lost. In the following sections, we will take a look at how to cope if borderline personality disorder has become a part of your life.

PART TWO

HOW TO COPE IF YOU SUFFER
FROM BPD

CHAPTER SEVEN

WHAT TO EXPECT IF YOU HAVE BEEN DIAGNOSED WITH BORDERLINE PERSONALITY DISORDER

So you have been diagnosed with borderline personality disorder. Perhaps this has come as a cruel shock. Or perhaps you may even welcome the diagnosis as an explanation to your previously unexplainable emotional outbursts and mood swings. It feel like a relief to know that this behavior is the cause of an illness, rather than another part of yourself.

Regardless of how you feel about your diagnosis, there is no doubt that living with borderline personality disorder can be a hellish experience, both for you and your loved ones. BPD can affect every part of your life, from your relationship to yourself and others, to your education, career and recreational life. Your tendencies to act out and behave in violent and aggressive mean that both you and your loved ones are prone to being hurt, both physically and mentally.

Learning to manage the disorder begins with understanding. By knowing exactly what to expect, you can prepare and develop coping skills to help you weather the emotional storm. Having a deep understanding of your illness and its traits will also help you communicate better with your loved ones about BPD, making it easier for them to assist you with the struggles you will face. We will address this more in Chapter Twelve, but for now, let's take a look at exactly what you can expect if you have been diagnosed with BPD:

How You May Feel Towards Yourself

If you have been diagnosed with BPD, you can expect to feel the following ways about yourself:

- Overwhelmed by the intensity of your feelings and rapid mood swings

- Lonely

- As though you are inherently flawed

- As though you are to blame for everything bad that happens to you

- As though you have a hard time deciding what you want in life, or even what you like or dislike.

- As though you are a bad person

- As though you are not a "real" person

- As though you are a child forced to live in an adult's world

- A though you don't know who you really are

- As though something you are unable to identify is missing from inside you

These negative feelings towards yourself can cause you to act out in the following ways:

- Keeping very busy so you are never alone with your thoughts

- Regularly changing plans, hobbies or even jobs as you struggle to identify who you really are.

- Overspending and/or binge eating

- Using recreational drugs and/or smoking

- Excessive use of alcohol to help dampen your emotions.

- Avoiding seeing things through

- Refusing to attempt activities you think you might fail or might otherwise cause you to feel disappointed.

How You May Feel Towards Others

Of course, borderline personality disorder also plays a huge role in the way you relate to the people around you. BPD can cause you to act with aggression and hostility towards those you love, causing them both physical and emotional pain. But again, understanding exactly how BPD can make you act and think can help you manage these outbursts and limit the damage to those you care about. Here are some of the ways BPD can cause you to think or behave around others:

- You may feel as though no one understands you and what you are going through

- You may inherently different from everyone around you

- You may believe that the world is a dangerous place that you want only to run away from

- You may believe that people are either completely perfect, or completely bad and hurtful, with no middle ground. (This is known as "black and white thinking.")

- You may fear your friends and loved ones will leave you forever if they get upset or angry with you.

These feelings can cause you to act in the following ways around other people:

- Getting extremely frustrated and angry with those around you

- Having difficulty trusting people, even those you love

- Wanting – and needing – to be close to people, but fearing they will leave you, so avoiding them.

- Having unrealistic expectations of your friends and loved ones

- Ending relationships with partners and friends if you think they might leave you

- Constantly looking for signs within your relationships that signal someone is going to leave you.

As you no doubt already know, borderline personality disorder can be exhausting. The constant swings from exhilarating highs to crushing lows can make it feel as though you as trapped on an endless emotional rollercoaster.

But the good news is, with treatment, most sufferers of BPD experience a complete or partial improvement of their symptoms. Many people find their symptoms improve markedly within a few years of their diagnosis. In addition, if someone experiences a complete departure of their symptoms, there is a good chance the symptoms will not return in the future. In the following chapters we will begin to look at the many tools and techniques available for managing borderline personality. While the road ahead is guaranteed not to be an easy one, there is hope. With patience and perseverance, you too can be one of the many people with BPD who go on to live productive and successful lives.

CHAPTER EIGHT

LEARNING TO CONTROL THE EMOTIONAL STORM

It is the "emotional storm" that most pointedly characterizes borderline personality disorder; that wild fluctuation of emotions you feel as though you have no control over. This emotional storm can leave you feeling utterly helpless, frustrated and/or detached from your body. When in the grip of the emotional storm, it can feel as though there is no way out, but the reality is there are many techniques you can implement to help you through the situation.

By studying the following techniques at a time when you are feeling calm and centered, you will be much more prepared and able to manage the emotional storm when it hits. Developing a "plan of attack" to deal with such a situation can help you feel more in control the next time your emotions threaten to overwhelm you.

Let's take a look at a few of the techniques that can be implemented when it comes to managing the emotional storm:

Identify Your Emotions

The first step in managing your emotions, it is developing the skills to recognize exactly what it is you are feeling. When you are in the midst of the emotional storm wrought by BPD, it can be difficult to discern just what is going on. You are literally in a state of chaos, and you may be experiencing a number of conflicting emotions at any one time.

If you are feeling emotionally overwhelmed and unable to pinpoint exactly what it is you are feeling, it can help to work through the situation a moment at a time. Focus on getting through one minute, then the next, then the next. Breaking the situation down into smaller, more manageable tasks can help it feel more manageable. Focusing on identifying a single emotion within the storm can also help to manage the overwhelm. Give a name to exactly what it is you are feeling. Is it anger, or frustration? Exhilaration? Grief? Try and identify the emotion without trying to find the reason for its appearance or bring it to a halt.

Here are some of the physical symptoms you will experience with a number of emotions which may help you identify exactly what it is you are feeling:

Anger

- Quickened heart rate
- Quickened breathing
- Tense muscles
- Tapping your feet
- Clenching your fists or your jaw

Sadness and depression

- Physical ache in your chest
- Decreased appetite
- Fatigue
- Insomnia

Anxiety and panic

- Sweating palms
- Dilated pupils
- Body aches
- Body temperature changes

- Chest pain

- Chills

- Choking sensation

- Dry Mouth

- Increased heart rate

- Nausea

- Shortness of breath

- Tingling sensations

Once you have identified exactly what it is you are feeling, you can begin to implement techniques for calming these emotions. See Chapter Ten for more details on calming specific emotions.

Accept Your Emotions

Now you have identified the emotions you are feeling, the next step is to accept them. This is a crucial step when it comes to calming the storm of emotions raging inside your head. This can be an extremely difficult thing to do, particularly if you have been suffering from the effects of BPD for a number of years. You will now have a great deal of resentment for the disorder, along with the emotions it causes you to feel. Accepting them may seem like an impossible task.

But it is important to understand that accepting your emotions is not the same things as approving of them or accepting that there is no chance of change. It just means that you keep yourself from trying to push away and suppress these feelings or deny what it is happening. By allowing yourself to feel the true intensity of your feelings, rather than battling to keep them away, you actually take away a great deal of their power.

Endeavor to just let your feelings "be", without engaging in self-criticism or judgement. See if you can focus on the present moment, without giving rise to thoughts of the past or future.

Try some of the following techniques:

- Imagine you are observing your emotions from the outside. After all, you are not defined by your emotions. You are not your anger, or your grief or your frustration, or anxiety. Attempt to view your emotions as what they truly are – something separate from yourself.

- Observe the ways your emotions come and go. It can be helpful to think of them as "waves"- imagine them ebbing and flowing, increasing and decreasing in intensity. This also strengthens your ability to see your emotions as something separate from yourself.

- Pay attention to your physical body. How do these emotions manifest inside you? Do they cause you to feel tension or pain? Where? Does this pain or discomfort move as the feelings increase and increase? Try and pinpoint exactly where you can feel the manifestation of the emotion. And what does it feel like? Is a dull ache? A sharp pain? A burning? A tingling?

- Tell yourself it's okay to be feeling these emotions. Accept them for what they are. Remember, accepting them does not mean you approve of them. And it does not mean you are giving them permission to be here forever.

- Tell yourself that just because you are experiencing these emotions right now, it does not mean they are reality. Your emotions are a result of your thoughts. And all thoughts can be changed.

Engage in Mindfulness Practices

Engaging in mindfulness practices can also be a great help in learning to manage the chaos of the emotional storm. Mindfulness is a form of meditation and that helps people manage their thoughts and feelings. It is used increasingly in the treatment of mental health disorders and is recommended by NICE (The National Institute for Health and Care Excellence) in the treatment of depression, among other illnesses. Thanks to the way it helps practitioners manage and become aware of their emotional states, mindfulness can also be extremely beneficial when it comes to treating borderline personality disorder.

The mindfulness state can be reached through a number of methods. Here are a few mindfulness techniques to try if you are new to the practice:

- **Standard mindfulness meditation:** Focus on your breathing. Feel the breath move in and out of your body and become aware of its rhythm. If you become aware of thoughts arising, simply notice them, then let them go by imagining them drifting away down an imaginary river. You can achieve the same result by focusing on a mantra (a repeated phrase), in place of the breath.

- **Sensory mindfulness meditation:** Pay attention to each of your senses. Identify five things you can see, five things you can hear, smell, touch and even taste. Challenge yourself to describe these sensory experiences in great detail. For example, rather than simply saying "I see a butterfly," describe to yourself exactly what it is you are seeing: "I see a butterfly with dark yellow wings and small semi-circular black spots. Its legs are moving slowly in a back and forth action." Apply the same level of detail to the descriptions of things you hear, smell, feel and taste. This is an excellent way to ensure you are engaged in the present moment, and not focusing on the past or future.

- **Bodily sensation mindfulness:** Close your eyes and become aware of the subtle sensations within your body. Do you feel an itch? A gentle ache? A tingling? Do not try to fight these feelings, simply become aware of them and allow them to pass. Work your way from the top of your head to the tips of your toes, mentally scanning every inch of the body. Paying close attention to what you notice, proving the same depth of description you would in a sensory meditation.

- **Emotional mindfulness:** Arguably the most beneficial type of mindfulness when it comes to managing BPD, this calls on you to allow and accept arising emotions without passing judgment. Rather than fighting your emotions, simply try to name them. Exactly what is it you are feeling? Anger? Jealousy? Frustration? Joy? Whatever it is you are feeling, accept it and then let it go. Imagine your emotion floating away down the river in the same way you would discard an errant thought during a standard mindfulness meditation.

Learning to Control Your Impulses

As any sufferer of borderline personality disorder knows, BPD is a constant struggle of battling your impulses. The sudden mood swings can drive you to impulsive, reckless, self-damaging behaviors ranging from self-harming to dangerous driving, to unsafe sex. You likely know these things are no good for you, but it can feel like the only way of easing the chaos inside your head. It can often feel as though you have no choice but to engage in these behaviors.

Though it may not seem like it in the heat of the moment, these impulses can be managed. Begin by acknowledging that these reckless, impulsive behaviors have a purpose. They are coping mechanisms that help you deal with distress, and should be seen as such, rather than a cause for punishing yourself. But as you no doubt are aware, these reckless behaviors can put both you and those around you in danger. It is important to find healthier and less damaging ways of coping with the distress BPD can cause.

In order to do this successfully, you must learn to tolerate this distress, rather than immediately seeking to relieve it. But building your tolerance, you will be able to step back and give yourself a moment to think when you feel the need to act recklessly, as BPD can so often drive you to do. By becoming able to tolerate distress, you will be able to "ride out" the experience, without resorting to damaging behaviors.

No doubt this sounds much easier said than done. So let's take a look at a few of the techniques you can implement to begin to build your tolerance to distress:

Lower Your Body Temperature: When we get angry and frustrated, our body temperatures often rise. Lowering your body temperature can help calm the anger within. Do this by splashing cold water on your face, standing in front of a fan or air conditioner, or stepping outside if you are in a warm building. The change in temperature will have the effect of cooling you down both emotionally and physically.

Engage in High Intensity Exercise: Vigorous exercise is a great way to ease many intense emotions. The next time you feel overwhelmed and about to act out, turn to exercise instead. Sprint around the block or swim a few laps. It can even be something as simple as doing a few jumping jacks or running or the spot for a few minutes. The increase in oxygen flow will greatly aid in managing your distress. Being physically exhausted also makes you far less likely to engage in dangerous and reckless behavior.

Focuses Breathing: Paying attention to your breath, much the same way as you would do in meditation, can be a useful technique in managing distress. Force yourself to breath in a rhythm, giving yourself five counts in, hold for two counts, then release. Repeat as many times as you need to.

Tense and Relax Your Muscles: When we are tense or stressed, our muscles can involuntarily become tense. But deliberately tensing your muscles and then consciously releasing it, you well be able to enter a deeper state of relaxation. Try tensing your fists as hard as you can and holding it for a count of ten. Keep squeezing harder and harder. On the count of ten, release your fists. You will feel your muscles become far more relaxed than they had initially been. If you are feeling distressed, try this technique in as many places around your body as you can. Tense each muscle and then feel them relax more deeply as your release the hold.

Find an Activity That Calms You: The next time you feel distressed and ready to act out, force yourself to engage in a different activity. This can be any activity you choose, as long as it is a healthy one that will not put yourself or others in danger. This helps by taking your mind off the negative emotion and forcing you to concentrate on the task at hand. It can be helpful to put together a list of activities you enjoy doing – they could be something as simple as taking a walk or reading a book, through to playing a musical instrument, doing a sport or baking a cake. The next time you feel distressed, you will have this list to turn to.

Do Something Kind: Though being kind and generous may be the last thing you feel like doing while you are lost in your own problems, engaging in an act of service is a great way to help your through your distress without resorting to reckless behavior. Bake cookies for someone, wash a neighbor's windows, or help out with tasks around the house. Not only will this distract you from your stress, it will have the added benefit of making you feel good about yourself, helping with your sense of self-worth. As with the above suggestion, when you are feeling good, it can be helpful to make a list of helpful tasks you can engage in that you can refer to the next time stress takes hold.

Keep Your Mind Busy: If you need a quick distraction from the chaos of thoughts inside your head, engage in an activity that forces you to keep your mind busy. Try saying the alphabet backwards or recite you times tables.

Utilize Positive Imagery: Imagine the way you would like to respond the next time you feel like acting recklessly. How would ideally like to manage the distress? Imagine what this would look like. Allow yourself to really feel the way this would feel. This exercise can be done both when you are feeling good and when the distress begins to take hold. By imagining the ideal outcome, you may be able to change the way you behave in reality.

Give Meaning to the Situation: We have already discussed the way reckless behavior has a purpose, in that it acts a mechanism in times of distress. But what other meaning can you give to the way you are feeling? Perhaps your battle with your distress has given you the strength to face it again next time it arrives. Maybe it has taught you how you *don't* wish to behave. Maybe you received help from someone unexpected and the situation allowed you to create a new relationship.

Make a Pros and Cons List: If you are battling with yourself about whether to engage in reckless behavior, such as going on a massive shopping spree or sleeping with someone you know you shouldn't, take a few moments to write down a list of the pros and cons. What will the benefits be to engaging in this behavior? And what are the likely consequences? The act of doing this will hopefully not only allow you to see the repercussions of your reckless actions but may also provide you with that moment of thought you need to remove yourself from the intensity of the situation.

DAVID LAWSON PHD

CHAPTER NINE

WHO CAN HELP YOU?

If you are suffering from borderline personality disorder, it is important to know that you are not alone. In Part Three, we will be looking more closely at how your loved ones can help you manage the illness, but it is important to acknowledge the vast array of healthcare professionals who are trained to help sufferers of borderline personality disorder.

While psychiatrists and psychologists are often the first people we turn to in the treatment of BPD, the condition can also be treated by GPs and nurses, along with occupational therapists and social workers who have undergone specials training. Some major cities worldwide also have specialized mental health services dedicated to patients suffering from BPD.

Finding the right health-care professional

Finding the right therapist to work with can be a challenge. With so many options out there, even knowing where to begin can be a challenge. While your GP will often be able to assist you in finding a therapist well-versed in dealing with borderline personality disorder, it is important that you play an active part in finding a person you feel comfortable working with. After all, for therapy to be successful, you will need to open up to your therapist and feel safe doing so.

So how do you being the daunting task of finding the right therapist for you?

Begin by narrowing down your options. You already know you want a therapist with experience treating BPD, of course, but think about what else you require. For example, how far are you willing to travel to get to your appointments? What is your budget? Do you have a preference for a male or female therapist? Apply these filters to your list of therapists to create a shortlist of potential candidates.

Next, take your time to read through the profiles of the therapists on your shortlist. Take note of not only what they offer professionally, but any information they might provide about their personal lives. It's good to use your instinct here – who do you get a good feeling from? Is there anyone who makes you feel uncomfortable?

Understand the different approaches each therapist takes when it comes to managing BPD. Is there a specific type of therapy you have been recommended by your GP, or one you feel would be most beneficial for you? Carefully examine the courses of treatment each therapist offers and learn as much as you can about each method of treatment.

Once you have found the therapist you feel may be right for you, take up their offer of a free consultation before committing to anything more long-term. It is important that you feel a connection to your therapist and that you feel they understand you. At the initial consultation, be sure to ask questions, in order to come away with all the information you need to make a decision. Here are few things you might consider asking:

- Are you experienced and comfortable in treating people with borderline personality disorder?

- Do you have any special training when it comes to the treatment of BPD? If so, what? How do you approach treatment?

- Are you comfortable with me expressing my emotions during our sessions? Do you feel comfortable with me raising sensitive issues in my life?

- How will you determine if your treatment is working?

- What will your next step be if the treatment is not successful?

- How often will we have sessions? How long will each session last?

- Does your treatment involve my partner and family? If so, how?

- Am I able to call you if I am experiencing a crisis? If not, can you provide details of someone I can call?

- What are you fees? Will they be covered by my health insurance?

As BPD often exists in conjunction with other mental health issues such as eating disorders, post-traumatic stress disorder, bipolar disorder and depression, it is important to keep your therapist updated on any new issues or changes in your behavior that may present themselves. In this way, you can both keep on top of any alterations in your condition and treatment can be adjusted accordingly.

As an adult, you should expect your healthcare provider to give you all the information and assistance you need to deal with your illness. You should be given the choice to make your own decisions when it comes to your treatment. Often you healthcare provider will involve your partner or family in this discussion. Be sure to ask questions about anything you do not understand.

Things You Can Do to Increase the
Likelihood of Success

To give yourself the best chance of defeating the BPD, you must take an active role in your treatment. Just relying on your psychologist, or other healthcare provider will not be enough to manage the emotional chaos than arises with the disorder. By taking the following steps, you will be greatly increasing the chance of successful treatment:

- Work with your psychologist or other healthcare provider, along with your partner and/or family, to make a plan for the management of your BPD

- Be sure to attend all your appointments

- Be honest and open with your psychologist. Tell them about anything that is worrying you.

- Be open to change with regards to your daily life. Allow your psychologist to offer suggestions, and do not disregard them without due consideration, even if they may seem uncomfortable at first.

- Be sure to do any "homework" set for you by your psychologist.

- Be honest when it comes to the way BPD affects you. Analyze your illness and understand the way it makes you act.

- Learn how to manage your impulses and emotions, and develop ways of coping, without resorting to self-harming or destructive behavior. (See Chapter Eight for further information.)

- Be patient and persistent. Keep trying different treatment options until you find one that works for you.

- Get as much reliable information about the disorder as you can. The more you know and understand about BPD, the easier it will be to manage.

- Design and implement a plan to get you through crises. Having a plan in place will help you think more clearly in times of distress. The plan should highlight things you can do to get through the crisis, along with things that should be avoided. (See Chapter Eight for further information.) Include things your loved ones can do for you, along with people you can contact in times of crisis.

What to expect with regards to recovery

If you are suffering from a physical illness, recovery is often a black and white thing. You are sick, and then you are healed. But, as you likely know, recovery is completely different in cases of mental illness. Vary rarely does recovery mean a complete elimination of symptoms. Is unlikely – thought not impossible – that you will ever be able to completely dispense with the need for therapy, medication or other treatments.

Nonetheless, many people suffering from BPD have seen marked improvements in their conditions through a variety of treatments. When dealing with borderline personality disorder, recovery can be measured in a number of ways.

When you are in recovery you will experience less frequent emotional outbursts, and these outbursts will decrease in intensity. You will have less incidences of self-harming and other impulsive, reckless behaviour. While it is of course possible that there will be relapses, you will be able to resolve these crises much more quickly than you did in the past. As your symptoms improve, you will likely feel more and more confident taking steps towards living a full and successful life.

CHAPTER TEN

USEFUL TOOLS

Learn How to Change Your Brain

As crazy as it sounds, learning how to alter the function of your brain is a key way of managing borderline personality disorder. As discussed in part one, BPD is often linked to neurological abnormalities. So what are you to do if your brain does not function in the same way as others'? Surely that is just something you have to live with, right?

Not necessarily.

Each time you engage in a healthy coping response, such as those outlined in Chapter Eight, you are developing new neural pathways. Skills and treatments such as meditation and mindfulness have also been proven to grown and strengthen brain matter. The more you practice, the stronger these pathways will become. Before you know it, the learned behavior will become automatic. With time and patience you have the ability to change the way you feel, behave and think.

Stimulate Your Senses

Engaging one or more of your senses can be a good way to manage the emotional challenges of BPD. As each person is different, it is a good idea to experiment with stimulating different senses to find out what works best for you. You may also find that what works for you changes depending on just what it is you are feeling. Something that is effective for you when you are feeling numb or empty may not work to calm anger or frustration. There are of course and endless array of way to stimulate your senses, but here are a few techniques to begin with. Start here and then experiment to find out just what works for you:

- **Sight:** Seek out an image that captures your attention. This may be something in your immediate environment such as a view, a piece of art, or an inanimate object such as a book or table. Or it could be an image you see in your imagination. Allow yourself to appreciate the colors and textures you see. Bright colors will have the effect of stimulating you if you feel empty or numb, while cooler colors can have a calming influence on anger or frustration.

- **Taste:** Stimulating your taste buds can help when you are feeling numb and empty. Try eating foods with intense flavors such as lemons, chilis, or strong-flavored mints. Alternatively, if you are seeking to calm your anger or agitation, warming foods such as tea and soup can help.

- **Touch:** If you are feeling numb, try holding a piece of ice, or running chilled or warm water over your hands. Gripping tightly to an inanimate object can also be helpful. If you need to calm yourself, a hot shower, warm bed or cuddles with a pet can be beneficial.

- **Smell:** If you are familiar with aromatherapy, you will know the immense power of scents. You will find essential oils available to manage any emotions. For example, scents such as lavender, ylang or chamomile can calm you, orange and sandalwood can have a stimulating effect, while rose, frankincense and basil can help alleviate anxiety. Also take the time to identify scents around your home that calm or stimulate you. For example, does the smell of clean laundry have a calming effect? How does the scent of freshly cut grass make you feel? What about the scents that come out of your kitchen? Pay attention to the way you feel when you smell different foods cooking.

- **Sound:** If you are struggling with emptiness or numbness, loud music, whistles or buzzers can help jolt you back to reality. To calm your emotions, try soothing music or natural sounds such as bird song, rainfall or ocean waves. If you don't have access to the real thing, there are many recordings available on places like iTunes or YouTube.

Activities to Soothe Your Emotions

While we have already touched on the role of activities when it comes to focusing your attention, specific activities can have the effect of soothing our emotions. Just like the sensory stimulation, different things will work for different people, so it is important to experiment and find what works for you. Here are few places to begin.

If you are feeling anxious, tense or panicked, try:

- Taking ten deep breaths, counting them out aloud

- Taking a warm bath or shower

- Engaging in mindfulness by making yourself a hot drink and drinking it slowly, paying attention to the smell, the taste and the feel of the mug in your hands

- Write down every detail you can about where you are in this moment. Include details about the room, the weather, the time, date etc.

- Go for a walk.

If you are feeling angry, restless or frustrated, try:

- Hitting a pillow

- Throwing ice cubes into the sink make them smash

- Tearing up a newspaper

- Doing some vigorous exercise such as boxing

- Doing a practical activity such as gardening or handiwork

- Listening to some loud music

- Focusing on your breathing. This will force you to focus on something other than your anger.

- Counting to ten before you react. This buys you a little time to think.

- Taking yourself out of the area. Take a short walk around the block, or even just remove yourself to a different from the person or situation that is causing you anger.

If you are feeling depressed, lonely or sad, try:

- Writing all your negative emotions on a piece of paper and tearing it up or burning it

- Listening to a piece of music or song you find uplifting

- Writing a loving letter to the part of you that is experiencing the sadness or loneliness

- Wrapping yourself up in a blanket and watching your favourite movie

- Cuddling a pet or soft toy

- Doing some exercise

- When you are not feeling sad or depressed, make a list of things you enjoy doing, such as playing a musical instrument, walking in nature, or watching your favourite TV show. The next time you are struggling, refer to this list and do one of the activities.

If you feel detached, disassociated or lost in your own world, try:

- Clapping your hands together hard and paying attention to the way it feels

- Chewing a chili or piece of ginger

- Splashing your face with cold water

- Walking barefoot and paying attention to the feel of the ground beneath your feet

- When you are not experience an episode of disassociation, write notes to yourself in places you will see them. The next time you feel detached, use these notes to anchor you in the world outside your head.

If you feel as though you want to self harm, try:

- Rubbing an ice cube over the place you want to hurt yourself

- Stick tape over your arm and pull it off

- Take a cold bath

Reduce Your Vulnerability

Give yourself the best chance of fighting negative emotions by taking care of your physical and mental well-being. Be sure to do the following:

- Do plenty of exercise

- Get a good night's sleep

- Eat a balanced diet

- Avoid excessive use of drugs and alcohol

- Practice relaxation techniques such as meditation

Psychoeducation

Psychoeducation is a useful tool that can be of great value to sufferers of borderline personality, along with their loved ones. It helps people with BPD and those around them understand the disorder at a deeper level. Psychoeducation programs cover symptoms of the disease, along with treatment options, recovery methods and available help.

Psychoeducation can take place either individually or in groups. It may comprise of written information-person meetings, websites, videos or discussion groups. Speak to your healthcare provider if you are interested in pursuing psychoeducation for you and your family.

Medication

Using medication in the treatment of borderline personality disorder has its roots in the 1980s. Since then, there has been a marked increase in the success of psychotherapy in managing the disorder. Thanks to this, many healthcare professionals believe medication, in conjunction with psychotherapy, is an effective way of managing the illness.

As BPD is believed to be caused, at least in part, by biological disturbances, such as chemical imbalances in the brain, many of the symptoms caused by these imbalances can be addressed through medication. Medication has proven to be effective in the rapid stabilization of emotional outbursts and aggression BPD sufferers can direct at both themselves and others. There has not been any form of psychotherapy to date that provides the same immediate response. In addition, medication has been proven to improve elements of BPD that are usually unresponsive to psychotherapy, such as paranoia, black and white thinking, high levels of suspiciousness and disassociation.

In some cases, the medication has such a profound effect on altering these biological processes that, in conjunction with psychotherapy, they decrease to the point of medication no longer being required.

There are four classes of medications usually used in the treatment of BPD:

- **Antipsychotic agents**

    These have been proven to assist with mood regulation and decrease the incidences of self-injury paranoia, hostility, black and white thinking and depression.

    Because of their ability to counter a wide range of symptoms, antipsychotic agents are considered one of the most useful classes of medications in the treatment of BPD. They are commonly used to treat other mental illnesses including schizophrenia and bipolar disorder, however, when prescribed at a lower dosage, they can also be extremely beneficial for sufferers of BPD.

- **Mood stabilizers**

    This class of medication is known to improve unstable moods, anxiety, irritability and problems relating to others. They do not however reduce black and white thinking, paranoia or disassociation; all common symptoms of borderline personality disorder. Because of this, many psychotherapists will prescribe both a mood stabilizer and antipsychotic agent.

- **Antianxiety agents**

  These have been proven to reduce anxiety, irritability, depression and agitation. They can also be beneficial for sufferers of BPD who have difficulty sleeping. However, thanks to their highly addictive nature, they are used with caution in the treatment of BPD. There have been several cases in which the use of antianxiety agents have been reported to increase impulsive behavior in BPD sufferers.

- **Nutraceuticals**

  This class of medications has been proven to reduce anger, depression and aggression.

The effectiveness of these medications will depend on several factors, namely, the patient's specific symptoms, the medication selected, and the degree to which the sufferer's disorder is caused by a biological imbalance. Because of this, medication which works for one person may not work for another. It make take some trial and error to determine which medication is right for you.

However, it is important to note that, many psychotherapists, as well as medical advisory group NICE are against the use of medication in the treatment of BPD. Medication can lead to addiction and may not be effective when a patient's disorder is caused by environmental factors rather than biological. For the same reasons, many patients are also resistant to taking medication to aid their condition.

Despite these conflicting ideas, the majority of therapists and doctors agree that the best way of tackling BPD is through a combined approach of medication and non-medical treatments such as CBT. Medication alone is rarely a suitable treatment plan.

Speak to your GP, therapist or other healthcare professional to discuss whether medication is the right treatment approach for you.

BORDERLINE PERSONALITY DISORDER

CHAPTER ELEVEN

SPECIFIC THERAPY SKILLS
FOR MANAGING BPD

These days, there are two main methods of therapy used to treat BPD: cognitive behavioral therapy and dialectical behavior therapy. Let's take a look at these two methods in order to understand their roles in the treatment of borderline personality disorder.

Cognitive Behavioral Therapy Skills

Cognitive behavioral therapy, or CBT aims to alter the way a person thinks and behaves. The effectiveness of this therapy relies heavily on a patient's connection and relationship with their therapist, along with their willingness to change. CBT is commonly used to treat a range of disorders including depression, anxiety, addictions and phobias.

CBT is generally a short-term treatment and, thanks to this, if often more affordable than other types of therapies. It usually focuses on helping clients deal with a very specific problem.

How Cognitive Behavioral Therapy Works

CBT operates on the premise that our behavior is heavily influenced by our thoughts and feelings. For example, someone with low self-esteem may believe that when they are in public, people are constantly judging them. As a result, they shy away from social occasions and prefer to spend time alone. Cognitive behavioral therapy aims to teach patients that they cannot control every element in the world around them, they are responsible for the way they perceive these external events.

One of the main goals of CBT is the removal of a patient's automatic negative thoughts and the replacing of them with something more positive and productive. These automatic thoughts, such as "I'm not good enough" or "I will never succeed" often have their roots in early childhood and, as the name suggests, pop into a person's head without them having any control over it. Someone experiencing automatic negative thoughts will generally accept them as true, thus the thoughts will have a great effect on their mood and can contribute to depression, anxiety and other emotional difficulties.

The first step of CBT therapy is to identify the automatic negative beliefs a patient is experiencing. This process is done under close guidance of the therapist and is important for learning how negative thoughts and beliefs can play a part in a person's behavior. This can be a challenging process, especially for someone uncomfortable or unfamiliar with introspection.

The second part of CBT asks patients to challenge and examine these negative thoughts, seeking evidence from reality to either support or refute their beliefs. For example, perhaps the person suffering from low self-esteem had an experience in which they were out in public and saw someone of the opposite sex laughing, while facing in their direction. At the time, they automatically assumed this person was laughing *at* them. But CBT calls the patient to examine situations such as this. Perhaps the person was laughing at a friend who was standing behind them. Perhaps the friend told a joke or pulled a face. In likelihood, it had nothing to do with the patient at all.

Doing this allows patients to look more objectively at the thought patterns that are contributing to their mental state. Once the patient is aware of the negative beliefs that come into their heads on a regular basis, they are able to catch themselves thinking these things, thus replacing the negative thought with a more positive one. For example, "I'm not good enough" can be replaced with "I am enough."

Through CBT, patients will also develop new coping skills to help them manage challenging situations. For example, patients with phobias will undergo exposure therapy, drug addicts may rehearse ways to avoid social situations in which there may be drugs present, and sufferers of BPD may work on building skills to help them cope with emotional outbursts.

The next step in the process may be rehearsing conversations with friends or family, in which the patient can implement the new beliefs and thought patterns they have been developing. By breaking the process into smaller goals this way, it becomes much more manageable.

While the therapist takes a very active role in CBT, the patient must be willing to put in a great deal of work, both in the sessions and in their daily life. They will often be given homework tasks to complete between sessions. CBT is much more structured and goal-oriented than psychoanalytic types of therapy, which can be quite open-ended. It is well-suited for people who want a short-term treatment to their emotional distress, along with skills they can use to manage their behavior long into the future.

Dialectical Behavioral Therapy Skills

Dialectical behavioral therapy, or DBT is a type of cognitive behavioral therapy that has been modified to specifically treat borderline personality disorder. Developed by Dr. Martha Linehan at the University of Washington, DBT focuses on skills specifically associated with the disorder such as mindfulness, controlling emotions, handling distress and cultivating relationships with others.

Often referred to as "talk therapy," DBT, like CBT, focuses on cognition – in particular, the way our thoughts and beliefs affect our actions.

DBT was the first type of psychotherapy proven to be successful in the treatment of borderline personality disorder. Thanks to its rapidly growing body of documented success, DBT is considered one of the best ways of treating borderline personality disorder.

DBT is based on the theory that the problem at the heart of borderline personality disorder is the inability to regulate emotions. DBT works on the premise that this inability comes about from a mix of biological and genetic factors and a traumatic childhood in which a child's caregivers either punished and trivialized a child's emotional needs or behaved erratically towards them. DBT aims to help patients build a skill set that will help them manage and regulate their emotions.

There are four main types of skills that a patient will develop while undergoing DBT. These are:

- **Mindfulness Skills**: This part of the process focuses on building meditative skills which allow the BPD sufferer to experience and acknowledge all the emotions and thoughts they are experiencing, without judgment. The patient is taught to simply witness and experience the emotions, giving a name to what they are feeling – "sadness" "frustration" "excitement" etc. – without labelling them as good or bad. These are considered the core skills a patient needs to succeed in managing their emotions.

- **Interpersonal Skills:** This part of the DBT process focuses on building skills needed to relate successfully with others. It teaches patients to communicate effectively and assert their needs and managing conflict within relationships.

- **Distress Tolerance Skills:** This section of the process trains patients to tolerate accept their distress, without resorting to reckless or self-damaging behavior.

- **Emotional Regulation Skills:** This focuses on increasing the patient's ability to identify and manage their emotional reactions to situations that may arise.

Structure

DBT is made up of specific elements that are introduced over the course of a year or longer.

These elements are:

- **Individual therapy sessions:** This uses CBT techniques such as cognitive restructural and exposure therapy in order to change patients' behavior and improve their quality of life.

- **Group therapy sessions**: These sessions provide skills training, teaching patients how to respond to challenging situations and problems faced in day to day life.

- **Phone calls**: These operate as "follow up" sessions in which the therapist checks in o the patient to discuss how successful they have been at applying the skills they have learned to life outside of therapy.

Thanks to the implementation of skills training in mindfulness, acceptance and tolerance of distress, DBT has been proven to be more effective in treating sufferers of borderline personality disorder than standard CBT.

Speak to your doctor to help you find the right therapy method for you.

CHAPTER TWELVE

GETTING HELP FROM YOUR
LOVED ONES

As any sufferer of borderline personality disorder will know, one of the biggest challenges of BPD is relating to other people. BPD can make you feel alone, attacked and unable to engage with those around you. You likely have a string of broken and damaged relationships behind you, and don't see any hope of improving the way you connect with others. Sometimes you may want nothing more than to hide away from the world and have everyone forget you exist.

But the reality is, the greater your support network, the more chance you have of defeating the disorder and going on to live a healthy and fulfilling life.

Understanding the illness and the way it can manifest is the key for both you and those around you. It can be incredibly distressing for your loved ones to watch you struggle with the effects of BPD. It can cause them to feel helpless and full of anxiety. Then, of course, there are the effects of your acting out; which naturally have the greatest impact of those you care about. Witnessing a manifestation of BDP, such as aggression, self-harm or even suicide attempts can be terrifying for those around you. As BPD can cause you to act aggressively and hostile towards those closest to you, the disorder can be frightening and frustrating for your loved ones when they are placed on the receiving end of your attacks. Assisting them in understanding what to expect from the disease, along with what they can do to help can go a long way to improving your relationship and ensuring you have the support you need.

What your family needs to know to help you with BPD

Your family will often feel angry and helpless at how you relate to them. When you strike out at them, they may feel emotionally – or even physically – wounded and will have to fight their own urges to retaliate.

But despite this, your family can be a great help and support when it comes to managing your BPD. After all, they love and are for you, and want the best for you. Speak to your healthcare provider about involving your family in your treatment and management plan. Ask your healthcare provider to give you written information about the disorder for you to show your family. The more they understand about what you are going through, the more support they will be able to offer.

When you begin treatment with a new psychologist or other healthcare professional, speak with your family members about which of them will be willing to be a part of your treatment. Ensure your psychologist is aware of which family members, or even close friends, they are able to speak with or contact with any concerns.

Family psychoeducation sessions can also go a long way towards building a deeper understanding and easing the distress that comes with seeing a loved one battle with BPD.

What your partner needs to know to help you with BPD

If you have been struggling with borderline personality for a number of years, you have likely seen the havoc it can wreak on romantic relationships. A BPD sufferer's intense fear of rejection, along with their inability to regulate their emotions can lead to one drama-filled relationship after another.

But BPD does not have to be a roadblock to having a successful relationship. There are many people with the disorder who have stable, loving and supportive families. The key lies in helping your partner understand what to expect, and how your disorder may manifest itself.

As with any relationship challenges, managing conflict becomes easier when you try to see the issue from your partner's point of view. This is especially important if you are suffering from a mental health disorder such as BPD which can cause you to think in ways that your partner will not.

To help them understand what you are going through, here are a few things it can be helpful to remind your partner of:

- It is important that they understand the way BPD P sufferers are highly sensitive to rejection and abandonment, both real and perceived. Explain to them the way even mild separations such as vacations or sudden changes in plans can spark your negative emotions and distress and the way having an important person disappear from your life even for a short amount of time can make you feel abandoned, lost and worthless. Accept that these concepts, while they may make perfect sense to you, might be difficult for you partner to relate to. That's okay. The goal here is simply to help them to understand how these situations make *you* feel and react.

- As you know, the challenges of BPD mean you are easily drawn into arguments, conflict and dramas. Ensure your partner understands the way your anger can creep up on you unaware. Help them understand that your BPD can make you very sensitive to the way you are treated. As this is never more prominent than in an intimate relationship, ensure your partner understands that your heightened sensitivity and outbursts are caused by your disorder, not by something they may have done or not done.

- Explain to your partner the way BPD can heighten bother positive and negative emotions. Tell them that even the smallest kind thing they do for you can cause you to react with intense joy and gratitude. But they must also be aware of the flip side of this; that even mild criticism a partner with BPD can result in intense anger and hurt.

- Help your partner understand your propensity towards black and white thinking. Explain to them the way it causes you to see things as either all good or all bad, and the way this can cause rapid fluctuations between love and admiration and intense dislike and disappointment.

- Explain to your partner the way BPD can cause you to misconstrue what others are saying to you. For this reason, it is important to make sure they know to communicate their meaning as effectively as possible. Explain to them the way you often have difficulty communicating through facial expressions alone.

The unpredictability of being a relationship with someone with BPD can cause your partner to have their own doubts about your relationship and their ability to handle it. Here are a few ways you and your partner can work together to make the management of BPD easier on both of you:

- **Hold discussions only when you are both calm.** As you are no doubt aware, when you are struggling with an episode of BPD is no time for rational discussion. But be aware that your BPD outbursts can also cause intense emotional reactions from your partner as they struggle to deal with you behavior. If you have something important to discuss, ensure you are both calm and control before you attempt to communicate.

- **Get information.** Help your partner find as much information as possible about what it is like to suffer from BPD. This will help increase empathy in the relationship, and help your partner understand the struggles you face on a daily basis. Help your loved one see that your challenging behavior is a facet of your illness, rather than a choice.

- **See a counsellor.** Seeking support from a mental health professional can be invaluable to both you and your partner. You may choose to attend therapy sessions alone or as a couple.

- **Work on your Communication.** Communication is vital in any relationship, but when a partner suffers from BPD, it becomes even more vital that both parties are able to communicate effectively. Ensure that all discussions you have come from a place of love and do your best to understand that what you may perceive as hurtful behavior is simply your partner trying to do the best they can for the both of you.

- **Tell Your partner to avoid blaming everything on your mental illness.** Help your partner understand that your illness does not define you. Make sure they understand that not every aspect of who you are can be put down to BPD. Help them understand that doing so can cause the disorder to become something of a put-down.

- **Ensure Your partner is practicing self-care.** Living with a partner with BPD can be an enormous challenge and it is important that you acknowledge the immense struggles your loved one is going through. Ensure you give them time to themselves, and that they have a network of friends they can rely on when things become overwhelming. As much as you might value your partner's support, accept that they need a life of their own. Allow them to prioritize time for friends and hobbies, both alone and with you.

What your children need to know to
help you with BPD

Being a parent is challenging at the best of times, and it can be an immense struggle when you are battling BPD symptoms as well. While all interpersonal relationships are challenged by borderline personality disorder, the relationship between a parent with BPD and their child can be one of the most difficult to navigate successfully. BPD can make it hard to be steady for your children and it can feel near impossible to be a good parent.

The sad reality is that many children with parents who suffer from BPD go on to exhibit attachment issues and other problems in adulthood. For this reason, it is crucial that parents with borderline personality disorder seek as much help as possible when raising their children.

Parenting with BPD is something that should be managed in conjunction with your therapist and/or doctor. But here are a few ways you can make the challenge less insurmountable:

- Arrange a professional family support service to visit you and your child in your home.

- Attend individual therapy sessions to help you manage your feelings, especially those related to being a parent and your fears surrounding your children's upbringing.

- Attend group therapy with you and your child to help build your relationship. Parents with BPD can often be detached and distant, leading to attachment issues in their children. Therapy sessions can be crucial in countering this.

- Have someone else care for your child for a period of time. Either put your child in childcare or another family member, allowing you to have a much-needed break.

- Just like when dealing with adults, helping your children to understand what you are going through can be of huge benefit when it comes to strengthening your relationship. Explain to them about your illness and exactly what it is you are going through, using books and stories where necessary. Teach your children about not only your own illness, but about mental health and wellbeing. This will help them understand your own erratic behavior and will also allow them to be more open about their own feelings and challenges. Engaging the help of a child psychologist can also be invaluable.

- If you have a baby, they should stay with you if you need to be admitted to hospital.

The best thing you can do for your children is to work constantly on your treatment, doing your best to get well, along with shielding them as much as possible from the negative effects of BPD.

PART THREE

HOW TO COPE WHEN YOUR LOVED ONE HAS BORDERLINE PERSONALITY DISORDER

CHAPTER THIRTEEN

MANAGING A LOVED ONE WITH BPD

If you have a loved one who is suffering from borderline personality disorder, life can be full of aggression, fear, crises and conflict. You might feel as though you're being held hostage, with a barrage of demands made against you, terrified that your family member will injure or even kill themselves if you don't appease them. Perhaps they are acting violently or asking to borrow money or your car again. Maybe they are bombarding you with endless messages and voicemails. Dealing with BPD can be an ongoing and seemingly unrewarding challenge.

Successfully dealing with borderline personality disorder requires you to build skills to deescalating crises and building independence in your loved one. Although it can often seem impossible, with the right tools and strategies, it is possible to help your loved one on make their way towards recovery.

Understanding what your loved one is going through can help make BPD more manageable for both of you. When you appreciate just what it is your loved one is experience, it increases both empathy and your ability to foresee crises, allowing you to better manage them. So what is it like to have BPD?

Begin by accepting BPD for what it is; a severe limiting disability. As you are no doubt aware, it is a disability that can affects sufferers' quality of life on many levels, including their romantic relationships, friendships and career prospects. The reality is that most people with BPD are severely unhappy. Thanks to the combination of chemical imbalances in the brain, along with deep-seated childhood traumas, a life with BPD is often one filled with great challenges. Beyond the mental symptoms themselves, BPD can also lead to broken education and few career options, drug and alcohol abuse and loneliness. This is especially true for people on the lower end of the socio-economic spectrum, as they usually have less access to treatment. Their hyper-sensitivity and tendency toward aggression can wreak havoc on every aspect of their lives. People with BPD are truly victims of their own illness.

Sufferers of BPD describe the disorder as akin to being on a roller coaster- both in terms of the dramatic emotional highs and lows, but also in their constantly wavering sense of who they are. BPD can cause a person to have violent fluctuations in their self-image, goals and aspirations, and even their likes and dislikes. It can be confusing, disorienting and frustrating. This feeling of being adrift can leave people with BPD frightened, in pain and defensive.

As you may already be aware, people with BPD can be extremely sensitive, with some people describing it as feeling like they are one giant exposed nerve. Seemingly small events of situations can trigger intense emotional reactions that are difficult to calm down. When in the midst of these intense emotions, BPD sufferers can find it hard to think straight. They may say hurtful things, or act in reckless or dangerous ways, leading them to feel guilty or ashamed once the violent emotions have passed. But these damaging behaviors are rarely done with the intent to harm. Rather they are done out of desperation.

People with BPD are at risk of creating havoc in their own lives and the lives of those around them. Thanks to tendencies to misinterpret situations, they are quick to anger and often strike out at those closest to them; namely, their family members, partners or children.

People with BPD, like any other illness, need to be treated with compassion and under-standing. But it is also important to acknowledge that they need professional psychological help. Offer your loved one all the support and care you can, but do not try and manage on your own.

CHAPTER FOURTEEN

HOW TO SPEAK TO SOMEONE WITH BPD

In general, people with BPD do not want special treatment. They just wished to be loved; an emotion which, thanks to traumatic upbringings, they may never have truly experienced. For BPDs simple things such as maintain friendships or cohabiting can be enormous challenges.

People with BPD exhibit heightened levels of sensitivity, meaning even the smallest criticism can cause great offense, leading them behave with aggression and hostility. In addition, they are prone to misconstruing things that are said to them and taking offense when none was intended.

These factors can make relating to someone with borderline personality disorder a complete minefield. While you want to treat your loved one the same way you would others, you must also be aware of the erratic behavior their disorder can cause.

Here are few ways to speak to and relate to a friend, partner or family member suffering from BPD:

What to Do:

- Ensure your meaning is as clear as possible. Do not rely on subtleties or facial expressions to get your meaning across.

- Offer ongoing and regular support. Listen to them, offer assistance and comfort when needed.

- Validate what they are going through. Acknowledge that, while you may not be able to relate to their experience, you understand it is very real to them.

- If you understand the way they are feeling, tell them. But if their feelings do not make sense to you, try to find out more. Ask questions. Let them know you really want to understand. Encourage them to tell you more about the things they are feeling and why.

- Give them hope by acknowledging that other sufferers of BPD have gone on to live long and happy lives.

- Acknowledge that the person is suffering and help them break their goals down into small, manageable steps.

- Have realistic expectations. The nature of BPD means setbacks are commonplace. Do your best to remain positive and encourage the person to do the same.

- If it is appropriate, ask them about their BPD management plan and find out what role you can play in implementing this.

- Communicate your boundaries clearly. Tell them what you are not prepared to accept, be it abusive language, violence, threats etc.

- If they are agitated, do your best to respond in a calm manner. If you feel in danger, remove yourself from the situation and call for help.

- Listening and reflecting on what you have been told is perhaps the most effective way of communicating with someone with BPD. Even though you may disagree with every word that comes out of your loved one's mouth, acknowledge that listening is not the same as agreeing to someone. You are simply accepting the person's emotions and perspective.

- Ask open-ended questions that encourages your loved one to share pieces of their life, such as "Tell me what happened today to make you feel like this?" or "How is your week going?"

- Summarizing back what you have been told. This helps someone with BPD feel heard and valued. For example, if your partner shares that she thinks you don't love her as much as you used to, you could say, "All right, you feel that I don't love you as much as I used to." Again, by doing this, you are not agreeing with the statement, you are simply acknowledging the emotions and perspective of the other person. Avoid the temptation to point out all the flaws in the argument remind yourself that the goal of this reflection is not necessarily to agree. It is not about proving who is right or wrong. It is about helping someone you love to feel valued and heard, and about deescalating conflict before it transmutes into a crisis.

- Focus on emotions, not words. BPD sufferers are prone to speaking in ways that may come across as hurtful or antagonistic, and it can be difficult not to focus on these words. But rather than pulling your loved one up on something they may have said, look beneath their words to the core emotion beneath. If you sense your loved one is struggling, ask questions such as: "It seems as though you are feeling hurt right now, is that right?" Asking questions such as these will validate your loved one and their feelings and help them feel as though they are being heard.

What Not to Do:

- Do not attempt to take control of the person's life. Allow them to make their own choices and simply offer your support. Do not let this become a source of conflict.

- Avoid being drawn into their conflicts with other people. As we will discuss further in Chapter Seventeen, people will BPD are skilled at manipulating those around them to engage in conflict with each other. Do not be drawn into their attempts to do so.

- Do not try and talk them out of their feelings. A BPD sufferer might come to you with a claim like "I am a terrible person." Flat out disagreeing with this with a comment like: "You're not a terrible person," has the effect of invalidating their thoughts and feelings. Instead, try to understand what it is that has made them feel this way. Ask questions and listen carefully. Find out if there was something specific they did to make them feel like a terrible person. From there, engage in practical problem solving – ask them what they can do to rectify the situation. Doing so gives the BPD sufferer a sense of being in control of their own lives and emotions.

- Do not attempt to be their therapist. Instead, assist your loved one in finding the right healthcare professional for them and offer your support throughout their treatment.

- Do not get defensive. While it can be challenging not to take accusations and criticisms personally, acknowledge that it is not about you. This is just a manifestation of the BPD. Remind yourself of this on a regular basis and do your best to see beyond the illness to the person you love beneath.

How to Communicate effectively during a crisis

When a loved one is in the midst of a BPD episode, they may become aggressive, insult you or hurl out unfair accusations. As human, our natural response is to become defensive and counter their arguments with hostility and aggression of our own. But when dealing with a BPD sufferer, acting such a way will only exacerbate the situation. It is important to remember that someone with BPD finds it difficult to see things from someone else's perspective. They have difficulty telling the difference between a minor issue and a full blown catastrophe. When you behave defensively, they see this as a sign that they are not valued. This will lead them to believe that you do not want to be around them, triggering their deep-seated fear of abandonment. This then leads them to act recklessly or in a self-harming manner.

Instead, when your loved ones become reactive, take time to pay attention to what they are saying, without pointing out the holes in their argument. While it is easier said than done, do your best not to take their attack personally. After all, it is not about you. If your loved one makes a point about something you did wrong, or something you could improve on in the future, acknowledge and accept their point, make your apology, and attempt to discuss ways you can improve in the future. When someone with BPD feels as though they are being heard and taken seriously, the situation is less likely to get out of hand. If, however if the conflict increases to points of threats, aggression or a tantrum, it will be most beneficial to walk away and attempt the conversation again when they have calmed down.

How to Identify an Emergency

While disparaging self-talk is a common feature of borderline personality disorder, particular among those suffering from 'quiet' BPD, the sad reality is self-harming and suicide is all too common among people suffering from this disorder. When you are around a person with BPD, it is important to be vigilant and aware of any attempts at self-harming that may be taking place. When someone with BPD is reactive, it can easily escalate to the point where they will consider self-harming. It is important, however, not to plant the idea of self-injury or suicide in their head by outwardly asking them if they are considering it. Instead, provide a space where they can speak openly about what it is they are feeling or experiencing. This will then allow you to make a decision about whether to seek professional help on that occasion.

Be aware that there are several subtle signs that may indicate a person is considering suicide or engaging in self-harm. These include shaving off their hair, isolating themselves from others, excessive scratching or a reduced appetite. These less overt symptoms represent the BPD sufferer's inability to discuss their emotions outwardly. Being alert to these symptoms and seeking help accordingly can stop a crisis from escalating and requiring serious psychiatric or medical attention.

All suicide and self-harming attempts should be taken seriously. Even if they are done to seek attention, they are still indicative of deep emotional trauma. While it is important to get your loved one professional assistance in any situation involving self-harm and suicide, seek help immediately if any of the following occurs:

- The person has deliberately injured themselves.
- The person is expressing suicidal thoughts or talking about killing someone else
- The person is acting in an aggressive and abusive manner
- The person has become disoriented; i.e. they do not know who they are, where they are, or what day it is.
- The person has become delusional or is having hallucinations

- The person has become severely affected by drugs and/or alcohol and is acting in a reckless manner.

If you don't believe the situation has escalated to the point of being life threatening, however, refraining from calling the emergency services. Doing so every time your loved one speaks of hurting themselves will signal to them that they have a great amount of power over you and that by threatening to self-harm, they can effectively put an end to any conflict or argument. Instead, when your loved one speaks about self-harming, ask them what they would like to do about the situation. Suggest calling their therapist or an emergency hotline or going together to the emergency room. Doing this gives the BPD sufferer back an element of control, which can assist in calming their runaway emotions.

What to Do When You Feel Overwhelmed

There is no doubting that having a loved one with BPD is a struggle. There are bound to be times when you feel overwhelmed and unable to cope. This is exacerbated by the fact that the person you love with BPD will generally be unable to fulfill the supportive role of parent, friend of partner, that they otherwise would.

Because of this, it is crucial to have a strong network around you of people you can rely on in times of exhaustion, stress and overwhelm. Allow yourself plenty of time to engage in hobbies and relaxation activities with friends who you can be open with. Ensure too that you have people you can speak openly to about the experience of living with someone with borderline personality disorder. This may be a therapist or other health professional, a support group, GP or religious leader.

Involving other people in your support and care of the BPD sufferer can also be invaluable. Caring for someone with a mental illness should never fall to one person alone. Ensure there are a number of people around you who are well-versed in dealing with the individual with BPD and are able to act calmly and rationally in times of crisis. The more people around the BPD sufferer who know effective strategies for dealing with their reactivity, the less likely it is that a crisis will occur. Depending on the situation, your loved one's friends, siblings, parents, children or extended family members are all people who can be turned to for support.

Manage your expectations with regards to recovery

When dealing with a physical illness, recovery is often very black and white. But recovery is completely different when it comes to mental illness. Vary rarely does recovery see the complete elimination of symptoms and it is unlikely that someone suffering from a mental health disorder will ever be able to completely dispense with the need for therapy, medication or other treatments. When dealing with borderline personality disorder, recovery can be measured in a number of ways.

A sufferer in recovery will experience less frequent emotional outbursts, and these outbursts will decrease in intensity. There will be less incidences of self-harming and other impulsive, reckless behaviour. While it is of course possible that there will be relapses, such crises will likely be resolved much more quickly than in the past. As their symptoms improve, your loved one will likely feel more and more confident taking steps towards living a full and successful life. Offering your support at every step of the journey will go a long way towards assisting this recovery.

CHAPTER FIFTEEN

BEING IN A RELATIONSHIP WITH SOMEONE WITH BPD

Often, people with BPD are very charismatic and energetic, so it is not difficult to be drawn to them. For this reason, many people find themselves in relationships with sufferers of borderline personality disorder. But the challenges of this illness mean a relationship with such a person is likely to be a cycle of perpetual arguments and dramas.

But while conducting a relationship with someone with BPD can be a challenge, if you have found a partner whom you love and care for, the relationship is likely worth pursuing. The key lies in knowing what to expect, and how your partner's disorder may manifest itself.

Understanding Your Partner

To really understand what is going on inside your partner's head, ensure you have read Part One of this book; a detailed overview of borderline personality disorder, its causes and the ways it can manifest. But here are a few of the traits of BPD that can be most prominent within a romantic relationship.

As people with BPD have such difficulty controlling their emotions, they often react with intense joy and gratitude if their partner does even the smallest kind thing for them. The flip side of this is that criticizing a partner with BPD can result in intense anger and hurt. As we have learned, people who suffer from BPD can be very sensitive to the way others treat them and even the smallest criticism can cause them immense amounts of hurt. Sufferers of BPD will experience often violent mood swings, which can be difficult to anticipate. Recognize that this is a symptom of the disorder, and likely not directly related to something you may or may not have done.

Sufferers of BPD fear abandonment and rejection, and this is never more heightened than in a romantic relationship. Experiencing even the smallest amount of conflict can lead your partner to believe that you are about to leave them. Sometimes, in order to avoid this rejection, they will pre-emptively end the relationship in order to be the one to do the "abandoning." Sufferers of BPD will have to work harder than normal to allow themselves to trust their partner and believe that they are not going to leave them.

You have probably noticed your partner tends to pick fights with you when things seem to be going well. People with BPD have often grown up surrounded by such trauma that peace and harmony in a relationship is completely foreign. In order to regain a sense of normalcy, they will seek to uproot this security through aggression, hostility and other damaging behavior. Peace and harmony can actually leave someone with BPD feeling empty and numb. In order to make themselves feel alive, they may attack you, or create conflict in another way. This helps them feel *something*, which, in their eyes, is better than feeling empty.

In addition, the BPD sufferer's propensity towards black and white thinking means they will often see you as either all good or all bad, often alternating rapidly between intense love and admiration to a crushing dislike and disappointment.

How to Cope

The unpredictability of being a relationship with someone with BPD can cause you to have doubts of your own. It may feel as though the more you love your partner, the less they seem to love you. All this conflict and confusion may have you doubting whether you have the strength to maintain the relationship. These concerns can be heightened by the fact that you don't have your partner to rely on or confide in. This can leave you feeling lost and alone. Implementing the following solutions can make living with BPD much more manageable:

- **Get information.** Learn as much as you can about what it is like to suffer from BPD. This will help increase empathy in the relationship, and help you understand the struggles faced by your partner on a daily basis. By familiarizing yourself with the traits of the disorder, it should become clear to you that your partner's challenging behavior is the result of an illness, rather than a choice.

- **See a counsellor.** Seeking support from a mental health professional can be invaluable to both sufferers of BPD and their loved ones. You may choose to attend therapy sessions alone or as a couple.

- **Communicate.** Communication is vital in any relationship, but when a partner suffers from BPD, learning how to effectively communicate is of utmost importance. It is crucial however that you take care not to say anything that your partner may perceive as a slight, or may make them feel unloved, or as though the relationship is about to end. Ensure that all discussions you have come from a place of love, rather than attacking your partner or seeking to put them down.

- **Ensure your meaning is clear.** BPD can cause sufferers to misconstrue what others are saying to them. For this reason, it is important to make sure you communicate your meaning as effectively as possible. Do not assume your facial expression is enough to convey what you are thinking.

- **Hold discussions only when your partner is calm.** Avoid raising important issues with your partner when they are suffering from an episode of BPD, such as exhibiting mood swings. When faced with decision-making in such a state, a BPD sufferer is likely to act rashly, without thinking the issues through. They are also more likely to be defensive or aggressive and may turn to self-deprecating or self-harming behaviors in order to help them cope.

- **Offer support**. We all need support from our loved ones from time to time, and BPD sufferers are no different. Make sure your partner knows you are there for them, in good times and bad.

- **Foster a sense of independence in your partner.** As we know, BPD can lead a person to greatly fear rejection. Even the smallest of separations such as a vacation or work trip can be a source of immense stress. But these separations can be beneficial for fostering a sense of independence in your partner. Make sure you have parts of your lives that are independent from each other; your own hobbies and circles of friends. While of course it is wonderful to have a partner with whom you can share so much of your life, having separate interests is great for your partner's sense of independence. If you are apart for longer than a few hours, it can be helpful to check in on your partner, to ensure they understand that the separation is only temporary and that they are not being rejected.

- **Avoid blaming everything on their mental illness.** Remember that your partner's BPD does not define them. Avoid linking every part of their behavior to the BPD. After all, it is just one facet of who they are. Doing so can cause the disorder to become something of a put-down. See past the illness to your partner's personality and avoid labeling.

- **Take threats of self-harm seriously.** Threats of self-injury or suicide should always be taken seriously with a partner suffering from BPD. If your partner begins to exhibit signs of self-harming or suicidal behavior, call their therapist or your local suicide prevention helpline. See Chapter Fourteen for further information on how to act if your partner is exhibiting self-harming behavior.

Practice self-care. Living with a partner with BPD can be an enormous challenge. It is important to allow yourself time to step back and relax. Ensure you have your own support network in place; people you can rely on if the stress becomes overwhelming. Prioritize time for friends and hobbies, both alone and with your partner.

CHAPTER SIXTEEN

PARENTING A CHILD WITH BPD

Raising children can be an enormous challenge at the best of times. Parenting a child with borderline personality disorder can seem like an insurmountable difficulty. While many of the techniques discussed in Chapter Thirteen, Fourteen and Seventeen will be of great value to parents of BPD sufferers, here are a few important points when raising a child with BPD:

Don't take it personally.

While the onset of BPD can be linked to childhood trauma, it is important to acknowledge that this is not always the case. While an examination of your parenting styles can be beneficially, refrain from placing the blame for your child's condition squarely on your own shoulders. Recognize that you did – and are doing – the best you could do in the situation. Children with heightened emotional sensitivity take a special kind of parenting and it can be an enormous challenge for parents to know how to respond effectively.

Practice emotional independence.

As a parent, it is easy to let your child's moods determine the way you yourself are feeling. Being emotionally codependent on your BPD child can lead to emotional burnout and distress. Foster your own emotional independence and work at growing your own tolerance to distress. You may find the self-soothing techniques described in Chapter Eight and Ten useful for not only your child, but for you as well. By building your own control over your emotions, you will be able to show love and support for your child, without letting your mood be influenced by his or her own.

Have your whole family learn skills
for managing BPD.

The more people you and your child have around you that are able to successfully manage the symptoms of BPD, the smoother the management of the condition will be. Becoming well-versed in skills such as DBT can assist the whole family in providing as stable an up-bringing as possible for your child.

See past the stigma.

While looking at your child's behavior through the label of BPD can help you understand their behavior, be aware that the disorder comes with a great deal of stigma attached. Look past the illness to your child's unique personality and acknowledge that the BPD is just a small facet of who they are. Separate their BPD symptoms from their personality traits and understand who they are beneath the illness.

Have the whole family agree on boundaries.

As we have discussed in Chapter Fourteen, setting boundaries with regards to acceptable and unacceptable behavior is crucial for the successful management of BPD. When the situation involves a child, involve the whole family, especially the BPD sufferer themselves, in setting boundaries. Be sure to discuss the values behind the boundaries – make sure everyone understands why certain limitations are in place. Agree on what the consequences will be if these boundaries are broken. It can help to even have a written contract which all parties sign. Doing this will help everybody feel more in control of the situation. Do, however, acknowledge that change can be difficult for everybody, particularly your BPD child. Do not attempt to implement all the boundaries at once, rather introduce them one at a time.

Do not make empty threats.

As parents, it can be easy to resort to empty threats such as "If you don't eat your vege-tables, there will be no dessert." While these may have worked for young children, making such empty promises to older children and teenagers, especially those with BPD, are meaningless. Fully acknowledge the consequences discussed in your boundary-setting session and follow through with implementing them if the boundaries are crossed.

CHAPTER SEVENTEEN

DISARM THOSE WHO ARE
MANIPULATING YOU

Reasoning with someone suffering from borderline personality disorder can be akin to reasoning with a child – impossible. It can be enormously frustrating and difficult not to get drawn into the provocations of your partner, friend or family member. But as you are no doubt aware, responding with hostility of your own is a surefire way to make the conflict escalate. In this chapter we will take a look at some of the techniques you can employ in order to disarm a BPD sufferer when they are acting with hostility towards you. These are crucial steps that can prevent your loved one's aggression from turning into a full-blown crisis.

Firstly, acknowledge that, as someone in a relationship of any sort with a person with BPD, you are, by default, part of the problem. Regardless of how well you handle your loved one's emotional outbursts, the very fact that you are there to respond and communicate with them means you are both a part of the issue, and also the solution. While you do not have the power to "fix" the individual with BPD, you can change your behavior towards them, in turn forcing them to change the way they behave towards you.

People with BPD will attack you in order to get one of three reactions from you: guilt, helplessness or hostility. As we have learned, people with BPD often grew up in a household full of conflict, so seek to recreate such an environment in order to feel a sense of normalcy. If a person with BPD succeeds at getting one of these three reactions from you, they will keep up the same behavior in order to get the same reaction again and again. Failing to get the desired behavior will usually see a BPD become more harmonious. However, if they have received the desired reaction from this particular person at least once in the past, they will continue trying for a long time before they change their behavior. For this reason, it is vital to do your best not to "reward" the bad behavior of a BPD by exhibiting the reaction they are seeking.

What not to do:

Of course it can be difficult to keep your cool and think clearly when faced with an emotional or physical attack from someone with BPD. The following steps can help you disarm your loved one before the conflict turns into a crisis.

- **Do not make undue sacrifices.** While you may well want to do everything in your power to help your loved one feel better, it is important not to do anything that is going to cause you to suffer in the long run. For example, do not stay up all night talking on the phone with them if you have work the next day. Do not lend them money you cannot afford, in the belief that they will have nowhere else to turn. Do not rearrange your entire schedule to fit in with their rapidly changing plans. Help your loved one by respecting your own needs.

- **Do your best not to get defensive.** While this is much easier said than done, avoid responding to their aggressive behavior with lines such as "I'm only trying to help, you know."

- **Do your best not to act hostile.** While this again can seem like an impossible task, responding to BPD aggression with hostility of your own will only exacerbate the situation. If you feel your own rage beginning to surface, take a few deep breaths to calm yourself, count to ten or remove yourself from the situation. Return to the conversation when you – and preferably also your loved one – are feeling calm.

  Do not allow yourself to feel guilty. When your loved one is assaulting you with a barrage on insults, it can be difficult to ignore their hurtful words. Acknowledge this is simply a manifestation of an illness. Do not allow yourself to feel responsible or guilty for making them feel a particular way. You cannot be expected to "fix" it, or to solve the impossible, unsolvable dilemmas brought about by the disorder.

- **Do not lecture them.** Sure, we all know drugs are harmful or reckless driving can put the lives of many innocent people at risk. But arguing these points will have no effect on someone with BPD. Remember, reasoning with them can be like attempting to reason with a child. They will only respond in an argumentative way.

- **Do not act superior.** One of the major struggles for someone with BPD is that they are attempting to exist within a dysfunctional social network. While this is largely brought about by the disorder, of course, you yourself, along with everyone else in their sphere constitutes part of this network. While this is not a cause for guilt or laying blame at your own feet, it is a reminder not to act superior, or believe that you are any better than the person with BPD.

- **Do not censor issues.** If difficult issues such as suicide or violence arise, do not attempt to suppress them or change the subject. Instead, do your best to address them in a calm and rational way. Enlist the help of a therapist or counselor if you feel out of your depth.

- **Do not attempt to deal with suicide attempts on your own.** When someone with BPD is a part of your life, you must be prepared for incidents of self-harm or even attempted suicide. If such an incident arises, it is important to get the person to a psychologist or other health professional as soon as possible. Do not attempt to deal with suicidal situations alone. See Chapter Fourteen for further information on dealing with emergencies.

What to Do:

- **Understand and acknowledge their strengths.** Though it may seem otherwise, many people with borderline personality disorder have a high level of interpersonal skills. This is evidenced by their ability to manipulate others and bring about the very emotional responses they are seeking. When attempting to disarm a BPD, be sure to acknowledge this strength. Understand that their reactions have likely come about through a childhood of being invalidated by their family and so they carry the underlying belief that their job is to ensure everyone continues to undervalue them. Counter this by finding and acknowledging strengths in the person (such as their high level of inter-personal skills). Rather than looking at their behavior as a problem of someone with BPD, see that they are in fact very reasonable and expected responses for someone suffering from this disorder. Acknowledge that it is not a case of them being immature, or deliberately malicious.

- **Keep Calm.** If you do not agree with something a BPD is saying or doing, tell them so. But do it in a calm and restrained manner, even in the face of their hostility. Do so without arguing about who is right or wrong. If you feel as though something you have said is being misinterpreted (a common occurrence when communicating BPD sufferers), gently explain what you meant, without focusing on the fact that the person with BPD misunderstood or made a mistake.

- **Be Honest.** If you have done something wrong or made a mistake, be honest and admit it. However, do not under any circumstances admit to things you have not done, just to pacify someone with BPD. While this may calm the storm for a brief period, it has the potential to lead to bigger issues in the future.

- **Set Boundaries.** To handle the aggression and acting-out of someone with BPD, it is important to set firm boundaries, and stick to them. By clear about what you will and will not tolerate, with regards to language, aggression and violence. If your loved one crosses a boundary, immediately remove yourself from the situation and refuse to engage with them any longer. Walking away when they engage in unacceptable behavior will make the connection in their brain that behaving in this manner will result in them being left alone. Because of the BPD sufferer's intense fear of rejection, this action can have a great benefit when it comes to them learning what behavior is and isn't acceptable. Be sure your loved one understands both the boundaries you have set and the consequences of breaking them. Help them to appreciate that you walking away does not mean you don't love them, but rather that you will not tolerate emotional abuse. You can also let them know that if they ever feel emotionally threatened by you, they are welcome to do the same.

- **Pay Attention to Your Tone of Voice.** Regardless of what you are saying, if you are responding to a BPD sufferer with anxiety or nervousness in your voice, they will be aware of it. This will render anything you say to diffuse the situation ineffective. Practice speaking with a firm, matter-of-fact and forthright tone. This both naturally boosts your confidence and removes a level of emotion from the confrontation. We often sound very different in reality to the way we perceive ourselves, so practice by recording yourself on your phone and listening back so you can hear exactly how you sound.

- **Disagree, Rather Than Invalidate.** As mentioned above, people suffering from BPD are often unconsciously inviting those around them to invalidate them. They often do this through making outlandish or wildly exaggerated statements. While it can be tempting to invalidate this statement by flat-out denying it, it is important to acknowledge that, on almost every occasion, this statement contains at least a grain of truth. For example, someone with BPD might say to you "Life is terrible." While your instinct may be to reassure this person that things are not that bad, recognize that for someone suffering from BPD, things most certainly *can* be that bad. So rather than invalidating their statement, acknowledge the truth of what they are saying, without accepting the exaggeration. For example: "It does sound like you've been having a difficult time lately," validates the truth within the statement, while refusing to agree that life is *always* that bad.

- **Accept That There Are Times You Will Feel Helpless.** The person with BPD may continue to make demand after demand on you to help them feel better, when the both of you know there is nothing you can do to improve the situation. In these cases, the BPD sufferer's goal is actually to *make* you feel helpless – and then make you feel anxious about your helplessness. To counter this, acknowledge that you are, in fact, helpless, but allow yourself to accept and be okay with this.

  For example, someone with BPD may come to you the night before an important exam and say "I haven't studied and I don't know any of the material. I am definitely going to fail."

In a situation like this, it is obvious that there is unlikely to be a positive outcome. You know that and so does the person with BPD. If you attempt to come up with a solution, the BPD sufferer will likely see it as rubbish, and it will come across as though you are treating them as a fool.

Instead, calmly respond along the lines of "I wish there was something I could do to help," acknowledging the problem but accepting you are unable to assist with a solution. Remember, honesty is crucial when dealing with someone with BPD

- **Respond Calmly to Illogical Statements.** There will be many occasions on which a BPD sufferer will make arguments that seem absurd or illogical. For example, they may say something along the lines of "I can't get by without cocaine."

  While to you, this may seem like an untrue statement, resist the urge to argue your point outright. People with BPD are not stupid. They likely know just how damaging cocaine can be. However, there is likely more than a little truth to their claim that they cannot get by without it. Arguing flat out against these illogical statements does the job of invalidating the BPD sufferer, something we must seek to avoid. However, if you truly feel the need to discuss the matter with them, to do so by including a caveat such as "I know you know this already, but…" Also, keep your statements short and to-the-point. Going into long-winded discussions about why cocaine is bad, for example, only serves to make the BPD sufferers look unintelligent. If they refuse to drop the subject or continue to argue, respond calmly with something like "I disagree with you," or "I'm not going to insult your intelligence by arguing any more about this."

- **Find the true meaning beneath hostile comments.** People suffering from BPD can make comments which sound outward hostile or aggressive but are often ambiguous. For example, they may ask bitterly, "Why do you always act like my mother?" While this can come across as a hostile comment, they may actually be making a comment on your caring nature. You can respond by simply acknowledging what they say to be true, for example, "Yes, I care about you very much."

While it is ingrained in us to notice body language and tone of voice, in such a situation, it is beneficial to do the exact opposite and pay attention purely to the words being spoken. This will help you see past the hostility to the true meaning beneath.

- **Be Conscious of Attempts at Creating Division.** There have been many occasions in which people hospitalized for BPD have caused staff on the ward to argue over the best way to treat them. This is a situation often unconsciously engineered by the BPD sufferer, though the technique of "mode flipping" (i.e., behaving in a pitiable, meek manner to one person and hostile and aggressive to another). This will undoubtedly lead to disagreements in the best way to handle such an individual. Sufferers of BPD are also prone to engineering such situations among family and friendship groups. The best way to counter such a technique is to be aware of it. If you find yourself arguing with a family member about your loved one with BPD, acknowledge that the situation may have been set up by the BPD sufferer themselves. Ask the family member with whom you are arguing what they are basing their opinion on. Calmly present your own arguments, and then "compare notes." Can you see any disparities or attempts by the BPD sufferer to create division? From here, you can agree on the best way forward, now you have all the information.

In such a situation however, it is important not to invalidate the BPD sufferer. For example, if they are trying to play you off against another family member, they may also make disparaging remarks about that person to you. If you stand up for this person and argue against what the BPD sufferer is saying, you are automatically invalidating them. If this situation arises, do your best not to respond emotionally and present any disagreements in a calm and respectful manner.

- **Own Up to Your Mistakes.** Being around someone with BPD is on ongoing challenge, and there are bound to be times in which you behave in ways you did not intend to. You may find yourself acting aggressively or saying things you did not mean. If this happens, own up to your mistake. Wait until you are both calm and apologize for your behavior. But be sure to apologize only for the damaging thing you did or said, *not* for the negative emotions that led to it. For example: "I'm sorry I criticized you, but I felt as though were automatically dismissing everything I said to you without taking it into consideration." While apologizing can be difficult, exhibit a strong sense of integrity and responsibility. Be someone your loved one can look up to and admire.

CHAPTER EIGHTEEN

BREAKING UP WITH SOMEONE WHO HAS BORDERLINE PERSONALITY DISORDER

As we have learned, people with BPD have a heightened sensitivity to rejection, whether real or imagined. And for this reason, breaking up with someone with BPD can be immensely difficult. When faced with abandonment, BPD sufferers can resort to impulsive, damaging behavior, self-injury and even suicide. Because of this, there are many people who never leave their unhappy relationships with borderline partners, condemning both themselves and their partner to a life of unhappiness and conflict.

Leaving someone with borderline personality disorder takes a lot of courage, but if you are unhappy in the relationship and you feel it has no future, it must be done. You cannot spend your life in an unhappy relationship and nor can you expect your partner to do the same.

Here are some important things to take into consideration when ending a relationship with someone with BPD:

Give yourself permission to end the relationship.

For many people, this can be the biggest challenge. They do not want to be seen as someone who would deliberately hurt another, especially someone who faces so many other challenges in their day-to-day life. Breaking up with. BPD sufferer can lead their partners to have intense feelings of guilt. There have been numerous cases in which people in relationships with BPD sufferers have seemingly willed themselves into illness, and eventually, death, in order to "leave" the relationship.

But it is important to remember that this is *your* life. If you are anxious and unhappy in the relationship more than you are enjoying it, that is a sure sign that you need to get out. Give yourself permission to put yourself first.

Be kind and succinct.

When it comes to ending the relationship, endeavor to do so in a kind manner. Tell your partner calmly and clearly that you have appreciated your time together, but that it has now come to an end. Avoid going into detailed reasons about why the relationship is ending. There is no need to lay blame or point out all the reasons you are leaving. While doing so may ease your own guilt a little, it will likely exacerbate your partner's sense of loss and harm their fragile sense of self-worth.

Allow Yourself to Mourn the Loss

When leaving any relationship, no matter how damaging, it is normal to feel a sense of loss and emptiness. Acknowledge that this is okay and give yourself permission to feel these emotions. Allow yourself to cry, to feel grief, to miss your partner. These are all normal experiences when a relationship is ending.

You may have been led to believe that making the right decision results only in "good" feelings, therefore, these negative emotions signal you have made the wrong choice. This, coupled with any guilt that may be arising, has the potential to have you questioning your decision. Remind yourself that you have made the decision that's best for yourself – and stick to it!

Set Boundaries – and Stick to Them

Once you have ended the relationship, it is in the BPD sufferer's nature to continue to call, text or attempt to visit you for months, or even years. This is due to their inability to accept rejection and their deep-seated fear of being alone. While this can be an immensely challenging period for you, the best thing you can do is not engage in any of their attempts at communication. Doing so will only prolong the pain of the situation for both of you.

In an attempt to get your attention, your ex-partner may fluctuate between accusations and hurtful comments, and heartfelt expressions of love. Remember, for many people with BPD, there is no middle ground – only black and white. And they will do whatever they can to try and regain control and win you back.

Naturally, refusing to respond to a BPD's attempts at communication can leave you guilt-ridden and fearful. You may worry your ex-partner will resort to self-harming or even attempt suicide. But accept that you cannot be held responsible for their behavior forever. You must begin to put yourself first. If you become fearful that your ex-partner may engage in behavior that is damaging to themselves or others, speak to their family members and/or therapist, then remove yourself from the situation as soon as possible.

Reclaim Your Belongings

The end of a relationship is something someone with BPD has a difficult time accepting. Because of this, they make seek to hang on to your belongings after the breakup, in an attempt to keep hold of a piece of "you." This is their way of not accepting that the relationship is truly over and of "keeping the door open" for far longer than you may wish.

If you are considering leaving a relationship, it is a good idea to remove any stuff you have from your partner's home beforehand. This will remove the potential for any bitter conflicts that can arise when you try and reclaim your belongings, along with the chance of anything being destroyed in your partner's rage.

Take Care of Yourself

Being in – and ending – a relationship with a BPD can have an immense effect on your own health and wellbeing. Living through months, or years, or emotional torment and manipulation can wear down your self-esteem, often leading you to believe the accusations flung at you by your ex-partner in the heat of the moment to be the truth.

This constant emotional stress can have a very damaging effect on not only the psyche, but the physical body as well. Stress has been linked to countless illnesses, ranging from heart conditions to migraines to cancer.

Allow yourself space and time to engage in self-care. Undertake relaxing activities such as yoga or meditation and make time for your friends, interests and hobbies. If you are struggling to get past your sense of guilt or loss once the relationship has ended, seeking the help of a therapist or counselor can have an enormous benefit.

Examine Your Own Attachment Issues

Now you have managed to step away from a damaging relationship with BPD, it may be a good time to examine your own issues regarding attachment and why you love the people you do.

As we know, people with BPD need conflict in their relationship to create a sense of normalcy and stave off feelings of emptiness. But it is also worth asking yourself what drew you to your BPD partner in the first place? Was it their charisma and energy? Or are you yourself carrying attachment issues that led you to seek out a potentially damaging relationship?

As people with BPD generally have a strong desire for both physical and emotional intimacy, they often tend towards insecure attachment styles, that can lead to damaging relationships. When they find themselves in romantic relationships, sufferers of BPD often experience chronic stress, abuse at the hands of their partners and unwanted pregnancies. Ask yourself whether your relationship with a BPD sufferer was a damaging one for both of you. If so, what role did you play?

We learn who to love and how to love from our parents and upbringing. If you grew up with parents who were absent or abusive in any way, these issues may have manifested themselves as an insecure attachment style, leading you to seek out relationships with people who will have a negative effect on you. In all likelihood, both you and your ex-partner have suffered trauma in your childhood, leading you both to form your relationship.

Perhaps as a child you were neglected by your parents, leading you to become a people pleaser. You may have learned that the only way to gain attention and praise was to behave in a perfect manner and suppress any negative emotions as doing so may have antagonized emotionally or physically abusive parents. People pleasers are often drawn to BPDs because they represent your *shadow side* – that part of your being that you suppress and prevent from seeing the light of day; namely your negative emotions such as anger, fear and jealousy. A person with BPD has no difficulty expressing these emotions, and by pairing yourself with them, you are allowing yourself to become "whole."

Or perhaps, like your partner, you grew up in a household of chaos and conflict and by seeking out a relationship with a BPD sufferer, you are simply recreating the tumultuous environment which feels most natural to you.

Working with a counselor or therapist can help you identify and remove your own attachment issues. By recognizing exactly what drew you towards your ex-partner in the first place, you can address these issues and save yourself the pain of repeating the pattern in future relationships.

CONCLUSION

While borderline personality disorder has the potential to wreak havoc on both sufferers and their loved ones, it is important to acknowledge that there is hope. Hopefully this book has shown you that, just as there are many different degrees of BPD, there are also many ways of tackling the disorder.

By working on their own emotional management techniques, and in conjunction with their therapists and loved ones, BPD sufferers have the potential to greatly improve their symptoms and go on to live their lives to the fullest.

While the road to recovery is bound to be a challenging one, vast improvement is possible.

There are many people with BPD who go on to live long, productive and happy lives, holding down steady jobs, meaningful relationships and loving families. There is no reason you or loved one cannot do the same.

BORDERLINE MOTHER

DAVID LAWSON PHD

INTRODUCTION

Fear; that stupid feeling you can feel in your bones that makes you feel helpless and afraid, that sense that is telling you to back off, to give up. Anger; yet another thing you can't control and you feel is getting the better of you. That anger is stopping you from opening yourself up to others, but you need them; you can't be by yourself because you feel alone and afraid. As you look into the world, you see the people and the relationships you want, but you are afraid and insecure. That kind of closeness is what you need – you can feel that deep inside your soul – but you do not know how to approach them. You feel damaged and uncertain. You find yourself in a loophole, an endless, vicious circle of emptiness and you don't know how you ended up here. You just feel that you need to get out. You are not alone, so don't be afraid.

If you think that this your fault, please believe it is not. You're just one of many people in the dark and desperate for light. The first thing you have to realize is that it's not your fault. You must not blame yourself. You are not guilty, but the fingers of destiny and the unfortunate set of circumstances that led you to see the world in the way you do, have caused you to feel guilty about everything. This book is here to support you, to be with you and to help you. Its purpose is to help you understand that you are not to blame for the scars on your soul. Its purpose is to show you the truth and the truth is simple. You're the victim of a toxic relationship. You can't keep friendships, you don't trust others and you don't think there are good days ahead. That's not true; you have to know that. This is the most important part of your healing process and a way to get back on track. You are only a victim of an unhealthy relationship caused by living with your mother who suffered from Borderline Personality Disorder. Your mother was neither guilty nor aware that you were suffering. She loved you and wanted the best for you, however, her condition is the main reason you cannot trust others now. Don't resent your mother. After all, it wasn't her fault that she had Borderline Personality Disorder. Deep down, she loved you and you need to know that. But unfortunately, because of her life and her condition, she was not able to show that love for you and that is why today you feel that you are different from others.

You can't trust others, you can't build a stable relationship, you just can't open up to anyone because you're afraid you're never going to be able to trust those who enter your life. It's a very heavy burden to carry. You probably spent your entire life, or at least a good part of your childhood, in the prison your mind built in response to your mother's actions. You never knew what kind of day was waiting for you. You constantly felt loved and unwanted at the same time. At first, you thought it was all your fault or that such a relationship between you and your mother was normal. It made you feel weird seeing other kids having no such problems with their parents. You probably didn't understand why every day in that toxic relationship was different. One day you were the best thing in the world for her, the next, you were the worst and guilty of many things. You were often criticized and were unable to understand why all of this was happening. This book will help you learn that the world is different from the one you know. That you don't have to be withdrawn, or an outcast, and that you are not unwanted. Your value is not less than other people's, you are no less important than others. This book will help you understand that there is a whole other world out there, and that you can build a normal and stable connection with people. That you can love and that you will be loved.

What you went through and what you experienced was very difficult. The pain of living with a mother who suffered from Borderline Personality Disorder is a topic that has not been sufficiently researched and which is controversial because some do not consider Borderline Personality Disorder a disease.

Someone wise once said, "all happy families are the same, but every unhappy family is different and unhappy in its way." What is most important about all this is the fact that you are not alone. There are millions of other people who are just like you. And they all feel like you; lost, unable to carry the burden they have been struggling with since the very beginning of life. And they also feel trapped, hopeless and they think there they are worthless and unworthy of other people's love and attention. That is simply not true.

All the children who went through such a childhood were in constant pain and suffering because they thought they caused everything that happened to them, including the humiliation, and the verbal and physical violence, but they were only victims, nothing more. Many of them – perhaps including you – may have wondered if life is worth living. Many developed suicidal thoughts because they were confused and frightened from the very beginning of their lives. The sad truth is that all the children who grew up with mothers who suffered from this condition are only victims. Not all stories end well, but for you, just by being here today, reading this, means that your story is not over yet. This means that you have succeeded in spite of everything you went through. You should be proud of yourself. Life is worth living, remember that. This book will help you open your eyes, to understand that this is a great pain, but that you can overcome it. You can have friends, normal social relationships, a normal life.

Until now, you've been living on the edge, constantly wondering "how and why." Although Borderline Personality Disorder has ceased to be a social taboo and is now receiving increasing attention, we believe you did not know all about this severe mental condition. Borderline Personality Disorder is na very controversial term. Not only are there many disagreements between scientists and researchers about how this disorder occurs and how it develops. There is even an idea that the disorder does not exist at all. Some classification systems do not classify it as a disorder; others find that people with borderline pathology are increasingly encountering it. In the sea of different definitions, it is very difficult to find the answer to the question of what is or is not a Borderline Personality Disorder. In this book we will explain why this is not just your problem, every child in the same situation goes through the same thing. The logical question, then, is why is this the case?

The child is quite dependent on the mother in those early days and needs his mother's support and love for normal development. If he does not get what he needs, he will not be able to adequately resolve the separation and independence phase. As a result, the child will not develop into a mature personality, but will always use some of the primitive defense mechanisms, will not perceive other people as whole (because he or she will not be developmentally rounded), and will slip between the idealization and the impairment of other important persons from his or her environment. In the borderline state, we always encounter the following triad – aggression, depression and a vague identity. An inner void can have at least two meanings, which are by no means contradictory. It can refer to the physical and the psychic. In the first sense, a person can be empty when, for example, they are hungry. In the second sense, emptiness refers to effect, feeling, or absence of feeling. Emptiness, in the psychic sense, is a term that confuses many. For those who feel it and the experts who deal with it, the very word "emptiness" indicates the absence of something. Since it is a shortcoming, it is difficult to give a precise definition of what exactly is missing. Some authors talk about "feeling empty." However, that phrase is contradictory. Feeling indicates bias, polarization and, to put it bluntly, something. The void indicates "nothing." How can anyone feel nothing? If he feels something, is it the same as not feeling anything? That all seems very confusing and it is.

It turns out that the answer to this question is both difficult and paradoxical. When one is not feeling, that person has not developed any emotions about anything. When, however, one feels nothingness, that inner "nothing" is very intense and quite polarized and represents "something." To feel nothingness is to feel a significant unexplained amount of something we have no say in, something dead in us, something that has died and left its bad aspects in our interior, or something that never even came to life to make us feel alive inside.

Although statistics show that there are more borderline organizations than ever, the question is how many diagnoses have been properly established. Does this question necessarily arise if one has in mind the many disagreements of scientists about "what is this entity if we can call it an entity at all?" The sources of suffering for borderline individuals are unrecognized to them. A feeling of emptiness that leads to forced action – "acting out" is a term that represents the repetition of unconscious childhood patterns to overcome them in the present. As these childhood problems are unconscious, acting out cannot be resolved. Being around people brings a kind of immediate relief from tension, and on the other side, BPD persons might see this interaction as unbearable.

While there are many disagreements about borderline issues, it would be good to try to systematize some of the backbones that most agree with and to provide some kind of picture of borderline issues.

The main problems are the instability of self-understanding, interpersonal relationships, and mood swings. A characteristic pattern is a behavior characterized by instability of interpersonal relationships, self-experience, emotions, and control of emotions, which can be identified as a pattern in early adulthood. The condition is marked by great effort in avoiding real or fictional relationships, bonding with others and engaging in close relationships. Interpersonal relationships are volatile and intense. The identity of oneself is impermanent and disturbed. Impulsiveness is present in at least two of the following activities, which are potentially harmful to that person: negligent, promiscuous and excessive sexual behavior, drug abuse, excessive eating or drinking or spending money. Suicidal tendencies or suicide attempts may be present. Instead of suicidal thoughts, the borderline person can self-punish himself in various other ways (varieties of psychophysical self-harm). There is a chronic sense of emptiness. The feeling of anger is intense, difficult or impossible to control and (given the previously described acting out) is unsuitable for a particular situation.

According to official statistics, this type of disorder is present in about 1-2% of the population. The diagnosis is twice as common in females as in men. It's about emotionally immature, unstable, capricious and quarrelsome black and white worldviews. Such persons often have a misconception of themselves and other people, and they are unpredictable and unable to control their overwhelming (often destructive) emotions. In the event of a failure in their essential activities (work, college, emotional relationships, socializing) they often tend to engage in self-destructive behavior. This disorder is quite common in combination with other psychiatric disorders.

Borderline organized personalities are difficult, both to themselves and their environment. An inability to control emotions; a black and white worldview and impulsive reactions lead to both destructive and self-destructive behaviors. Although borderline people are not necessarily "giving up" people, relationships made with them are chaotic, intense, often short-lived, and usually very turbulent. They try to enter into relationships with others to regulate their tension and that can often fill others with a sense of emptiness. Borderline people can be in a state of idealism and euphoria, and others may think for a moment that they have succeeded in finding an ideal partner. But soon they can feel severe disappointment because the other person cannot patch up the gaping emptiness and chronic unfulfillment. Then there is the devaluation of the other person and, often, the search for someone new, the "ideal other," who unfortunately they will not be able to find. For every child, this is a terrible condition to grow up in. But you must understand, this is a very difficult social problem, mainly because the relationship between you and your mother is supposed to be the purest possible relationship. And this is not some kind of easily recognized condition. A BPD person lacks insight and the ability to see reality as it is. As such, he needs the help of another compassionate being to overcome difficulties and strike a balance in the chaotic world. Mother loves you and that is the main problem; no one who is looking can know for sure what is going on and you are trapped in the web of mixed emotions. That is why you feel like you are beneath everyone and that kind of feeling is quite normal; you simultaneously resent your mother but you love her too. We know that your self-confidence is shaken, but you can and will get better.

Your mother's condition is a very difficult mental state. This issue is so complex that many psychiatrists are unable to make the right diagnosis. Although this condition was first mentioned centuries ago, it was not given much importance. It is a great triad that develops in a person that can destroy a child. Your mother is an important part of your life; there is no doubt about it. This is why this is a very important topic. Everything begins with the mother. Each child looks for a warm hug, a nice word, a kiss, and tenderness. Showing tenderness and closeness to the child also helps these children understand what love is and to convey that love to their children when they become parents. This also applies to all other aspects of life, such as romantic relationships, partnerships of all kinds, and friendships. This is the primary reason you are unable to connect with people. In Borderline Personality Disorder, the mother is both addictive and aggressive and often has no boundaries. In moments she cannot see the difference between good and bad and you are the victim. To one who is only a child, anger and love are often torn out at the same time. You likely never understood it as a kid. We believe that one of the main problems for a child growing up in such a relationship is that the child cannot understand what is going on around him. The child has just arrived in the world, and is getting to know the world as he grows up. We think that the main problem is that the child cannot understand and compare.

This is precisely why the child gets a distorted picture of the world. We will give a banal example of the ability to understand and compare. We believe that the ability to compare is the ability to differentiate between different things. For example, someone may say that one cup is good or that it is bad because he has seen other cups. As he watched the cups, he developed the ability to figure out which cup is good and which is bad. It's the same with a child. But as a child, metaphorically speaking, you couldn't see other cups and that's the main problem. Your cup was your mother. You didn't have another mother. So you couldn't understand anything. For this reason, you and many other victims have developed a feeling that you are not worthy, that you are weak, that others are better.

You had to endure verbal and psychological violence. And you didn't know what was going on. You later learned to love your mother no matter what. Because after all, she's your mother who knew how to show you love from time to time. But you can help yourself, and you will. This book will help you to understand your problem, to confess to yourself that you have a problem and help you not to be judgmental to yourself. You can even help your mother. Although therapies can often be very long and difficult, research agrees that therapeutic assistance is beneficial for most borderline persons. Many therapies, however, are incomplete, and a "full recovery" does not always occur. However, by caring for and understanding the therapeutic relationship, borderline individuals often move towards a better, more integrated and fuller life. Just remember, you are here still, and by reading this book you are making a decision to heal your traumatic experience and to move on. That is priceless, and that is why you are a natural-born fighter and you will win in this fight also.

CHAPTER ONE

UNDERSTANDING THE BORDERLINE MOTHER

How do you understand someone who does not understand himself? Understanding a mother suffering from Borderline Personality Disorder is not easy. These are people who in many cases are unaware of their problem. They are high-risk, always conflict-ready, and difficult to reach. The usage of the term Borderline Personality Disorder (BPD) started in the 1930s, and the name was symbolically coined by Adolf Stern as the disorder is on the border between psychosis and neurosis.

Towards the end of the seventeenth century, English physician Thomas Sydenham wrote a frequently quoted sentence about a number of his patients in a letter: "They love the same ones beyond measure but they also hate them for no reason." He described their sudden outbursts of anger, pain, and fear. Of course, the disorder that Sydenham described was not called Borderline Personality Disorder (he choose the term "hysterical" for women and "hypochondriac" for men), but his description was a good prediction. Even today, the symptoms he cited are the two most important symptoms when making a diagnosis of Borderline Personality Disorder.

So this condition is not new. Symptoms have been reported earlier, but only in the last few decades have they become more significant. The severity of this condition is so big that it requires deep analysis.

The borderline condition is characterized by unsuccessful separation from the mother, which developmentally would normally occur at an early period. This failure to separate often comes because the mother (probably due to her problems) did not respond positively to the child's attempts to become independent, and to experiment with the world. The mother tends to be dismissive, depressed, or even angry when the child begins (naturally and developmentally normal) to separate from her and tries to get to know his wider environment.

'e can say that early traumatic experiences and genetics are major factors in the development of Borderline Personality Disorder. All those suffering from this condition say they feel a void. It's a void they can't even describe to themselves. The main problem is that they are trying to bridge that gap through aggression, possessiveness or self-destruction. This is a very big problem, and it is of great importance when people suffering from this condition are mothers. The main problems are the instability of self-understanding, interpersonal relationships, and mood swings. A characteristic pattern is a behavior characterized by instability of interpersonal relationships, self-experience, emotions, and control of emotions, which can be identified as a pattern in early adulthood.

If the mother cannot understand herself, how can she understand the child? A mother with this condition is in a terrible position; she is both an aggressor and a victim. She is considered an aggressor because this condition leads to terrible behavior and a lack of empathy towards the child. Then, because of her condition, she terrorizes all the people around her and the child is best suited to serve as a pressure valve. On the other hand, the mother is also a victim because when the aggression, panic or other behaviors pass, she suffers, because she knows she has hurt the child. She suffers deeply and sincerely because she is aware that in the onset of anger, she hurt the innocent child she loves. Then in every way, she tries to make up for that outburst towards the child, so she acts protectively and she is then full of love for the child. This lasts until the next attack caused by the condition, so the terrible cycle repeats. This leaves the child very confused and sad because he does not know or understand how the mother who loves him now hates him again. Of course, in this sad story, the child is the biggest victim, but we have to be objective; in most cases, the victim is also the mother who suffers because she hurts the child and cannot control herself.

Although this condition is followed by unstable emotions, and a tendency to experiencing strong euphoria and intense disappointment, borderline individuals are, in fact, mostly dysthymic. Dysthymia is a chronic, non-psychotic depressive disorder that lasts for at least two years and is characterized by a depressed mood and overall loss of life satisfaction. Therapies for people with these problems are, for the most part, long and difficult. The basic things that a therapist should offer to a borderline person are empathy (compassion), acceptance, as well as showing that he or she will be there and will stay with the client, will not leave him or impair him, and will be able to tolerate his sudden mood swings, anger, and often hatred and other self-destructive manifestations. Therefore, both the therapist and the client must "endure" the therapy. The shift is slow, but if a person is determined to accept help, they will, step by step, build up broken parts of their personality and reorganize early traumatic experiences. Borderline Personality Disorder is consistently inconsistent and stable in its instability. A BPD person lacks insight and the ability to see reality as it is. As such, he needs the help of another compassionate being to overcome difficulties and strike a balance in the chaotic world.

It is important to recognize this problem and help your mother, because the consequences are dreadful unless both mother and child are helped in time. One of the basic characteristics of Borderline Personality Disorder is emotional deregulation. Mothers with this disorder experience major mood swings accompanied by intense and sudden anger, often directed at their loved ones. In some cases, they have a personality that is "high risk" for conflict. This means that they have recurring patterns of behavior, where they focus their anger on specific offenders, which prolongs or escalates conflicts. If a child is a target, he needs to understand what this is all about. This is a major mental health problem that affects the relationships of millions of people every day. The main problem regarding Borderline Personality Disorder is related to living with a person who suffers from the disorder, especially when that someone is a person you depend on; your mother.

Causes of personality disorders are almost always associated with genetic predispositions when combined with the environment during childhood. The biopsychosocial approach to discovering the causes of personality disorders, i.e. the correlation of an individual's genetic, social and psychological background, is increasingly emphasized. Early childhood experiences have been shown to play almost the most important role in the development of the disorder. Excessive criticism, lack of attention, neglect, physical or psychological abuse, and many other childhood circumstances can be the trigger for a personality disorder that is already present in a person's genetic background. Often, different combinations of personality disorders also occur, so borderline personality disorder often occurs in combination with affective bipolar disorder.

The situation with the most consequences when it comes to Borderline Personality Disorder is certainly when the mother suffers from this disorder. This condition has devastating consequences on the children and if it's not properly recognized and treated it will most likely develop into the same condition in the child, or it will ruin the child's self-confidence for life.

Continuous entanglement in chaotic interpersonal relationships is one of the most recognizable features of Borderline Personality Disorder. In chronic avoidance of loneliness, these individuals often engage in dysfunctional relationships, despite intense feelings of victimization from partners.

So we know what it is like to live a life with the mother who suffers from this condition. She is constantly on edge; she loves and hates her child at the same time. If the relationship between mother and child occurs in the classic "nuclear" family, the child will often be forced to watch the constant verbal (and sometimes not just verbal) argument with the father. The child will often feel helpless and afraid in early childhood, but in the later years this will encourage rebellion within the child or the child will become lonely and associative, unable to trust anyone, and if the things escalate, that child will develop ideas that life is worthless and the idea of taking his own life and intensive thinking about suicide will occur. Yes, the pain is enormous and pressure is great, but you must understand that this is not your fault. You must see the problem with open eyes and be able to see the wider picture. Your mother may have scared you for life but do you still love her? Probably you do because you must understand that she did not ask for this, no one wants to be mentally ill. But the damage is done already, and you must go on.

The same thing will happen if the child is raised by a single mother who suffers from this condition, with the difference that mother may have numerous sexual partners and that can cause a whole new wave of traumas.

A mother is the beginning of everything. Even if she psychologically harmed her child, it is only a consequence of her poor childhood or poor relationship with her parents. A mother who often leaves her child with relatives, takes it too early to kindergarten, or needs more space for herself, her career or hobby can have a negative influence on the child. In adulthood, that child will have difficult relationships with the opposite sex: first, they will love to madness, then they will hate fiercely. In such cases, it is impossible to build a healthy relationship. In families where the child has been a judge in a quarrel between mother and father, later he will feel disrespect for himself, and for him, the lives of others will become more important than his own.

Children of single mothers often struggle to build their family because of feelings of guilt relating to their parents. Girls often have inappropriate relationships with men, and young men who are sensitive to women's suffering choose a woman who pities them and then suffer a lifetime of lack of love. If the mother cares for the child both physically and emotionally, the child will surely grow into a healthy person. Otherwise, they will not respect themselves; they will always place themselves in second or third place. The influence of the mother on the mental development of the child is one of the most significant and perhaps the most exploited topics in psychology. But this should not be surprising, given the fact that the quality of that emotional connection depends on what kind of relationship the child will have with himself and the people around him.

Children recognize and experience this connection with their mother primarily through the emotions they have about her. For example, a child who falls and scratches his knee generally runs toward his mother, knowing that she will help him feel better. This is because the mother is the primary source of security, and the father is a "knight in shining armor" who fights for the family and protects it. However, if we look at the mother with a personality disorder, we can almost certainly state that she had a traumatic childhood. Personality disorders originate from unstable family environments, with frequent losses and multiple parental substitutions in which deep and lasting relationships were not possible. Many of them were born as unwanted children and were never fully accepted. Others had parents who were ambivalent and hostile, who were lied to, physically beaten, or sexually abused. The role of trauma suffered in early childhood, as noted by some authors, is considered to be a key factor in the development of Borderline Personality Disorder in future mothers.

1.1. So what is so particular in understanding the mother with a borderline personality disorder? We have to analyze two questions. First; what is the role of the mother in the family and the child's life? And second; what is the core of Borderline Personality Disorder?

The role of a mother is crucial for the child. Many childhood scholars, especially those with psychoanalytic orientations, emphasize the importance of the mother in the development and upbringing of the child. First, there is an unbreakable biological bond between mother and child that grows into a deep emotional relationship. So that is the main problem for you; the biological bond is created by nature and you are unable to resist that bond. The love of a mother is a special kind of love. When someone rejects you, it can have severe consequences but we hope that you will learn how to cope with them and help yourself and your mother. Studies have shown that various anxiety states of the child, which can manifest even into adulthood, have a prenatal origin. More specifically, they are associated with the secretion of the maternal stress hormone, cortisol.

One aspect of the protective function of the mother is physical, that is, the child must be bathed, nourished, fed. Another form of protection is psychological, which is reflected in the child's safety when they are together. This form of protection is of great importance for the mental health of the child, as it is precisely the first emotions that are exchanged with the mother. Breastfeeding is not only about satisfying the urge to eat, but also about creating effective attachment. Attachment, as author and researcher Bolbi calls it, even influences the child's future partnerships. The baby cries, his mother takes the baby in her arms, gently rocking him and saying, "I'll kiss it better." The baby calms down from his mom's kiss and smiles. We know this situation; every mother has experienced it several times. A close relationship with the mother is the main driving force behind the baby's development in the womb and during the first six months after birth. Scientific research has confirmed that the unborn baby responds to the mother's mood and emotions. When the mother is upset, her fetus is upset as well. When the mother experiences short-term shock, the fetus remains cramped and disturbed for hours afterward. During all nine months of pregnancy, the baby is in inseparable physical and physiological contact with the mother. This cannot change abruptly after birth. When the baby comes into the world, she is not yet in the environment, but she perceives

light, hears voices and feels pleasure from her mother's touch. That is why the physical c
ness of skin to skin in the first hours after birth is so important. It remains important for many
months to come. A mother's love is a fundamental physiological need that ensures development, as is food.

Regarding the other question, the answer is very difficult. Arrieti calls borderline personalities "tornado personalities." She says that they often live in an atmosphere of "disaster and
doom," chronically dissatisfied, disappointed, with a constant sense of deprivation, but at the
same time they show resilience, a sense of humor and "phoenix phenomena" (persistently
"getting up" after frequent "falls"). They complain about alienation from people, they are
desperate for the meaninglessness of living, it is easy to recognize them by the leitmotif of
their verbalization; "There is a great inner void in me."

You cannot look at a mother with this condition only as the offender. She is a victim too,
because she is not incapable of loving. On the contrary, she suffers. She suffers terribly and
later she tries to repair everything with the child. So you may have experienced another
trauma. Mothers bond with children and there is no exception. She may later try to keep the
child, to not let him grow up because she wants him to be with her forever.

Only the aggressive type of mother will cause the child to develop anger. But you need
to know that these cases are common and you are not alone. This consequence has affected
many people and in this story, they are all victims. If you are a survivor of this trauma, be
strong, encourage yourself to seek professional help and overcome the problems that have
arisen because you will realize that you are no less important than others. Your worldview
will open up, but you must know that nothing was your fault, and it was not your mother's. If
you understand and forgive, you have already taken the first step towards healing. Only great
people are forgiving and you must be aware that no one wanted this to happen. Not you, of
course, and not your mother.

CHAPTER TWO

HOW IT HAD TO BE

If you remain in the stage of remembrance and keep looking over your shoulder, you will grow old alone looking into the past. It's not a good place, it's called the past for a reason. What you need to know first and foremost is that the past must be left behind. As long as you look out the window of the past, you will remain there forever. If you look and wonder what could have been different, you will miss a lot. First of all, you will miss the future. Worst of all, you won't be aware of the present. Many opportunities will pass, trains will come and pass and you won't see them. You will look back. That's why we tell you to stop looking at yesterday. Remember – yesterday ceased to exist today.

It was not easy in the family you grew up in. It is hard for you, we understand. Your main problem is that you wake up every day with the same question popping into your head. And you're not the only one. Many others who have survived a mother with Borderline Personality Disorder may be having the same or similar thoughts. When you open your eyes after a bad night's sleep – because we know that every night is a challenge for you – you ask yourself, "Why me? Why are others happy and I'm miserable?" and so on. That little voice becomes your constant companion. When you lie down to rest, the voice does not allow you to relax and calm down because it reminds you that your childhood left a wound on your soul that will be waiting for you in the morning. That little voice doesn't go away. It will be there every morning. You have to wake up from reality, you have to wander off from yourself, you have to stop the issues that bring you back to the past. Because that reality that is like a nightmare – with the difference that you know everything is real and that there is no escape; you have to wake up. This book is here to help you understand who you are, to understand that life can and should be better.

We know you've never been like other kids. Your role in the family was to be a metaphorical punching bag. You served as a bucket for emptying someone else's emotions into. Your mother hit you with her unstable emotions because of her disorder. She emptied her frustration through you. You looked at your friends who were simply children. Your friends enjoyed their childhood, being loved constantly while you were caught in a swirl of emotions. In the holidays, your Christmas tree was probably beautiful one day and destroyed the next. Being a sponge to your mother and absorbing all her bad feelings was, unfortunately, your role.

You deserve to be loved as a kid. You were loved but you were also constantly the best person for your mother to unload her frustration on. Your father either objected, and you witnessed terrible quarrels and physical altercations between your father and mother as your father tried to share that burden with you. Maybe you had a father who decided to stay away and to not interfere. Maybe you resent him for that. There was no one to defend you. While you were trying to understand the world, no one understood you. It's a terrible pain. You felt betrayed, especially when you compared yourself to other children and listened to stories of happy families. But your family was different. You kept repeating the same pattern that you eventually adopted because you didn't know you that you needed something different. In a way, you laid your head before destiny and reconciled with it. You knew every new day was a challenge and you didn't know what was waiting for you. You used to be able to watch TV and play and sometimes you had to sit while crying in the dark wondering why. It's a question you still haven't resolved today. It's a question you have to clear if you want to get ahead and beat this. We are sure you want to help yourself because you are reading this book. That's why we're sure you'll make it. We'll look at what your family was supposed to be like. What did you miss in your childhood?

2.1. What does a healthy family look like?

Family is an irreplaceable environment in which a person forms himself as a person, in which he lives and satisfies some of his most important needs. The family is such a social community that every individual feels the need for because it is the foundation of the whole of human life. That is why it is of vital importance for every member of the social community.

During childhood, the child needs to be given as much love as possible, since this later reflects on his life in adulthood, his interaction with the environment, and affects his openness to others, and love and understanding for another. By satisfying the child's need for love and tenderness, a sense of security, safety, acceptance and belonging in society develops. From these feelings, a sense of self develops. Parents' behavior serves as a model for children to strive to identify with. Therefore, mutual respect, mutual assistance, and love between spouses and parents and children, which is characteristic of most modern families, is an important encouraging example for a young being. Of several factors that influence the development of a child and the formation of a person's personality, the family is one of the most important.

Family and family education represent the first and fundamental stage in the development of a child and his or her personality, and they cannot be replaced by anything. The family differs from other social groups by the social role it plays in the life of each individual, in that it provides a much more concrete impetus for the development of man as a human being. It also differs in the functions it performs, which are not primarily aimed at society, but also individual members. The individual today feels the need for the family as a community. In all societies so far, the family in its most generalized context is formed based on the specific social institution of marriage, which indicates that the family is a socially regulated community of opposite sexes within the allowed form.

In a family where each parent plays their part, the emphasis is placed on the children and the children themselves learn through that love to return the same love later to their children.

If we want to understand the importance of the modern family in personality development, we will explain its most frequently mentioned functions and especially the educational function, as well as some of its characteristics and development throughout history. The family is a specific bio-social community of people. It plays a very significant role in the development not only of man, but of society in general. Family is a mediator between society and the individual, but the family performs more functions than any other social group. By forming a family, a person is perceived as a social being in such a way that his life has a completely different sense of purpose compared to when he had no spouse or children.

All household members under one roof are family. It is also a group of people with common ancestors, common descent. The word "family" today refers to different terms. In the broadest sense, it is an inseparable whole of persons connected by marriage or adoption or the birth of an individual who inherits lineage, gender, and dynasty. In the narrower sense, the word "family" means relatives living under the same roof – or even simply a father, mother and children.

That feeling of warmth is irreplaceable. It brings a sense of security in which you know that someone will always protect you, no matter what. You know you can share your problems and you know that someone will stand up for you and show you the right way. Family makes us who we are. We gain our worldviews through our family values. We learn from our parents. Although there are exceptions, numerous studies have shown that many children will imitate their parents. Children want to repeat their parents' patterns of behavior. That is why when children witness violence in their family, they see it as normal behavior.

But through this book, you're hopefully already beginning to realize that this doesn't have to be you. Just because you witnessed violence as a child, you don't necessarily have to be a bully to your children and loved ones. You need to understand that all this is very bad. Some children have been in bad families and grow into great parents who never show violence because they realized that it was bad, and that just because they went through it, their children don't have to. Your kids don't have to be victims. There are many examples of bright and caring parents who were strong enough to not let their childhood fears and the traumas they endured affect their children.

Every family goes through different stages. The family encompasses two types of interrelated but distinct relationships in which biological, psychological and social elements intersect: satisfying the sexual urges and emotional needs of people, giving birth to and raising children. Although these categories may also take place outside the family, they mostly occur within the family.

2.2. Home family

A family begins when two people decide to live together. This stage is characterized by teaching partners to be a dyad/twosome, which involves setting internal organization and boundaries. The difficulty of this phase is that it is not just two individuals, but two products of their family backgrounds that nurture different cultural values and have different expectations. In partnership at this stage, it is important to be flexible so as to reach a consensus on issues of money, religion, recreation, friends, household chores, and shared free time. The problems specific to this phase of family development are the establishment of rules and conflicts that accompany this process, the distribution of responsibilities, lack of respect for diversity, and difficulties forming family boundaries.

2.3. A family with a very young child

The second stage involves the pregnancy and birth of the first child when the parental roles are established, which involves the distribution of care, authority and power, and participation in the upbringing process. This life stage is also characterized by the development of patterns of emotional attachment of a child to the mother in the first years of the child's life. This is different from the first months of life during which the child is dependent on the mother in terms of satisfying physiological needs. The problems that arise during this period are conflicts of responsibility, unwillingness to play a parental role, and a pushing of the external boundaries of the family system.

2.4. A family with a preschooler

This developmental phase begins after the couple's adaptation to the formed triad. This phase is characterized by specific tasks concerning the psychosexual development of the child and adapting the child's upbringing to his age. This process should take place in the protective and safe atmosphere that parents provide for the child. At this stage, the child goes through significant stages of psychosexual development, and parents exert an influence on his or her need for tenderness, rejection, defiance, and affection, etc. At this stage, parents introduce the child into the world of interpersonal relationships, shaping his personality, educating him and being a model for the child.

2.5. A family with a school-aged child

In this life cycle, the child begins the process of socialization, acquires working habits and learns responsibilities. Differences in parental involvement may cause difficulties in the child's adaptation to the new circumstances. At this stage, the relationship to external systems and the permeability of family boundaries are examined, on which the external impact of the school and the wider social environment will affect the family. The most common problems of the family in this life stage are problems related to the learning and behavior of the child, school phobia, etc. In the background of these problems are the most common unresolved parental or marital conflicts.

2.6. A family with an adolescent

The time of adolescence of the eldest child is characterized by the adolescent's need for a greater degree of independence and acceptance of new values outside the family while testing the limits of parental authority. The rebellion against parents by which adolescents develop their own identities can become a problem, which may be a continuation of earlier emotional and developmental difficulties that have not been adequately addressed. This period is also characterized by a review of the permeability of borders. If the boundaries are too closed and the family does not allow external influences to penetrate, family relationships are networked and the rules become rigid. Such family dynamics do not provide an opportunity for adequate development and the differentiation of young people. If the family boundaries are too open to allow uncritical penetration of outside influence, the family runs the risk of losing its identity. If the family cannot change, it faces the problem of adolescent-parent conflict.

2.7. The departure of children from their parents

The time of separation of children from their parents may be considered the most stressful event in the life span of a family. Children need to leave, and parents rethink their roles, often unwilling to adapt to new circumstances. Parents try to keep their children in the family environment, unaware of the serious difficulties their endeavors can bring. Therefore, the family, in contrast to its function, becomes a risk factor, not a child and youth protection factor. At this stage, the family most often faces the problems of delayed separation of young people from their parents, insecurity, and fear of independence.

2.8. The postpartum family

This phase of family development is characterized by an "empty nest" in which the partners are alone again without children in their homes. After many years during which the primary preoccupation was the upbringing of children, partners face the need to re-adjust to new life situations, change the way they communicate, and regulate closeness and distance in the relationship.

2.9. An old family

This phase is characterized by aging parents, which leads to a change in self-image, the challenge of coping with health issues, and loss of one or both partners. Age contributes to social exclusion and the also leads to the efforts of elderly parents to break the boundaries of their children's family system, which can most often be recognized in their attempts to engage in the care of grandchildren. Each stage of family development has its specificities. The time of transition from one life stage to another is a source of internal stress as the transition requires a change in the way the family functions. At each transition point from one life stage to another, the functionality of family relationships from the previous period is reviewed. Going through the trajectory of one's development, the family goes through developmental stages to adapt to the requirements of the life cycle in which it is located.

These processes, shaped by the beliefs and value system of previous generations, customs, secrets, and myths, create a family culture that defines all-important issues of one family, including how to emotionally bond and separate members.

But in a dysfunctional family like yours, problems have been created that are now yours.

2.10. A functional family

The term "functional" refers to something capable of fulfilling its purpose or function. However, it is not possible to reach a definitive definition of a functional family by a pure analogy, since the assessment of whether a family is functional or dysfunctional depends on the goals the family sets for itself, the value system, the life cycle and the satisfaction of economic and cultural needs. Just as the modern family questions the comprehensive definitions of the family for a variety of reasons, so can a "functional," "normal" or "healthy" family be viewed as a social construction determined by continuous change in a world that is also constantly changing.

Also, our personal experience, language, and professional orientation influence the perception of this term. You can see that the functionality of a family depends not only on the relationships that exist between family members but also on the relationship between family and society. The primary social task of the family is to ensure the socialization and humanization of man, that is, to create the development of those traits in the personality that will allow for good adaptability, but this should not necessarily mean a conformist attitude towards society. All authors who have dealt with family functionality point out that those functional families should have a solid parental alliance. Parents use authority based on maturity and fairness with understanding, respect, cooperation and a warm relationship.

A functional family, among other things, is largely determined by cohesion, a shared home, communication between family members and interactions between generations. Of course, a family in a formal sense can exist without all these determinants, but then it loses its psychological meaning. It is precisely the family of communities where there is a sense of belonging and solidarity. Each family will be all the more content and functional if there is a willingness on the part of those who join such a community to fulfill and mutually fulfill important human needs (closeness, trust, cooperation), and not only to achieve specific goals (reproduction, economic security or gaining social status).

A functional family has a flexible structural power with shared authority, clear family rules, unbroken generational boundaries and a style that fosters association. Family members have their individuality and ability to determine closeness and distance, can tolerate disagreements and uncertainty, communicate freely and spontaneously, and accept the diversity and sensitivity of others. Humor, tenderness, and care are integral to the family atmosphere. Conflict is openly discussed and problems are identified and resolved. Given the different understandings and definitions of the functional family within system theory and theoretical models of systemic family therapy, an overview of theoretical and clinical points of view can be summarized in four major concepts in defining family normality:

According to this concept, whose origins are in the medical model, a normal or healthy family is one in which there are no symptoms or disorders in any family member. The limitation of this approach lies in the fact that it is based on the absence of pathology (negative criteria) and ignores indicators of positive functioning. Healthy family functioning is more than the absence of symptoms or problems. Similarly, another limitation of this concept stems from the realization that there may be some simple correlation between family functioning and the health of the individual. It would be wrong to assume that every individual disorder is related to dysfunction in the family, as well as to assume that a healthy individual necessarily comes from a healthy family.

2.11. Normal family as average (normality as mediocrity)

In this concept, which has a foothold in the social sciences and is formed based on statistical indicators for presenting reality, the family is normal or healthy if it is typical and if it is in line with what is common and expected for ordinary families in a given context. A limitation of this approach is the ability to fall into the trap of equalizing optimal functioning of the family with severely dysfunctional ones, as they both deviate significantly from the normal distribution.

2.12. Normal family as optimal (normality as optimal)

This approach defines a normal family through optimal functioning with ideal features, which is a utopia. The limitation of this concept stems from the fact that the norms of an ideal family are socially and culturally constructed values that "prescribe" what families should be. However, patterns that are optimal for one family may not meet the standards of the ideal in a given environment, which does not mean that that family is not functional.

2.13. Normal family relationships (Normality as a process)

This approach, which rests on general system theory, defines the normality of the family through the normality of family processes. Unlike other approaches that look at normality statically, this approach does not think of a normal family as an immutable, timeless entity. Seeing normality as a process that varies depending on the internal needs of the family and the external needs of the wider systems constantly questions both continuity and change throughout the life cycles of the family. If we take into account the concepts of a systematic approach to the family that we have discussed in the previous section, then it can be said that functionality has the meaning of usability of the family pattern (the way the family functions) in achieving family goals. Therefore, normal family functioning is a process that takes place over time in a particular socio-cultural context, and through which, through developmental interactions, the basic tasks of the family are accomplished.

Such a functional family is characterized by the connection of members to a community characterized by a mutual relationship with trust, closeness, mutual care and support. There exists a balance between autonomy and reciprocity, and an environment in which there is an appreciation of individuality and intimacy, which has a respect for individual differences and autonomy. A functional family gives impetus to individual maturation care, socialization of children and cares for other vulnerable family members. There is organizational stability with clear roles and boundaries, adaptability, capacity for change, flexibility concerning internal and external demands, effective methods for coping with stress, open, clear and warm communication, effective and creative negotiation and the ability to use a wide range of behaviors and strategies in conflict resolution. The generally accepted belief system of a functional family enables trust and connection with past and future generations, and there exists adequate resources for basic economic security and psychosocial support through a network of extended family and friends, the community and wider social systems.

This definition of a functional family needs to be complemented by the trait of such a family that it can grow, despite any difficulties it encounters. A healthy family is always looking to expand their experiences. The difficulty is seen in such a family as a way for the family to increase its experience and growth. A healthy family, therefore, has the resources to solve their problems. Joy and humor are the strengths of a healthy family. Humor alleviates tension, allows for communication without confrontation, and adds emotional intensity to problematic situations.

2.14. A dysfunctional family

The term "dysfunctional" refers to something that works wrong or doesn't work at all. Unlike functionality, it is much easier to understand what the term dysfunctional is in one family system. If we started from the assumption that any change in the life cycle of a family brings stress, then a dysfunctional family would represent that family that is unable to adapt to the new living conditions and cannot cope with stress without major consequences. In such families, there are extremes in the connection of its members, so that the boundaries between the members are deleted or the members are very far apart. The borders to the "outside world" are also not permeable. The dysfunctional family is most often either isolated from the outside world without a formed family identity with inflexible and strict rules, or the boundaries are so open that anything that comes from the outside world is uncritically accepted.

The roles in dysfunctional families are not clearly defined, so often children assume parental roles. Communication is vague, confusing and contradictory, messages are not listened to or accepted and there is only minimal verbal exchange with frequent mystification. Such a family always delays problem-solving. The family is constantly in a state of crisis that is not recognized until one or more family members have a symptom or when the family threatens to break up.

2.15. Symptoms of dysfunctional families:

A dysfunctional family can be characterized by lack of empathy understanding, and sensibility towards individual family members, while on the other hand there is an expression of extreme empathy towards one or more family members who have a "special status." Other symptoms include denial (refusal to acknowledge the existence of undesirable conduct) inadequate or non-existent personal boundaries, disrespect for other people's borders extremes in conflict (or too much strife or insufficient discussion between family members), unequal and unfair relationship rules towards one or more family members due to their gender, age, ability, race, economic status, etc., and high levels of jealousy and other controlled behaviors. Dysfunctional families may also include divorced parents, parents in constant conflict or parents who should have separated but did not (at the expense of their child). Dysfunctional families lack time spent together, especially recreational activities and social events ("We never do anything as a family"). They may also be characterized by unacceptable sexual conduct (adultery, promiscuity or incest) and an environment in which children are afraid to talk about what is happening at home (inside or outside the family), or otherwise feel afraid of their parents and other family members. Family members may not acknowledge each other, and (or) refuse to be seen together in public (either unilaterally or bilaterally). It is also important to emphasize that dysfunctional patterns at one level (e.g. maintaining an unstable marriage) can also be dysfunctional at another level (in this case the subsystem of children).

If we include wider social systems in the assessment, we can also identify their dysfunctionality concerning the family (e.g. schools or kindergartens), so interventions sometimes need to be addressed not only to the family but also to wider systems that can be a source of dysfunction. When a family is faced with a crisis or becomes aware of the presence of symptoms or dysfunctional relationships, then it must be willing to change.

It is a common belief that the parents' love for the child is instinctive, biologically given and that it manifests itself at his birth. In reality, the birth of a child begins a process in which a long-lasting and stable emotional connection between the child and the person caring for him or her is gradually developed. This process of shaping emotional closeness, the most important part of which takes place in the first year of a child's life, is called the daily love of mother and child. In professional literature, this is the so-called "emotional attachment". Because the mother typically spends the most time with the child in that earliest relationship, we will hereafter refer to the mother, although the primary caregiver may also be the father, grandmother or someone else who is the closest to the child.

Early childhood is very important; we might say essential for the child. A strong emotional attachment and communication between the child and the mother develops most intensively in the first year. A child's need for such a relationship is of evolutionary origin and is part of a survival system. An infant who is unprotected and helpless in his or her immaturity is more likely to survive if protected by one person's proximity. Separation from this person causes intense fear in the child. The fear of separation first appears at the age of 6 to 8 months and is most pronounced by the 18th month.

Fear is also an indicator that the child has established this important emotional closeness with one person. A child needs to have a calm, stable and sensitive person with him/her who will be able to respond to his/her needs and provide him/her with security and love. If not, the infant and toddler will not develop well, not only emotionally, but also intellectually and physically. The mother-father relationship is extremely important, so too the father's feelings towards the child, which greatly influence the quality of the mother's role.

Experience shows that no pressures are good. If the mother is in circumstances that are difficult for her, she may have repulsive and aggressive feelings towards her child. This is a taboo topic. And it is in this situation that the mother needs the understanding, support and assistance of the family and a professional, a person to whom they will be able to express their feelings and thoughts without condemnation. Here, the crucial role of the father and the wider family is to support the mother-child relationship with patience and understanding. The love and security that a child experiences in their earliest childhood are an important prerequisite for the later development of a normal and healthy personality. In this earliest emotional relationship, basic personality traits are formed, which are difficult to change afterward. These experiences depend to a large extent on how much the child will be capable of love when he or she grows up and how they will experience themselves and the world around them (the so-called basic picture of the world); whether he thinks it is good and deserves the love of other people or is does not deserve it; is the world around him good and ready to help when needed? These first contacts with the environment largely depend on how much later, in childhood and adulthood, he will believe in himself and other people and be able to achieve in life what he wants and what makes him happy. The love and security gained in the early years is successful in prevention of later disorders: behavioral disorders, delinquency, addiction, violence and abuse, and other evils of the modern age that afflict parents. The development of brain structures and the way of raising children at an early age are physically connected.

Attachment issues arise when a mother does not respond to the need of a child who is seeking her. These mothers reject the child's need for attachment, dislike intimate, face-to-face contact, especially when the baby wants it. They can talk about their baby in warm words, be a play partner, be diligent about feeding and sleeping, but when a child shows a need for physical and emotional closeness, it becomes threatening for them (because they may have felt left out during childhood). Such children show little or no caution to strangers and only become upset when left alone. They show a lack of collaboration, exploratory behavior, and empathy, have poor relationships with peers, avoid close emotional attachments, feel that emotions are not important, resulting from a defensive self-protective adaptation to expecting rejection by the mother in stressful situations. Avoiding affectionate adults shows fear of intimacy, and lack of confidence in people. Such people may feel uncomfortable when close to others, and become nervous and repulsive if they get too close. Anxiety attachment arises as a result of the mother's behavior in which she sometimes responds to the child's need for closeness and is available and sometimes unavailable. As a result, these children perceive the mother (or other attachment figure) as inconsistent, at times supportive, at times unsupportive, causing them to become insecure and fearful, and perceive all adult figures as unreliable. As a consequence, children's confidence and self-esteem as well as motivation to explore the environment will depend on the support and approval of the mother. This dependence on others hinders the development of adequate emotional connections and leads to emotional instability and sensitivity to stress.

So with these examples and information, you are slowly getting the information you already know deep down. You now know all the major facts. But you must realize that just because you have missed a lot you mustn't look back in anger. Focus on tomorrow, focus on the future.

You were a victim in a family that did not fulfill its purpose. Instead of happiness, you got sadness and now you look at the past and that disturbs you. You must have asked yourself a thousand times "What am I doing here?" Because of your lack of love, you began to doubt yourself; you began to disbelieve in better. Don't despair; you must never give up hope. Hope and will are your salvation. And the understanding you need you will gain by reading this book. You will understand what your recovery path is. There is a way; you must never give up on yourself. This book will give you guidelines for recovery and a better life.

You have to know one more thing; no one succeeds alone. We all need people around us who help us to see that path of recovery. You will find your way. You've already taken a step toward recovery with this book. Believe in yourself and let this book be a guide. In that way, that little voice in your head that accompanies you to bed every night and wakes you up every morning will start to fade and eventually it will completely disappear.

CHAPTER THREE

THE MAIN STYLES OF A BORDERLINE MOTHER

3.1. *The unfortunate truth*

Every disease is the same in one respect. Every illness, whether mental or physical, occurs in many variations. So it is in some ways useless to cut off a branch when the disease is at the very root of the tree. The disease is in the person. People are not afraid of illness, people are more afraid of the healing process. This is not due to fear of medicines, but because most people think they are relieved of their moral obligations due to illness. This condition is very specific. There is a fine line between a sense of morality and aggression in Borderline Personality Disorder. Thus, Borderline Personality Disorder is no different to other illnesses in the sense that it can occur in different forms. The most sensitive group are mothers because their role in society is essential. The mother is the one who instills moral values and makes a man from a child.

3.2. *Specifics of BPD*

Your pain is what makes you different, more specific, and your suffering is great because you grew up in such a situation. You have no one to complain to about it because you don't think anyone understands you. That's where you have made a mistake. You are afraid of disappointing others because you feel you are less valuable. All these feelings in you are caused because your mother suffered from Borderline Personality Disorder. You need to understand that your mother showed symptoms of her condition and that they were different depending on what variation of her condition appeared.

The pain you carry within yourself is the result of variations on the conditions your mother struggled with. So again, do not blame your mother; she did not choose to have this condition and she did not want you as her child to be injured in any way.

3.3. The main styles of a borderline mother

It can be concluded that there are several types of borderline mother, the main ones being:

1. Discouraged borderline

2. Impulsive borderline

3. Petulant borderline

4. Self-destructive borderline

3.4. Depression and anger

The first type of borderline mother is the so-called "discouraged borderline". That kind of mother is often very needy and dependent. The main paradox is that this type of borderline mother is particularly dangerous because even though they are needy and dependent and even insecure, they simultaneously harbor a lot of anger in them. They have a strong desire for acceptance and approval, but they are also very insecure and they have feelings of inferiority, so they are both depressed and they have a sudden outbursts of aggression. If they don't find proper approval, they will become marginalized and seriously depressed. That depression is not a joke. If they are not treated well it could evolve into suicidal thinking and possible tragedy.

In this case, you probably dealt with so many bad things. You probably had to go through a lot to please your mother because you were afraid of what would happen if you weren't with her.

3.5. Pure rage

An impulsive borderline mother tends to be very charismatic, energetic, and they are very good company. People love to be around them because their impulsive behavior can be very appealing to people. But the downside of this type is their need to be the center of attention. The mother with this type of Borderline Personality Disorder will be fun, but she is also "the drama queen." She will often heavily neglect the child's needs because she must be the center of attention. This type of mother will be abusive, self-centered, and she will act rashly and she will not care for possible consequences.

In this case, you suffered terrible consequences because you were a victim in every way. To deal with this type of mother is extremely difficult. But you endured, you're still here and that's the most important thing.

3.6. What went wrong?

The petulant borderline mother can't be pleased. She will always complain about everything because she is always right. She has a constant need to argue, to fight, to have an outbursts of anger, and that kind of behavior is a living nightmare. She will provoke conflict without any reason. She is stubborn and she doesn't know to say "I'm sorry." In that kind of relationship, the mother will set up a task and she will have an outburst of anger towards the child and that child will never get recognition for any effort. It will become a person with no self-respect because in this type of relationship the child will always be the "guilty party." Later in life, this will result in major consequences for the child. They will become a person who doesn't trust anyone, who doesn't appreciate himself and a big hole will appear regarding social relations and contact.

"You are not good, you know nothing, you are not worth it, you are wrong." If you heard a lot of these words during your childhood and grew up while trying to please your mother without success, no matter how good you were for everyone else, then you are the victim of this type of Borderline Personality Disorder your mother suffered.

3.7. Please don't do this

The self-destructive borderline mother is her own worst enemy. She tends to all kinds of dangerous behavior. She lacks a stable sense of self, she is also dependent and she has a constant fear of abandonment. This type of borderline mother will often try to get away from her inner problems by experimentation with various drugs, alcohol and other risky behaviors. She will always be bitter, moody, and filled with anger that she can't properly express. That is what leads to various types of arguing, and provoking others. The child will suffer a lot because it can't control this kind of behavior and that will lead to fights and abandonment. A consistent pattern of neglect and abuse will occur and it will result in loathing.

"I want to kill myself; my life doesn't mean anything... Mom, don't please, I love you" is a common phrase that characterizes this variation of Borderline Personality Disorder. You probably had to hide drugs, alcohol and other destructive substances because you feared your mother would abuse them.

3.8. Look up and never look back

Today you have to take a different attitude, no matter how much you have suffered through life. Many people like you are still struggling with this and trying to understand how and why. You have to stop this and tell yourself loudly, "The world changed me and because of that I suffered, today I want to change myself and because of that I am wise."

Life has shown you his teeth, you've survived terrible things, now it's time to fight back and take a stand.

It doesn't matter that they say, "It's easier to make a strong kid than to repair a broken man." No matter how broken you feel, you can be again yourself.

The scars you wear are a reminder how many times life tried to break you, but every single time you survived – because you are a warrior.

CHAPTER FOUR

TYPES OF ABUSE

It's not the point of this chapter to serve as a painful reminder of what you've been through. This chapter should serve as a guide for you to see what other types of abuse exist, besides the ones you survived. The purpose of this part of the book is not to make it difficult for you and make you experience bad memories, but to show you that you are not alone. That there are many others who have experienced what you have, and that abuse can take many forms.

Abuse is not only what you see with the naked eye; it can be much more complex than broken bones and bruises on the body. Although less noticeable, psychological violence against children leaves much more severe consequences, which often come to light several years after the abuse. It can permanently damage a child's mental health and have serious consequences for his or her personality and that is the case when it comes to abuse from a borderline mother.

Emotional abuse is the most insidious, and even the most dangerous, when it comes to a child's development. It gradually kills the child's feeling of being wanted and loved, their sense of their own identity, security, reality, and relationship with the world. The possibilities of neglect and abuse of children are very diverse in both ways and intensity. Emotional neglect and abuse are far more common in everyday life than physical and sexual ones.

Every day, the child is felt by various actions and words that he or she is guilty and responsible for all the inconveniences, failures and dissatisfactions of the parents, that at his/her birth he/she began to endanger the life of the family. A young child cannot grasp the illogicality and unreasonableness of these remarks and accusations – he or she begins to feel guilty and sometimes even encourages this abuse through his or her behavior.

When a mother does not intentionally show love to a child to punish him for his misconduct, it is a form of psychic violence. These actions are often accompanied by a verbal message such as "I no longer love you because you were naughty."

4.1. The six most common forms of child abuse by a borderline mother

<u>Rejection</u> involves a large group of heterogeneous behaviors that (intentionally or unknowingly) send a message that a child is unwanted, unloved, bad, wrong. Child abuse or neglect of a child's emotional needs is a common form of emotional abuse against children. Telling your child to get out, calling them derogatory names, making a child a "scapegoat or black sheep" in the family, and blaming them for family problems are common forms of rejection. Refusing to talk to or hold a child, and refraining from cuddling, touching, kissing and hugging has the same effect.

<u>Constant criticism:</u> ("You never try ... You don't do anything right ... How many times do you need to be told? ... What is your problem? ... Will you ever remember it? ... I worry what will happen to you ...") Examples of constant criticism include:

- Comparison of the child to peers at the expense of the child

- Telling the child it's ugly

- Yelling or swearing at the child

- Misrepresentation and use of labels such as "nerd," "idiot," "jerk," "fool," "whore," "incompetent," "slug," "drug addict."

- The constant humiliation of a child through a joke

- Constant teasing of a child for his physical appearance

- Regret that the child is not of the opposite sex

- Refusal to hug or express love physically ("Too tired, nervous, not comfortable, tired, doing something alone, boring, hard ...")

Abandoning a child can include:

- Excluding a child from family activities,

- Treating an adolescent as a child

- Removing a child from the family (sending to relatives, boarding schools, camps...)

- Allowing a child to make decisions that are not appropriate for his or her age

- Refusing to spend time with a child or play with him

Ignoring is a form of rejection, but unlike rejection, there is no (conscious or unconscious) intention. Ignorance is common in adults whose emotional needs were not satisfied as children, and as a result, they are often completely insensitive to the needs of their children. Such parents are unable to connect with the child or provide adequate care. They sometimes fail to notice the child's presence at all. Many times such parents are only physically present. Failure to respond to the child's requests for connection or lack of interaction with the child psychological abuse. It can also include:

- Non-response to a child's spontaneous social behaviors (smiles, handshake, giggling, questions...)

- Not paying attention to significant events in the child's life (birthday, school events, New Year's, sports competitions ...)

- Refusing to talk about school activities, or the child's interests...

- Planning activities or vacations without children

- Failure to provide adequate health care to the child

- Non-involvement of the child in daily activities.

Intimidation: Borderline mothers use threats, shouting, and physical punishment to inflict serious psychological harm on their children. Separating a child to criticize and punish or ridiculing her for expressing emotion is abusive behavior. Threatening children with cruel words, beatings, abandonment or death is unacceptable. Witnessing domestic violence is also one of the worst forms of abuse of a child; the child does not have to be directly exposed or be the physical victim of that violence for damage to occur.

Child isolation: A parent who uses isolation as a form of child abuse may not include the child in age-appropriate activities, may keep the child isolated in their room without adequate stimulation necessary for the child's development, or may prevent a teen from socializing and having extracurricular activities. Requiring a child to spend time exclusively in his or her room, denying meals with his family, or separation from the rest of the family and peers can be destructive to the child. Some parents may allow their child to use drugs and alcohol, witness the cruel treatment of humans and animals, watch inappropriate sexual content, witness or be guilty of criminal activities (theft, assault, prostitution, gambling). Encouraging a minor child to engage in activities that are illegal or potentially dangerous is child abuse.

It doesn't matter that the definitions of violence against children are numerous, they all inflict pain, physical or psychological damage, endanger the health and physical or mental integrity of the individual and impede the normal development of a minor.

The most common and visible form of violence against children is physical violence. It comes in many forms, most commonly: hitting, slapping, burning, throwing on the floor or downstairs, tying to a radiator or closet, denying food, locking in an attic or basement, administering toxic substances, alcohol or inappropriate medications, biting, attempts to drown or choke a child, etc. Physical abuse is most often accompanied by emotional abuse and neglect. There are numerous consequences of such abuse.

Mental abuse or emotional deprivation is a relationship or behavior that neglects, threatens, underestimates, offends or verbally attacks a minor's personality and displays negative feelings about them. The forms of emotional deprivation include the denial of parental love and emotional support, rejection in the form of indifference and lack of attention, rejection by shouting, attributing blame to the child for problems, the transmission of negative messages that offend the dignity of the child, etc.

Emotional violence leaves a big mark on the victim. If it is longer lasting, it is more destructive than physical violence. Emotional violence is reflected in the permanent omission of expressing love and attention to children, as well as in verbal outbursts that humiliate and hurt children.

The forms of emotional abuse are: ignoring, rejecting, terrorizing, isolating and socializing, verbally injuring (belittling and insulting inappropriate terms - eg, a nerd, cattle, fat), verbal intimidation, attacking the most important values (beliefs, religions, races...) monitoring, tapping, eavesdropping on phone calls, etc.

Emotional abuse in a child victim creates confusion, causing the abuser to further abuse him. The goals of emotional abuse are to develop anxiety in the victim, to create dependence on the abuser, to weaken the physical and mental capacity to resist, provoking self-blame, etc. The most difficult form of emotional abuse is when the victim takes on the role of their abuser and begins to abuse herself, degrading herself.

It is clear that you have been through a lot, you have not really known yourself all your life and you have suffered many forms of abuse. Reading this book is your first step to recovery. The journey is long but the choice is yours and remember that even the longest journey begins with a simple step. If you have taken it, it means your journey has started and that is great.

Probably this brought back some bad memories, but as we wrote, it was not our intention. We intended to encourage you to learn and to break through the imaginary wall you created in your head. Most victims do this, almost always unconsciously, intending to forget bad memories and get away from problems. It's a good solution for a short time but causes problems in the long term. Denying and building walls only deepens and aggravates your mental state. So you have to go through this chapter to realize that you are not alone; that abuse is a phenomenon that affects many. It's not just children; unfortunately, abuse is a widespread phenomenon that affects all age groups. You had to go through all this again to break through that wall, to read about what you always held in denial.

In your case, it's a lot harder because the abuser was your mother and you were just a kid. You were incapable of understanding, you didn't understand why this was happening, you didn't know how to cope with abuse from the one person you love the most in the world.

You were ashamed, sad and you couldn't confide in anyone. You were afraid to open up to someone, even if that person was your closest friend. You were afraid to say that you were in pain, that you couldn't deal with it anymore. You didn't understand why, when you did everything right, instead of praising you would get taunting, yelling, and other humiliations.

But you have to snap out of it, you have to be strong. Because of this abuse that you have suffered, you have developed some behavioral patterns. These are just habits. You have become distrustful, pessimistic, unable to fit into the world. But this is just a defense mechanism that your mind has developed to protect yourself from what you see as a potential danger. Of course, you don't want to be hurt, you don't want to interact closely with people because you were hurt. Your behavioral patterns are created to protect you.

But these are just habits. Habits can be changed. Here you have to look at the whole problem like a true visionary. Only then will you be able to break through the great wall between you and the rest of the world.

That abuse formed your habits. Habits are part of automatic actions from our daily lives, even though we are sometimes not aware of them. They are like a hidden memory bank that tells us what to do. This is why Aristotle regards habits as "second nature" which brings us back to our "primary nature" or instinct. The difference is that habits are learned behaviors while instincts are innate. Habits allow us to perform multiple tasks at once and to do so efficiently and accurately. Because of this, a person can type and talk at the same time. This is because typing has become a common practice that does not require thinking to perform. This makes it easy for young people today to type a message on Twitter while simultaneously watching TV and talking with friends.

You should be brave in dealing with new situations. Get used to the unknown. Learn habits that will help you with the new circumstances. These may be similar to those you already have but should be adapted to your current assignment. A person playing basketball can easily switch to volleyball, as the habits developed in playing one sport can be transferred to another.

The study habits that researchers develop in their field can help them gain knowledge of other fields with less effort than individuals who have not developed these study habits. People can get used to expressing certain positive behaviors in different social situations, such as suppressing anger, showing solidarity and generosity. Indeed, some describe moral values as "ethical habits." These habits are a means by which people preserve the values of society as they prepare for what the future holds. They protect against the trauma of sudden changes. Habits allow people to learn quickly, respond with understanding, and effectively adapt to new developments. Past actions become an automatic response that requires no effort or attention, freeing the mind to deal with more important concerns.

Giordano Bruno was burned at the stake for opposing a geocentric view of space. Much later, Galileo was placed under house arrest for the same views. Many scientists faced hostility over proposing ideas that were contrary to what people knew. But innovative thinking is essential to discover. But what is essential in all of this is that habits can be changed. People can adapt their habits. Your defense can be transformed if you are willing to fight. That same habits will help you. But you must be persistent and you must break that wall, you simply must open your mind and think outside the box.

If they had not thought outside the box, Einstein would never have come up with a theory of relativity; Columbus would have never discovered America or Vasco de Gama discovered the Cape of Good Hope.

There's an old Native American proverb that talks about choice, or at least that's how we interpret it. The little Indian boy asked his father, "Dad, am I good or bad?" The father gazed in the distance and then looked at him and told him, "My son, in each of us there are two wolves, one wolf is good and the other evil." The little son then asked his father, "Well, which wolf prevails, Dad?" The father answered, "Son, the wolf we choose to feed prevails." So the choice is yours, you can either hide behind the victim mask or you can break those imaginary chains and be your own person. We know you will make the right decision.

CHAPTER FIVE

TYPICAL BEHAVIOR OF A CHILD WITH
A BORDERLINE MOTHER

We have come to the part of the book where you will be able to see how children with borderline mothers behave.

A large number of children who have undergone this type of trauma exhibit different patterns of behavior but there are common traits to them all children. As a child of a borderline mother, you only see the world in two colors, unfortunately. You see the world in white and black. You have to know that the world has many colors. A variation of black and white can only create gray. A gray world is not a place for you and it is not a place for other children. The voice that wakes you up and tells you that you are small, that you are not worthy, that others are better, is wrong. Tell it to leave.

One day you will wake up and realize that there is no more time to do the things you have always wanted to do. You will indulge in that annoying little voice and let him beat you. So immediately tell him to leave. Do it now and continue reading this book and looking for answers. Remember, the answers are there, you may just need to dig a little deeper. They are hidden as obvious truths and they can be learned by those who want to know them so much that they are ready to dig. This book is, therefore, a great step for you.

You are now thinking that you are safe where you are and you are afraid to go further because you think that if you stay where you are, there will be no pain. In a way you are right, there really will be nothing. But not in a good way. You will be on the bad side of this story, you will not move anywhere and you will stay in one place forever. You will be simply stuck. A ship is safest when it is in port, but the ship is not made to be in port. The ship was built to sail, to move away from the shore and go on to the open sea. A motionless ship will never help people and eventually, the rust will do its thing and the ship will perish even though it never set sail. The same thing applies to people. Your open sea awaits you. New people are waiting to come into your life. People who can give a lot and who will give love to you.

Even though you may not be aware, you are already walking towards the answers. Reading this book will reveal to you the truths that have always been distant to you and that you thought were hidden. They were never hidden, but you were afraid to ask; you were afraid because of everything you went through. To see that you are not alone, we will show you how children behave when abused by mothers with Borderline Personality Disorder.

The baby is small and innocent and the earliest attachment should be just with the mother. This is the main problem. When a mother is suffering from Borderline Personality Disorder, this bonding between mother and child does not go well. So from the very beginning of your life, just like many other children, the problem arose immediately.

5.1. Children who are abused by their mother with Borderline Personality Disorder vs other abused children.

Borderline Personality Disorder is such an insidious condition that it leaves children who have been abused in such relationships with specific problems. Mothers with Borderline Personality Disorders initially show much less desire to connect with their children. They are cooler from the start, distant, and less concerned about their children. Such mothers provide much less smiles and much less play for their children, they do not touch them and there is no integration.

To make matters worse, mothers with Borderline Personality Disorders often have a problem identifying their child's emotions and responding appropriately to the child's needs. This deprives the child of safety, comfort, and the security needed at the beginning of life.

How can you grow up and become more social and eager to get to know yourself and the world around when you there were completely different problems for you to face at home? You had no compassion because your mother couldn't give it to you. Remember this, your mother was ill. You were drawn into abuse without the will of the abuser. There was no conscious reaction and desire to abuse.

The general types of abuse can vary and the abuse itself can be mental, physical and even sexual. Some children suffered more than you and some of them less. But there are two big differences between deliberate abuse and the abuse that comes from a mother with BPD. The first difference is that these children are abused with intention. So the abuser wanted them to suffer. It can be a comfort to you that you were not abused because your mother wanted to abuse you. Her actions and anger towards you were not intended to hurt you. She hurt you a lot, but she didn't want to and you have to understand that. She deeply loved you but couldn't show that because of her condition. Her sadness, anger, and frustration were not created by her desire but by her impulses. Because of this, you have to forgive her; you will realize in time that she never wanted you to suffer.

The other difference is that, because of the complexity of the situation, you are hurt much more deeply than other children who have been deliberately abused. Unfortunately, you have had constant abuse and with far greater consequences because you have never been able to get answers for your questions and have never been able to connect with your mother in the right way.

5.2. Your behavior

You likely act antisocially, are distrustful and have an "always on the lookout" attitude. It's your defense mechanism. As a young child, you wanted answers and couldn't find them because your behavioral mechanism was not set up properly. As parents pass their behavior on to children, so do children form their personality because it is a natural process. You lacked those emotions and now you don't know how to approach a person properly. As a kid, you always looked to lean away so someone else wouldn't hurt you. That's why we compared you to a ship standing in the harbor. You've never had a real interaction and it's the same as a ship that has never sailed. As you grew, you grew further away from people, maybe you hid behind a hobby to fool yourself into thinking you did not have a problem. You didn't interfere too much in human relationships and didn't talk much. You felt that your opinion didn't matter and that nobody cared because you developed a sense of being of less value. Deep down, you were afraid of being hurt. That's why you run from reality to imagination. You created the world within yourself and you put a wall around it. In that world, there was only room for trying to close the emotional hole that had arisen. You've probably tried music, writing, painting or just fantasizing. Later, you began to fear love because you never got any. You refused any loving relationship because you saw your mother and that close relationship in all things and it reminded you of her. You were afraid that if you embarked on another relationship that required closeness, you would again feel like you were a little helpless child. That's why you broke up or ran away from them.

You still feel the same today. You're scared of people. You are afraid of interaction in every way. That's why you're in a vicious circle and you can't get out of it. We tell you, you can. You are in a vicious circle and inside a big wall. It's time to tear down that wall and move on.

5.3. The consequences of the abuse itself

Childhood abuse has an impact on five significant, interconnected areas: neurological and intellectual development; school success and life expectancy; socio-emotional development; social relations and behavior; mental health as a whole. In each of these areas, the consequences can be immediate and/or long-term. Abuse and neglect in most cases happens to children repeatedly, and the consequences depend on the age of the child – the victim. In terms of socio-emotional development, decreased self-control, increased dependence on other people, depression, lower self-esteem and a sense of inability to control life events occur. Social skills and social perceptions are poorly developed in the area of social relations.

5.4. Aggression

Aggression is always there because you are deeply angry with yourself that you cannot do better and that you know your life is passing by and you are helplessly watching. Your frustration and anger turns into aggression because aggression is your pressure valve.

Aggression and delinquency, psychosomatic disorders (allergy, asthma, and indigestion) occur. Children develop various defense and adjustment mechanisms: dissociation (denial and repression of feelings and events), self-blame, idealization of the abusive parent (resulting from the fragmentation that leads to the inability to evaluate themselves and others) and self-destructive behavior (self-harm, alcohol, drug use, sexual risk behavior).

5.5. Panic

Panic is something that is also your companion. Children who grew up with a mother who has Borderline Personality Disorder often feel panic and anxiety. It's a side effect of the fear you have come to expect.

Feelings of discomfort, anxiety, fear, hopelessness, confusion, loneliness, and anxiety are also prevalent. Post-traumatic stress reactions may occur. The long-term consequences of the abuse are difficulties concerning fundamental trust in others, independence, and personal effectiveness. Men often become abusers of their partners and their children, while women enter into partnerships in which they act as victims and may abuse the children. Most research has addressed the characteristics of abusive parents with BPD. Parents who were abused in 30-40% of cases were found to be abusing their children. An intergenerational chain of abuse is not necessary if the child has received, with a realistic experience of parenting behavior, sufficient social and emotional support from the wider and immediate environment.

5.6. You don't have a complete personality

You're not whole. You feel that deep inside. You know you're missing something. You need something else to be whole. You tried to find yourself in other people. You tried to imitate others because you don't want to be you. He would rather be anyone else. This is because you do not love yourself and do not believe in yourself.

Studies have shown that child neglect can be more pernicious than outright abuse, and that neglected toddlers fall into the most vulnerable category: the most anxious, careless and apathetic, distrustful, withdrawn, insensitive to grief and potentially aggressive. Children who are actively denied parental love and attention develop a labile ego structure, later susceptible to psychic crisis or breakdown. A retrospective analysis of individual cases indicates that childhood neglect, which occurs in early childhood, increases the likelihood of severe depression later. Children of mothers with BPD, who have not learned to create a warm and safe climate in the family, immediately after birth, develop an insecure parental attachment relationship.

5.7. *Your mother didn't even know what she wanted from you*

Your mother suffered a great deal in herself. And there were times when she wasn't aware of it. It's scary and sad. She didn't know what was real and she couldn't define herself, and you went into this whole story to be her valve and that is what caused your present behavior.

Such mothers are often unrealistic when it comes to what they expect from their children, and if the child's individual growth does not match the mothers' egoistic aspirations, the frustrations and feelings of parental failure can lead to abuse. In this case, children are faced with painful stages of adaptation to stress, which is reflected in their emotional and social growth and development. In later life, these result in difficulties concerning others, as they tend to expect abuse and destruction in every object relationship, become insecure, closed to new experiences and new acquaintances, less curious and less willing to learn from their peers. According to statistics, abused children have difficulty mastering school materials, and about 65 percent of these children repeat the first grade.

5.8. Feelings of guilt

You're just a victim. You are the one who is not guilty, the one who is innocent. If we look at this situation more broadly, we will find that conditionally speaking, it is difficult to see the culprit. If you are looking for a culprit and resent your mother, we will tell you right away, the culprit is your mother's condition; the culprit is not your mother. However, to make matters worse, you are the one who has developed a sense of guilt and shame. You feel guilty because you think that you have caused this behavior of your mother. Now we tell you to stop it, don't condemn yourself because you are not guilty. You have nothing to be ashamed of. Just think; is it logical to be ashamed? How logical, if you think a little better, is it to be ashamed that in some ways life was not fair to you and your mother? You feel ashamed to share it with someone, but if you were to share it, you would not get mockery but compassion. Think of it this way, you didn't write a petition for someone to give birth to you, you didn't write a petition to come into this world, you couldn't choose where you were going to be born, who you were going to grow up with. Does it seem clearer to you now why must open yourself up?

A victim who has experienced recurrent traumas of childhood abuse by a BPD mother feels guilty, ashamed, fearful and distrustful, is insecure and hesitant in decision making and has a sense of personal lack, and as she loses her sense of worth, is socially isolated from other family members and society.

Because children are the best imitators of their parents, long-term abuse in an atmosphere of broken marital and family relationships negatively targets them – that violence is effective and is an acceptable way of resolving conflict. As they grow up, these children can become rude spouses and parents who often abuse their partners and their sons and daughters. Galdston (1979) states that one who has long been exposed to physical abuse in childhood can become a person who practices sadomasochistic sexual acts concerning a partner. The abuse that takes place in the family environment of deeply disturbed relationships, pervasive fear and totalitarian control, seduced by violence, threats, and punishment, leads to the child feeling helpless and seeing greater harm in himself than in the abuse itself (Herman, 1996).

5.9. Consequences of abuse - drugs and alcohol

You don't like reality. You are disgusted with reality. You hate the image of this world and yourself in it and that's why you need to change reality. The distortion of reality is easiest if you put yourself in a state where you will lose that line between reality and imagination. It's a very thin line. Unfortunately, imagination and reality are most easily combined through the abuse of alcohol and drugs. If you have tried this way to ease the pain it is not difficult to understand why this is so. However, you are likely well aware that when the effects of opiates cease, all problems return and start hitting you like a freight train. You are only destroying your health, and problems remain. The key to the solution is hidden and lies in having the courage to face your problems. You must know that you can do this and that by talking about your problems, you will find the help you need to be a fully functional person and have a good and fulfilling life.

Mental health facilities and psychological counseling centers are full of people who have endured long-term, recurrent trauma in childhood. Research shows that abused children can meet diagnostic criteria for disorders such as addiction and substance abuse (alcohol and other psychoactive substances), personality disorder, various types of phobias, anxiety, post-traumatic stress disorder (which can lead to permanent personality changes), dissociative disorder, eating disorders (anorexia and bulimia), suicidal behavior, and even the most severe psychiatric disorder – psychosis. Much more often than their other peers, such children appear as delinquents, being potential perpetrators of rape, robbery, crime, and other misdemeanors. From all of the above, it can be concluded that childhood trauma impairs the achievement of developmental goals and tasks, and the lasting consequences it leaves leads to long-term psychological trauma. A BPD mother's relationship can have a very adverse effect on all aspects of an individual's life.

5.10. **You have become skeptical about life itself**

It's quite understandable that many children in such a situation may become very skeptical of life. This is not surprising because the simple fact is that, metaphorically, you have not been dealt good cards. Life has played with you, but stop wasting your time looking at those cards. Time passes as you analyze them. Instead, try to play the best you can with those cards.

Such children can become moody, irritable, and resentful, can seem exhausted and be withdrawn. In contact with family, peers, and friends, they can become aggressive. However, children who are merely innocent bystanders of such violence can also suffer the consequences. This causes them great fear, which causes their ability to learn to decline, so they can also become potential victims of various types of social predators.

Life does not ask you to be the best, but it asks you to do your best. So never give up because there is always a place when the tide will change. That is why, like the boat we mentioned, you must sail into life.

CHAPTER SIX

WHICH MASK ARE YOU WEARING – THE CONSEQUENCES IN ADULTHOOD

We'll start this chapter with a trivial question. Ever wondered why superheroes wear masks? Superheroes wear masks to hide their identities, hence to protect themselves. And you probably put on a mask too. But there is a difference between you and them. Superheroes invent identities to defend the costume. And you? You invented a costume to defend your identity.

Imagine dividing the world into people who love the color red and people who love the color blue. There is no intermediate space, there are no other colors. You divide yourself to see the world in just these colors.

6.1. Colors are important

But there are so many colors out there. We know that there are not only red and blue colors; we actually have a wide variety of colors and it is also possible to love multiple colors at once. The same thing applies to people. The world is not just black and white, and therefore neither are we. There are indeed 50 shades of gray. This is not to say that we all suffer from Borderline Personality Disorder, but rather that we can be different depending on the situation itself, the people we associate with, and our needs at any given time. The different faces, or masks, we portray represent our different versions of ourselves. They represent our capacity for adaptation, which is the only constant in a changing world.

6.2. How does your face develop and what does it mask?

Putting on a mask is, unfortunately, a side effect of your trauma. You created that mask because you think that you will be protected from possible abuse. You simply choose to hide and we understand why. Your mask was a necessity for you because you didn't want to reveal yourself to others. The fear of hurting was and still is, too great. But you must take off your mask. Your identity isn't something you need to hide. That mask is preventing you from having a close relationship with anyone and the sad truth is that the mask is destroying you, so take it off.

Why?

In childhood, we are like unformed clay. You can often hear people mourn their childhood because at that time they felt most like their true selves. During this period we are what we are at our core and we act that way. Children act following their feelings and needs. They have no inhibitions. As we grow up and become aware of other people, others' expectations, and our own, we develop the need to belong, to fit in and to protect ourselves. We change and a greater number of our selves emerge. The experience shapes our faces, to enable us to cope with the world in the best and most adaptable way.

6.3. The endless loophole

Life presents us with an everyday masquerade in which we wear a different suit depending on where we are going. The masks are similar. Our experiences play a large role in the emergence of our masks. From it, we gain a picture of ourselves and how the world sees us. Masks often arise as a product of seeing some of our weaknesses and the need to replace that weakness with something better. Unlike our different faces, that have their essence in ourselves, the mask is an artificial creation, without the material that exists in us; something we make from other people's material to replace the parts of ourselves that we do not love. It can be seen as a form of compensation; we compensate for our shortcomings by adopting certain traits and abilities that manage to cover those cracks we found in ourselves. But, unlike compensation, where the acquisition of skills and abilities represents a certain development of ourselves, the masks do not have that developmental direction, they do not represent mastering new skills but pretending to possess those skills or pretending to think in a certain way all to escape from what we are. That is why a mask is worthless and you are mistaken by wearing the mask.

6.4. A school example

Do you remember yourself in adolescence, when the need for belonging and acceptance was the strongest? You may have become a fan of cars or heavy metal music overnight, just because these were things that interested your peers. You put on the masks of a girlfriend or guy who didn't mind anything in a relationship, just so someone wouldn't leave you. And all that had its purpose. In adulthood, through additional experiences, deeper relationships, and a deeper knowledge of ourselves and the world, you become great at masking your true self. The masquerade of life has a practical application, because there are times when we do need to adapt to our surroundings. The question is, what happens when we no longer recognize we are wearing the mask?

6.5. The mask is not real

Ever since the beginnings of the world, masks have been created by people like you; people who felt that their personality wasn't complete. You hide behind someone else, but you know that is not you.

6.6. Let's go back a little

Long ago, when going to war, warriors dressed in special costumes, and smeared colors on their faces. Such behavior aimed to make warriors from ordinary workers, citizens. To accomplish their task, to go to battle, they had to become someone else, someone they probably hadn't been before. Today, we don't have to go quite that far; but we could consider makeup as a similar preparation for battle with the world. But what is the point of it? In a new situation, when we do not know what awaits us, putting color on our face is a shield for us – just as knights had shields, so today we use masks to protect ourselves.

6.7. What are you protecting?

You wear a mask to protect your ego, but also that child's uninhibited part of yourself, your true identity, because the world is not only your playground, it is the playground of all people and no one is guaranteed comfort and safety. Look at all the superheroes hiding behind the mask. Their initial experiences were not great, they were hurt, weak, they did not like how others saw them, or how they saw themselves. And then they would put on a costume, put on a mask and become someone else, someone better, stronger, faster – heroes. It is the same with you. You put on your warrior colors when facing the world, to lift yourself up, to pat yourself on the back and to say "I can do it." But now is the time to forget about the mask. We know that you adopted the mask, because thanks to it, you do not stay in bed every day thinking that the world is sad and ugly. However, that is not the answer.

6.8. Why are you hiding?

The mask represents an escape from reality, and with that escape comes problems of identity and acceptance of oneself, which results in dissatisfaction with life. Prolonged use of the mask leads to a loss of health. In addition to the feelings of loneliness it creates, the mask makes it impossible for us to connect with another person. It isolates us, even though it may have once been a function of actually bringing us closer and attracting people. Think of a school bully. Psychology tells us that in many cases the aggressive behavior of such children is a mask and that they feel smaller than poppy seeds. They use that mask of a bully to protect themselves and to gain a sense of power that they lack.

But in adulthood, when that mask is easily translucent or when aggression no longer leads to the status of strength but is rather seen as something bad, that mask creates more problems than benefits. The mask loses its adaptability, and the person who has been using it for so long faces a crisis where she is required to redefine her understanding of herself and what is expected of her, as well as the mechanisms she has used to meet her needs. Changing such content is not easy, and often people don't even try, but rather bang their heads against the wall hoping that it will break the wall rather than their head.

6.9. Why do we protect our masks?

As we said, we wear masks to protect our ego, and our true personality. But if you continue to do so, eventually, your true personality will fade. You will become that mask and you will forget who you really are. That is why you need to throw that mask away and start to rebuild yourself. This is one of the most important things that you must do to help yourself.

6.10. Masked love – another example

When do we hide from the world? When we think we are not good enough or when we think we are not worthy. We all use masks from time to time, not because we are corrupt and insincere, but because we want to be loved and allowed to love. In the early days of your relationship, you may have shared everything your partner likes, only to slowly relax over time and allow yourself to be different because you felt comfortable enough to show him that you had different interests without fear of rejection. Why do we do this? Why don't we immediately say, "I'm weird about chocolate, I don't like to share." Because we want to be loved by that person, we want to hold that image of the ideal for as long as possible. It has its function, it allows us to see each other a second time, a third and a fourth, and so on until the time when more masks are not so necessary and it is okay to show your face.

6.11. Identity crisis

Our different versions of ourselves, our faces, all exist at the same moment, but they do not all occur at once. There is cognitive processing of the situation and an assessment of which version is now appropriate. In addition to how our brains work in such a complex way, the priority you give to a particular version or a certain understanding of yourself influences when which version will appear to you.

The fear of loneliness and the need to be loved pushes us to the brink of our capabilities and willingness to use whatever means we can think of to fulfill our goals and needs. One would think that, from so many versions and faces, our system would overheat and explode, but, the more complex you are as a person, the more different you are – the more peaceful you are.

The mask and faces are not the same. The mask is an artificial creation, and the face is a part of us - not the separate part we put on when we go to fight criminals. Masks are not necessarily bad for our health, they have an adaptive role as our faces, it is only a matter of assessing to what extent it is useful to have a mask, and when it is better to show your face. In your case, it is time to show your face to the world.

6.12. You don't need to be someone else

Every day we learn something new about ourselves and the world. And with that, our color palette is expanding. Think of it as having an endless stack of cards and constantly pulling out a new card for a new situation. And for each new situation, we might craft a new version of ourselves. Consider the many different faces you exhibit throughout your life: the person who jumped over the kindergarten fence with their childhood companion and swung in the middle of the night on a swing, and the one who diligently goes to college and listens with serious facial expressions is the same person, as is the one who goes to work to do responsible and sometimes daunting work. And while it is the goal to seek the true version of ourselves, you must accept the existence of all those versions and to develop a sense of wholeness. Because with that feeling that you are one whole, not separate parts; you will be able to feel fulfilled and, without feeling guilty or divided, at every opportunity will actually be you and not someone else. The mask is a defensive mechanism, nothing more. You suffered a lot and you needed a mask, but now your identity is at stake, you must protect you. Don't hide in the dark, you need light to heal. You need your identity back.

CHAPTER SEVEN

LEARN HOW TO DEFEND YOURSELF AGAINST THEM

Normal and disruptive are two concepts that are never clearly demarcated. It is difficult to determine where one begins and the other ends. The most common issues when it comes to mental health are realism, self-control, self-esteem, the ability to have close relationships, and the desire for self-realization.

People with Borderline Personality Disorder suffering from anxiety, loss of touch with reality, depression, among other symptoms. Treatment involves therapy, which may include medication or psychotherapy, which involves verbal and/or non-verbal communication.

7.1. About everything

Mental disorders can occur in people of all professions, classes and cultures. Race, gender, money, and socio-economic background do not prevent or cause mental illness. This is why your mother also has this condition.

What is most important to you is to learn how to behave properly with your mother. This is very important because if you do not learn how to behave well with a mother who because of her condition has great problems, the damage in your relationship will be increased. But you also need to understand that it's important to build a defense mechanism. You have to learn to defend yourself and somehow balance yourself in this difficult situation.

We know that you feel anger and that it is not easy for you; we know that great damage has been done and that you have no more desire to be anyone's valve. You were a victim and you carry your scars with you. But you have to learn how to defend yourself. This way you will protect both yourself and your mother. Remember that your mental health is the most important thing and only if you are completely healthy and protected you can help your mother and yourself.

7.2. How to approach this problem

The most important thing is to try never to argue with your mother. You have to learn to restrain yourself and ask questions slowly and meaningfully because only in this way will you be able to defend yourself.

7.3. Specific examples

We think it's best to start by showing you some specific examples of conversation. That way you will be able to understand how you need to put yourself in this situation and learn to defend yourself. In most cases, this is not at all easy.

This is the basic thing to know when it comes how to help your mother suffering from a mental illness such as Borderline Personality Disorder. When talking to your mother, you have to act this way.

What you want to say: "Can't you see that you need serious help?"

What you should say instead: "Do you agree that you have been sleeping badly lately? Maybe we should make an appointment with a doctor. You want me to call him?"

It's not uncommon for people who are sick to be completely unaware of it. People who do not want help often refuse good advice. Therefore, starting from what they are aware of is a good start.

Below is another example. We hope that through concrete examples you will best understand how to successfully and positively interact with your mother.

7.4. Example

What you mean: "Did you take the medicine? Did you take the medicine? Did you take the medicine?"

What you should say instead: "Do you want me to help you organize your medicine box so you know when and what to take?"

You must never feed on your mothers addiction, her depression, or her aggression. You must never start arguing or let your her see your own aggression because she is ill, remember that. Any of your behaviors that she takes as an invitation to a quarrel will cause her to react badly, and again you will suffer more because of it.

7.5. Here is another specific example

What you mean: "You have no reason to be depressed!"

What you should say instead: "If you and your psychiatrist agree, I'd love to attend one of your conversations to better understand what's bothering you."

Even if the river of pain is pouring from you and you want to blame her, you must not show that aggression. That is why you should take this approach in such cases.

7.6. Another example

What you want to say: "Snap out of it!"

What you should say instead: "It's not always going to be this way."

Giving hope is your priority, especially for someone suffering from depression. When it comes to depression, the patient believes that it will last forever. During those dark moments, you must be optimistic and supportive. This does not mean that you should be a psychiatrist to your mother, but you can encourage her and help her accept the fact that you are not her enemy. Show her that you understand her. It will develop some kind of empathy within her and your relationship will become much better.

7.7. Understand the nature of mental illness

Mentally illness can be difficult to understand by those who have not experienced it. It is much easier for many of us to learn how to deal with irrational delusions, fear, hallucinations, and sadness than with irrational anger.

Mental illness can be frightening when we witness it in our loved one, particularly when a person with a disorder of consciousness screams and gestures as though they are preparing to attack. In every situation, the possibility of violence must be objectively assessed. If your mother shows signs of aggression, never feed that aggression. We know it's very difficult, but you have to do it for yourself and your mother.

7.8. The optimal approach for you

First of all, you need to control your emotional attitude. If you are both tense, go to different places first and calm down. At least try to relax. Here are some tips:

- Count slowly to 10;

- Breathe deeply and slowly;

- Walk (around the room, down the street);

- Try something else positive and enjoyable;

- Take a break (do something around the house).

The situation is easier to control, with clear and calm behavior. Communication is very important when emotions heighten. A mentally ill mother needs you to express confidence. Often, a firm and soothing voice allows you to quickly dispel your mother's irrational feelings. Remember that behind anger and confusion, there is often internal trouble and fear lurking.

7.9. *Give your mother space, be careful and safe*

When communicating with an angry person, you must be present. You shouldn't be hugging her, but you have to be there. Do not block the exit from the room, but stand so that in the event of an emergency you have the opportunity to move away. When a mentally ill person is disturbed, beware of any contact if you are not entirely sure that she will like it.

As your mother's anger is usually caused by a specific event, be as careful as possible with her. Gently try to discover the source of the anger. Do not ignore or minimize the alarm. Help your mother focus on what will help her cool her anger. Initially, it is necessary to find a way to calm down and later, in a calm state, to find out the cause of the anger.

Do not allow your mother to cross the line of acceptable behavior. If she raises her voice, throws things, threatens you, breaks furniture, or worries neighbors, you must confidently object and say that this is bad behavior.

7.10. *Basic rules for combating a BPD mother's anger:*

- Do not lose your composure, speak calmly and clearly;

- Stay calm, do not show your fear, as this will only make the situation worse;

- Give her the opportunity to leave;

- Do not touch or approach your mother until she has approved it;

- Try to objectively evaluate the possible outcome;

- Try to determine how angry and unreasonable she is, whether it is a manifestation of the disease or if there is another reason to consider;

- Do not discuss nonsensical ideas;

- Help her decide on further action;

- Protect yourself and others from possible violence.

If irritation and anger are common components of your mother's behavior, and she regularly releases aggression, then wait for the anger to pass, before attempting to discuss the matter wth her.

7.11. You need to follow these four rules:

1. Do not irritate your mother, as this will cause even more aggression.
2. Unleash your negative energy through workouts, chores, or just go and yell out in a hidden place.
3. Calm yourself by watching television or reading a book.
4. Give your mother medication prescribed by a doctor.

To reduce the likelihood of repeated anger attacks, you must first understand that a mentally ill person is an ordinary person with characteristics such as self-doubt and low self-esteem. Treat your mother with understanding; like any sick person, she needs compassion and support. A mentally ill mother is also disorganized physiologically and spiritually. You don't have to scold her for that; try to communicate more optimistically, put kindness, warmth, and respect into the conversation.

7.12. Things you must never forget

Remember that someone suffering from a mental disorder may get confused, and their feelings and contradictions increase. If your mother does not turn to anger, you must communicate with her more often about the problems and difficulties she encounters. There is no need for long conversations; speak slowly and clearly. Let your mother be alone, take a break from others. If the situation gets out of hand, call an ambulance or police immediately.

7.13. What else do you need to know?

The medical definition of Borderline Personality Disorder tells us that it is a mental illness that is mainly characterized by a disorder of attitude towards reality, a disorder of thought, sensory deception, and a disorder of emotional expression. These symptoms can appear either individually or in different combinations. In the initial stages of the disease's development, intellectual ability is maintained, although over time certain cognitive deficits may develop. The disorder affects the basic functions of behavior.

Such a person may consider her most intimate thoughts, feelings or actions to be known by others and in this connection may develop delusional interpretations in the sense that natural or unnatural forces influence her thoughts and actions, often in a bizarre way. Thoughts are often dominated by peripheral and irrelevant concepts that are otherwise inhibited in normal mental activity.

Borderline Personality Disorder is caused by imbalances in the metabolism of the so-called neurotransmitters found in certain brain regions. The mechanism of neurotransmitter operation could most simply be illustrated as a fast data flow between two nerve endings. In this way, the two endings are in communication with each other, and as a result of a large number of such neural connections, total brain function is created. The metabolism of these substances is very lively and precisely regulated, and a certain disturbance in their metabolism is the cause of the condition.

Current knowledge indicates that there is multifactorial causation in the onset of psychosis, and we know from this that the disease is not only hereditary or genetically determined, since in only 48% of cases of identical twins do both members suffer from this condition. The disorder is not sampled solely by environmental factors, and we can say that the condition is caused by genetic predisposition, and in combination with environmental factors.

Borderline Personality Disorder is not a product of desire, insolence, or inactivity. Factors that increase the likelihood of psychosis are a genetic predisposition and accumulated stress events, and excessive alcohol and drug use.

7.14. What does all of this mean?

This means that Borderline Personality Disorder is one of the most complex conditions and this can have catastrophic consequences. So you have to direct your behavior as we showed you in the examples. Don't yell, don't show aggression, and try as hard as you can to support your mother. We know that you feel angry, but remember that everything you went through was just a result of your mother's condition. If you want to help yourself you have to help her too. Only in this way, will you help yourself. Forgive all the insults and all the humiliation. Let the knowledge that your mother didn't want this help you. These are all just life circumstances and for you to learn how to treat your mother and defend yourself properly you must accept that. This way you will be able to move on and have a good and healthy life.

CHAPTER EIGHT

HOW TO HELP A CHILD COPE WITH A BORDERLINE MOTHER

Many things have been taken from you; we will not pretend that is not the case. You have been thrown into the mud from the very beginning of your life and your life circumstances have forced you to become a person who is afraid of interaction. They have caused you to become a person wearing a mask, a person who does not trust others and who thinks that he is not good enough for others.

You have had many challenges throughout your life, you have suffered a lot. There was never enough attention, love, compassion, and tenderness for you. You as a child needed to be loved. You were loved, but you were also distressed due to life circumstances. As a kid you needed love, you needed attention, you needed a hand you could take. You needed a foothold in life.

Unfortunately, you didn't get any of this. From birth you were thrown into a whirlwind of aggression and you could never understand why this was so. We have talked about everything you went through. But one thing is clear and worthy of note – you are still here, you are reading this because deep down you know that you can bring your life back, that you can live better and you have made your decision. You deserve a medal because you didn't give up, you didn't let that stop you, you moved on. Everything that life threw into your face, you threw back at life, put simply, you managed to defend yourself.

8.1. How to deal with a mother suffering from Borderline Personality Disorder

In this story, children are the main victims because they need help and they should not have to pay for what is not their fault. If we look at all this objectively, we can see it is not their mother's fault either but the fault of fate. Many children suffer daily and should be motivated by what you have gone through and what you have overcome. And one more thing is very important; who is a better person than you to understand the pain and suffering of other children who are going through life with a mother with Borderline Personality Disorder?

Your "friends in pain", the children who have been through the same abuse as you are experiencing social anxiety.

8.2. What is social anxiety?

When children experience social anxiety, they are afraid of situations where they have to interact with other people, and they are afraid of situations where they would be the center of attention. They are often worried that others will think badly about them or that they will do something shameful.

Social anxiety is mainly seen in older children and teenagers but can be diagnosed even in children as young as four. It occurs as a consequence of poor relationships between children and mothers.

Some of the signs of social anxiety in children are:

- They are shy or withdrawn;
- They have difficulty approaching other children or joining groups;
- They have a limited number of friends;
- They tend to avoid situations where they notice that they might be the focus (such as not wanting to start a game even when the teacher asks for it; not answering questions in front of other children, etc.).

8.3. They think bad things will happen

School children with social anxiety usually have a fear of reading aloud in front of the class or answering questions in front of others. Sometimes they start avoiding daily activities such as going to school (feigning illness, etc.). School children avoid or rarely perform in front of peers or seniors. They often have a worse concentration than other children. Also, it is not uncommon for them to avoid birthday parties or visiting friends; they rarely initiate the first game or call to go to the park. Young children have a fear of new things, are irritable and cry often, they refuse to speak, and often withdraw from the group.

Some children with social anxiety monitor group events very closely, but never join in. Children with anxiety lack the confidence to try new things, and sometimes they are unable to cope with daily challenges. Some anxious children are prone to angry outbursts.

As with adults, social anxiety in children can also have physical symptoms such as nausea, abdominal pain, redness, hand tremors, and the like. It is not easy to notice social anxiety at this age. The reason for this is because children are small and often obedient to institutions (which is a desirable situation, right?), so perhaps less attention is paid to something that "doesn't look like a problem." Also, children may not be able to talk about it. In most cases, younger children do not have a well-developed set of words to explain what is happening to them, what they are afraid of, and what they are worried about.

8.4. Shame or social anxiety

Shyness is not a problem itself; many shy children make satisfying, long-term friendships. But the problem occurs when it prevents a child from engaging in daily activities such as class discussions with older children or fun events with kindergarten children, or making lasting friendships along the way. In this case, the problem must be resolved.

How can we help a child who has a social anxiety issue because of their mother's influence?

There are many things you can do at home with your children, or when you are in another social setting, or whenever you talk to them about their disturbing emotions.

At home (by father or family member):

Try to prepare your child for situations that are scary or worrying. Act out the situation in the house and practice things that would make it easier for him/her in their next encounter with the unwanted situation. Encourage your child to do some "detective work." For example, if he thinks everyone will laugh at him if he answers the questions asked in a class or kindergarten, ask "how do you know that someone will laugh at you?" It can also help to talk to your child about some of the times when you, too, felt anxious in social situations. This can help your child feel that it is perfectly okay to talk about how he or she feels. They will consider it supportive. Gently encourage your child to join a particular social situation and start new activities. Assess the situation yourself but try to avoid ones that can make the problem worse;

Do not force your child to talk or do things in front of others unless he or she wants to. If your child has an anxious reaction to this situation, do not immediately lose patience, but try a second time with a little more preparation. Do not punish your child for "failure" or push him or her into any given situation.

Inform the teacher of your child's anxiety problem. It is also important to note what you all do at home with your child to address social anxiety. In this way, educators can get involved in the problem and there is the possibility that they will try to provide the child with consistent support as much as possible.

When talking to your child:

Whenever your child completes an activity he or she found frightening, let them know that you think they are brave. Praise him quietly and when you are on your own; make it a very important thing that he has been able to accomplish this task. This helps to nurture children's self-esteem.

Avoid labeling your child as "shy." If others comment on your child's behavior in social situations and front of him/her, you can always respond "he relaxes with people he knows well." Even if you feel frustrated, avoid criticizing the child or displaying any negative behavior related to their social anxiety.

8.5. Kids need help

You know what social anxiety is. You went through all this yourself. All that you have gone through, the abuse and lack of support you received led to symptoms that can be called one general and abstract name – social anxiety.

8.6. Hard life

Much is said about violence; what happened, who committed it and who suffered from it. Society is often urged to report every form of violence as soon as it is encountered, but do we know how to recognize a victim of violence? How do we recognize a child who lives with a mother suffering from Borderline Personality Disorder? And how do we help him or her cope?

8.7. What is violence?

We all know what physical violence is – bruises, torn skin, and hiding injuries. But it is important to know that violence does not have to be physical.

Violence can also include calling someone derogatory names, insulting, ridiculing, intimidating, mocking, expelling from a group, spreading rumors, ordering, cruel criticism and blackmailing.

Psychological violence can be brutal and can cause a child to lose faith in himself completely. Victims are afraid to seek new friends for fear of being rejected again, so they choose to be alone, withdrawing into themselves.

The younger the child, the more likely it is that nightmarish fears, urination, stuttering and sucking of the thumb will occur as a result of the abuse, so extra attention should be paid to this, whether it is happening to your child or a child in your area. Older children experience self-harm – suicidal thoughts occur, and the parent may notice that the child is beginning to lie, as well as developing alcohol and drug problems.

Although victims are mostly withdrawn, silent and submissive, there is a possibility that the consequences of the abuse may be manifested differently. The victim may lose her sense of empathy for others and become a bully herself. Victims experience aggression, and the child usually tries to make up for the loss of control and helplessness by responding with aggression of her own.

8.8. Silence is a problem

Children often choose to remain silent, and violence can be difficult to prove. Children are silent and suffering, and any long-term stress has serious health and psychological consequences. Eating and sleeping disorders occur, and it can be observed that children have frequent headaches and abdominal pain. When a child suffers from violence, extreme and frequent mood swings, changes in habit, and low self-esteem can occur. The victims remain silent and fear that if they admit they have been abused and abused, it will be worse. The children fear that the abuser, in this case, the mother, will find out and become even more brutal. It is important to teach children that there is no excuse for violence. No one should endanger one's right to a dignified life, no matter who it is.

8.9. A no-win situation - what's going on in the victim's head?

Violence emotionally disables a child, creating a feeling of helplessness, hopelessness or despair. Violence can make children believe that they will never escape the clutches of the abuser. Victims can often be identified by a constant state of alertness, to the point that they are never fully relaxed, and are jumping at every sound. Victims have difficulties in social relationships; suffer from social anxiety, tension, and depression, which can continue to be expressed throughout life.

8.10. These are children's jobs

As stated above, victims of violence feel guilty and live in fear. If a child happens to trust you, do not let him down, accuse him of lying, or tell him that the problem will be solved by itself, but rather do your best to help him.

If you suspect that a child has been abused, broach this issue indirectly to gain the child's confidence. Avoid statements that start with "You," as they may indicate in the child's head that they are wrong. Also, pay attention to the tone you in which you are addressing your child. If you are too serious, she may give you the answers she thinks you want to hear. Speak in a more relaxed tone, which will encourage the child to reveal all the details.

8.11. How to deal

A child abused by their mother is the most difficult category of abuse when it comes to getting them to talk, because of the deep love children have for their mother. But children should be encouraged in every way to publicly say "my mother abuses me." Unfortunately, this rarely happens because of the child's unwillingness. Without real help, therapy, and counseling, a child can not only cope with the betrayal of his mother because he is in a subordinate role.

8.12. Tips for children

If this book ever gets to you, kids; to those of you who are suffering, contact a social work center. Tell your teacher at school, tell your neighbor, tell another family member what's going on.

You can only help yourself by seeking to spend as little time as possible at home. This way your interaction with your mother will be less. You can turn to the other parent and ask him or her for protection. It is important not to retreat into yourself, there is no way to saving yourself there. Life has already made you a "little soldier" so be brave and be a hero. Come forward and say that you are a victim of violence. If you notice this happening to someone else, tell everyone you believe can help. Tell your parents.

Don't run away from problems thinking they will magically disappear. Stand up boldly and say out loud that there is a problem. If you don't, there will never come a day when everything will stop and as you get older you will only suffer more. You will miss out on a lot of things in life and you will not even have a chance to see how beautiful life can be.

Once you know what violence is, how it manifests, who perpetrates it and how it affects the victim, go one step further and report it when you encounter it. We must not allow young lives to go out in front of our eyes just because we have made a conscious decision not to interfere. Every child deserves to have a happy life.

8.13. How can you help your child withstand the pressures of a mother with Borderline Personality Disorder?

You know best how it feels. You had to take it all yourself. That is why you are the perfect "savior" for children who need help because they live with a mother suffering from Borderline Personality Disorder. It's easier for you to recognize these kids than those who did not walk the same path.

It can be a comfort to you, knowing that you can help them. Maybe that it is one of the purposes of your life. It can help you to heal yourself and the altruism in you can greatly help these children.

You must be good and healthy first. You can only help others by first helping yourself. So don't give up and we're sure you won't. You're a fighter and that's a simple fact. You have struggled your whole life and now that you are "born again" you can speak publicly about this problem, you can advise these children, you can prevent other children from going through what you went through. In that fact lies the only beauty of what you went through. You can stop other kids from going through it. Think of all the ways you can contribute to society. You can save many and there is your power. So you have to persevere in your fight. You've already woken up and are eager to help, and tomorrow is when you can be the one to help others. It's a wonderful thought and a wonderful thing to think about. That you, from the sacrifice, may one day be a savior. That's beautiful.

CHAPTER NINE

HOW TO OVERCOME THE TRAUMA OF THE BORDERLINE MOTHER AS AN ADULT

The cause of most psychological, emotional problems is trauma. In your cause, it was the trauma you went through due to your mother suffering from Borderline Personality Disorder. But being stuck in trauma leads to the emergence and persistence of negative symptoms such as anxiety, depression, despair, anger, helplessness, hurt, pathological possessiveness, feelings of guilt, etc. All these feelings at the level of intellect are accompanied by negative beliefs such as: "I am not worthy, Life is meaningless, I will never change, and no one will love me" and other pessimistic thoughts.

It should be emphasized that these negative emotions, as well as negative beliefs, are only symptoms of trauma, that is, indicators that trauma is still within us, that it is still activated and that it significantly affects our perception of ourselves, other people, life and the world at large. It is important not to be ashamed of your trauma because you have figuratively gone through hell. Now you have to understand what is stopping you and not letting you live life like other people. What is that little voice in our head we were talking about?

9.1. What is trauma?

Trauma is an experience of defeat, a subjective experience that involves the simultaneous experience of being threatened (emotionally or physically) and the experience that there is nothing we can do about it; that we cannot escape or avoid a situation that threatens us. Simply put, trauma is a situation in which we experience danger, and in which we judge (truly or falsely) that we do not have the resources (capacity) to protect ourselves. Trauma can be a situation that happens to us personally, but it can also occur by watching other trauma survivors. Observing people experiencing trauma can also be traumatic for the observer, especially if he or she identifies with the person experiencing the trauma.

9.2. Big and small traumas

Most people think that trauma necessarily involves experiencing some extremely bad and extremely intense experiences such as rape, war, natural disasters, etc. But many small traumas also paralyze and damage the person. Traumatic situations can be, for example, a car accident, situations involving separation from loved ones, a change of environment, all kinds of emotional, physical and sexual abuse, intimidation and harassment at work, etc.

9.3. How does trauma affect the psyche?

Trauma always occurs in a specific context, in a specific situation, and at a particular moment in time. All the traumas we have survived that we have not got rid of remain in our memory and affect us as if they were happening now and here. Whenever we find ourselves in a context reminiscent of the trauma, some of its characteristics result in the activation of trauma. When the trauma is triggered, unpleasant symptoms occur, including primarily negative emotions (anxiety, depression, anger, etc.) and bodily reactions (strain, spasm, desire to escape, numbness, etc.). At the moment when a person first experiences trauma, he or she experiences shock because, as a rule, the traumatic situation occurs unexpectedly. In a moment of shock, a person usually does not feel intense emotions, is not aware of their bodily reactions and thoughts. Symptoms of trauma begin to manifest themselves only when a person comes out of shock and that is after a certain amount of time that the person has spent safely, outside of a situation in which he or she has experienced trauma.

A good example is a soldier who has returned from the battlefield, and is now in a safe environment; he feels the symptoms of trauma (he can't stand loud sounds, has nightmares, is anxious, depressed, withdraws from people, etc.). Non-resolved trauma is reactivated over and over in all situations reminiscent of the event. What is it that reminds a person of trauma? A person is triggered by any situation that is either reminiscent of the original trauma or is a situation in which the person has the experience of being trapped. A person who has experienced trauma but has not resolved it chronically suffers from symptoms of anxiety and depression. These symptoms indicate that the trauma is still active, that it is not resolved, and that the person is making strong efforts to suppress the traumatic experience. Anxiety and depression are indicators that suppression is unsuccessful, and unsustainable in the long run. When a person can no longer tolerate anxiety or depression, he or she often takes some substances that increase the suppression of trauma and its unpleasant symptoms. A person may resort to alcohol, drugs, cigarettes, antidepressants, sedatives, etc.

9.4. Why does trauma persist and create unpleasant symptoms?

Even if the trauma took place twenty or thirty years before the present moment, how is it possible that it affects us now and here? Trauma is written in the body, that is, in memory, which triggers some bodily reactions. These bodily reactions are survival instincts. All animals (including humans) have survival instincts that are very powerful and that are triggered in situations of survival or danger. Trauma cannot exist without the activation of survival instincts. These instincts serve to keep us in a dangerous situation and allow us to survive the danger. Safety is a top priority for our bodies. The problem arises when we remain stuck in instincts that have activated. The traumatic situation has passed, we have survived, but the instincts remain activated and the body acts as if the danger is still there. Activated instincts create symptoms.

Our body expects us to release trauma, to resolve it. But we are not always able to do so. When we are unable to release trauma, it becomes trapped in the body, forcing us to suppress the painful memories. Anxiety and/or depression occur as a signal that suppression is unsustainable. Then the person tries to suppress the anxiety as well and consequently, the anxiety intensifies. Then the person may resort to drugs, alcohol or drugs.

9.5. Suppression maintains trauma and its harmful effects

As long as we suppress the trauma and its symptoms, we cannot get rid of the trauma. It affects our experience of ourselves, others and the world we live in. Secondary negative symptoms may also develop under this condition, which is usually some type of depression.

9.6. Can we permanently clear the trauma and its symptoms?

To clear the trauma, the person must first agree to it; by his own will decide that he wants to get rid of the trauma and its symptoms and take responsibility for his feelings and the changes that will occur. When a person does this, they are ready for the process.

9.7. What does the process of trauma purification look like?

The process of cleaning trauma does not involve talking about trauma or reliving the trauma. We can talk about trauma for years without any result, and the same goes for reliving emotions that are just a symptom of trauma. The process of trauma purification involves a person experiencing some of the trauma symptoms and activating the trauma through them. This does not mean that the person will relive the whole traumatic experience; it is not therapeutic and does not produce the desired results. Rather, it it is about activating the survival instincts underlying it. When instincts are activated, we can then turn them off, deactivate them. When we shut down instincts, all trauma symptoms disappear permanently, as do all accompanying bodily symptoms.

9.8. How do we know that trauma has been deactivated, purified?

When the trauma is deactivated, the person is unable to reactivate that trauma. When a person re-imagines a traumatic situation or finds himself in a similar situation, he feels nothing, is often unable to even remember the trauma; it is simply gone. When the trauma clears, all the negative symptoms that it created disappear permanently.

When we clear the key traumas, the person not only has nothing to suppress (thus no longer feeling anxiety or depression), but has access to certain conditions that were previously blocked. We call these natural state resources. These resources are love, self-love, freedom, a sense of our boundaries, security, etc.

Each person walks through life collecting different experiences. Life is about gathering experiences and applying them and exploiting them in future situations. That's a real skill. We all love it when it we experience positive and happy experiences, those that bring us peace, satisfaction, pleasure, joy and put a smile on our face. We enjoy them and want to be constantly in the state that happy experiences bring us. But what happens when we experience a distressing, negative experience that we feel has characterized us and causes negative emotions that we cannot possibly get rid of? Most people like you are trapped in traumas of the past, dating back to childhood. You've survived much, much more than a soldier in the war, but now it's time to let go of the trauma. We have said many times that you have to let go of your memories – that little voice in your head has to go away. The biggest problem is the transfer of memories and a return to the past.

9.9. Transferring memories

Emotional memories are stored in our cells. When they are negative, they often remain unclear. This usually causes many physical and mental illnesses to develop. Our cells are always being renewed. Different cells are renewed at different speeds. Liver cells take 6 weeks to recover, while skin cells take 3 to 4 weeks. Our eye cells are completely renewed every two days.

9.10. The cells are complete

However, old memories remain in our cells. These old memories can cause decaying diseased patterns within the cells. And before the old station dies, it transfers its memory to the next station.

9.11. How to break that vicious circle?

The memory must be detected first. Some people know which trauma is keeping them captive, while some are unaware of it, that is, they have forgotten or suppressed it. But they feel the impact on their health, despite being unable to remember. But that's where your biggest asset lies; you know your trauma: your childhood and your mother with Borderline Personality Disorder.

9.12. How to overcome traumatic events

The general concept that trauma can still bring about positive change is a common theme that emerged in religious and philosophical teachings thousands of years ago, but it wasn't until the mid-1990s that the term "post-traumatic growth" was coined by psychologists Richard Tedeschi and Lawrence Calhoun. Tedeschi and Calhoun argue that post-trauma growth and recovery occur in five general areas:

- Respect for life

- Relationship with others

- New opportunities in life

- Personal strength

- Spiritual change

In addition to these five factors, there are many other items developed by these psychologists to determine an individual's progress in the area of the personal, observing others, and the meaning of events while dealing with the consequences of trauma. This approach involves dealing with post-traumatic stress, but also offers a new lens through which an individual can explore himself in the shadow of trauma.

This approach entails, first and foremost, empathy for patients and an understanding of their condition, rather than alleviating their suffering and moving on to proposing practical solutions. Most often, the help of a psychologist/psychiatrist/psychotherapist is sought after a traumatic event has occurred. Psychotherapy can help you see that things like this are true and possible:

- I found that I was stronger than I thought.

- Now I know I can handle it better.

- I have changed priorities about what is important in life.

Learning and growing from our own experience allows healing to take place in "real-time" – we are not just talking about it, we are getting into it.

Here's an example we believe you will see yourself in. A patient called Tanya (35) suffered psychiatric abuse from the age of 8 to 13. Tanya constantly felt lonely and distrustful of others and started the process of psychotherapy. In several psychodrama group therapies, Tanya experienced the support of group members by having people in the group stand behind her, hands on her shoulders in support, as she talked about her traumas. She received hugs when she cried or felt scared. Group members contacted her between sessions to see how she was feeling and progressing. At the end of the three-month therapy, Tanya said, "Because the members of my group were there for me, and they supported me when I was crying and when I was in pain, I was more likely to be able to count on others during difficult times."

9.13. What other methods can help overcome traumatic events?

Post-traumatic Stress Disorder is not a terminal illness. It can be treated with experiential methods such as group therapy for psychodrama, which deals with trauma in progress. As clients collectively build the strength to cope with their trauma, they realize that they can become winners in dealing with it.

Psychotherapists also recommend that story writing be used as an experiential strategy for identifying, clarifying, and solidifying post-traumatic recovery. Because every time we describe the events of our lives, we provide and discover the basic patterns of their meaning. It is the meaning of our experience that shapes how we feel, think and react.

No matter how difficult things were and the events you went through, it is important for you to understand that post-traumatic recovery and growth is a normal process that may be an opportunity for you to build a new life.

"These are wounds that never appear on the body, but that are deeper and more painful than anything that bleeds," wrote Lorel K. Hamilton. When we are physically wounded, the world sympathizes with us. We get sick leave, social assistance, and medical care. Unfortunately, when our emotions are hurt, most of this is missing. We have to create it ourselves.

Emotional trauma forces you to be your own hero. Here are six tips to help you do just that and let go of a bad childhood, your mother and that little voice in your head.

1. Give Priority to Taking Care of Yourself

For many of us, it is natural that we care most about our loved ones. We often do this at the expense of fulfilling our own lives. Unfortunately, you cannot pour from an empty glass. Caring for yourself must come first, especially for those who care for others. Look at yourself honestly, carefully and with love. Determine your needs. Do you need time in silence every day? Counseling or group therapy? Useful service work? An artistic expression? Relaxation? A weekend trip to reconnect with your spirit? Give these needs priority. Fill them without remorse.

2. Become Grateful

When we struggle with emotional demons, it can become natural for us to focus on the darkness in our lives. Instead, turn your eyes to the light. As often as you can, take a break to identify the five things that you are grateful for. They do not have to be deep or significant. Just be good enough. For example, I am currently grateful for water, sun, music, bed, and the internet. This exercise is simple but very effective. It changes our worldview. The world around us starts to look brighter, happier and more forgiving. By acting in the world with gratitude, we can transform it into the place we want it to be.

3. Respect Your Body

When emotions are challenged, it is normal for us to allow our physical health to deteriorate. Unfortunately, this is the opposite of what we need. When our body is healthy, our mind is clearer. Emotions come under our control. Our spirit is capable of dealing with the world better. Make sure you sleep enough. Stay hydrated. Exercise in a way that suits you, moderately or rigorously, indoors or out, alone or in a group. Eat the foods that supply your body with the nutrients it deserves. Stay away from the scales. This is not about how you look or how your clothes look. What matters here is how you feel.

4. Build a Support Network

The worst part of any trauma is the feeling of being alone in it. As human beings, we are not created to face challenges ourselves. We need emotional support. Because of this, there is a support group for almost every major emotional challenge. From depression to addiction, incurable illness to sexual assault, there is certainly a group with people like you. First, you enjoy the warm relief that you are no longer alone in your fight. Then, allow them to share their experience, strength, and hope.

5. Communicate Honestly

Bad will and intolerance grows in you as long as you keep them. If you have a problem with a loved one, let them know. Tell her how she hurt you. Put your feelings on the table, calmly and kindly. This is how you give yourself the freedom to forgive. Remember, forgiveness is not about the other person. It's about your decision to let go of the hurt and get on with life. Don't let the other person's unkindness have power over your heart for a day.

6. Write your story

When our hardest feelings remain in us, they become stronger. There is something liberating in the decision to put them on paper instead. Use the pen to regain power. Let the words flow, and then read them to yourself. This is how you allow your mind to create new insight and perspective. You also allow your emotions to be released from your brain and body and find a new home on paper.

"Anything human can be mentioned, and anything that can be mentioned is manageable. When we talk about our feelings, they become less burdensome, less poignant, and less scary. The people we confide in with this important conversation can help us know that we are not alone," Fred Rogers wrote. If you are injured, do not hide. Fight. Connect with others and connect with yourself. Love yourself enough to heal your wounds.

Your trauma is great without a doubt. But you have done a lot of things for yourself just by reading this book. Now you have to persevere. The most important thing is that now, more than ever you believe in yourself, we believe in you because you have almost come to the end of the book. You are aware of yourself and the confusion that has occurred. Now is the time to "feed the good wolf," to rise above what was and to leave the past where it belongs.

My grandmother once told me something that I still carry with me and that takes me through life and now I will share it with you. She said to me "Son, you are a blacksmith of your fortune."

CHAPTER TEN

START YOUR HEALING PROCESS

You've come to the last chapter of this book. Congratulations on your persistence and for the fact that you have started your healing process. This has been a long journey.

You would never have read this book if you did not want deep answers. You wanted to find out if there was a way to live better, to be a better person. Not to be the one hiding behind the mask because he is afraid to show himself and have a normal interaction with others.

All your life you've stood by and watched other people happy and content with their lives. You tried to get away from others, you had no one to turn to because you didn't trust anyone. The sad truth is that this is a very sensitive topic without many people being aware of how painful and severe it is. Borderline Personality Disorder is a condition that is difficult in itself, and when the mother is the abuser and the child is a victim, as in this story, it becomes an even more difficult topic.

Now that you know everything, your path to healing can begin. But there are a few things you need to do to finally move forward and start a new happy part of your life story.

10.1. Forgive your mother

To forgive means to get rid of the hurt and the need to punish the one who hurt us. Don't hold on to the past and resent your mother. We kept saying – she never consciously wanted you to be hurt. To forgive involves letting go of anger and feelings of shame, as well as getting rid of the need to talk again about a painful event and how to hurt we are. Forgiveness has nothing to do with the person who hurt you, forgiveness is what will bring you relief and deliverance and what allows you to continue on your path to what you want.

To forgive does not mean to forget, because it is impossible, and the mere memory of the event serves us not to make the same or similar mistakes in the future.

10.2. Spiritual prerequisites

First of all, it must be understood that at the spiritual level, each injury has long been agreed upon. We agreed with the people who would hurt us long ago, before coming to this planet, what they would do to us and what we would learn through that lesson. Of course, there is spiritual amnesia and we are not aware of it throughout our lives, but that does not mean that there is no prerequisite.

In my experience, the people who hurt us are our most important teachers and the people who have enabled us to grow the most. A lot of people in this form get their "wake up call" and thus begin their spiritual growth.

10.3. Forgiveness is a process that takes time

It is one thing to make a mental decision to forgive, and it is quite another to truly forgive, to get rid of toxic feelings and replace them with compassion. Spiritual bypass happens when, knowing that it is good to forgive, we neglect to be deeply hurt on an emotional level. We must process and release all emotions associated with the event. That is why it is important to face our feelings we feel and release them. Forgiveness takes time; it is a process.

10.4. Giving up judgment

To truly forgive someone, we need to completely give up condemnation, what we believe to be just, unjust, bad and good, and look at the whole story from a higher perspective. Understand that it happened to us because our soul has chosen such a lesson. Not only did we choose, but we also needed to grow, so it was important to learn. Forgiveness is one of the most powerful things we can do for ourselves and it brings about a great transformation when it happens.

10.5. Pitfalls in the process of forgiveness

The whole process of forgiveness is hampered by what is called the "victim concept" that can be found in almost every one of us. It is necessary to recognize this part of yourself and to change it gently. Our ego loves to be right and that is why we remain stuck in our anger and feel injustice for longer. The trap we often fall into is that we think we would never do something like that. Getting rid of expectations from others but also from ourselves is perhaps the most beautiful gift we can give ourselves because all disappointments come from it. If we drop expectations then there will be no disappointment.

10.6. To forgive means to give yourself love

Forgiving someone means actively applying love for oneself. And as you have probably experienced, the most difficult person to forgive is yourself. So give special attention to this process and get yourself out of the door, stop expecting perfection from yourself, give yourself permission to make a mistake and just be more laid back with yourself and others.

10.7. At every moment, each of us does the best we can

The truth is that the person who hurt us is a being who has also been deeply hurt and who did not know how to do better than she did. This is a person who has not healed their wounds. It is the same with us; until we heal our wounds, we hurt ourselves and others. Essentially, each of us does the best we can in the circumstances.

10.8. Let go of the past

Do you regularly lose yourself in sad and bitter thoughts about past events in your life? Do you often find it futile to try because everything will "turn out bad again?"

We humans are always on the lookout for patterns in our experience. In this way, we make sense of everything that happens to us and the world around us. This system works pretty well for most things and has been the driver of our evolution. It helps us to decide more easily what action i.e. action to take when confronted with a new situation and experience.

10.9. Why is it so difficult sometimes to let go of the past, even when we try?

In some cases, we may have problems with the disagreement between the facts as if it were some "system error" that appears in our mental software. This usually happens when it comes to strong emotions. Most likely, we will remember very clearly and vividly the things we have strong feelings about. These patterns will, therefore, make our choices stronger than others.

So, if some disturbing or sad events or situations from our past are also very emotional for us, they can grow quite big in our heads, making us hyper-sensitive to similar patterns in the present. We make a connection between things of the past and things that seem similar to us in the present, even when they are not very similar. It's like "cleaning everything with the same cloth."

For example, someone who was previously in a very unhappy relationship may find themselves in a situation of fear and anger, even when the present relationship is good. They create the wrong link between the old and the new situation based on the learned pattern of connections from the past that can cause unexpected difficulties in the current relationship.

To let go of the past, you need to change how you feel about those events. Of course, we cannot undo what happened in our past. So, are we doomed to live with such "broken links" and their unintended consequences forever? Are we stuck surviving what happened over and over, wishing it was different? Of course not, because even though history cannot be restarted, we can change how we feel about it. And we can do this by eliminating the emotional toll on past events, emotionally distancing ourselves from them all. This involves making an emotional change within us and finding a healthier, more positive view of those events of the past.

When you start living day by day and when you learn to fully indulge, you will experience a range of benefits. Nobody likes bad times because they harm our mood and mind. All of us have a past filled with bad memories and days that we may regret, but it's never good to think about the past. When you learn to live in the present and let go of the past, positivity and hope will come into your life.

10.10. Avoid bad moods

We all have bad days and times when we are not in the best of moods. Living in the past can cause a bad mood, and this attracts and spreads negative energy. That's how you create a negative and unhealthy environment, and no one wants to live that way.

10.11. Start living a new life

Have you ever caught yourself living in the past, thinking about bad memories, situations, and problems? This happens occasionally to everyone, especially when we are doing something that reminds us of the past. It can be frustrating! That is why it is important to combat this mindset. You need to forget the past and continue living. Life always goes on.

10.12. Relieve stress

Stress is the worst and strongest enemy. With a hectic lifestyle, stress can rarely be completely resolved. Still, that doesn't mean you don't have to try and try to eliminate stress. One way is to stop living in the past. Doing so will remove one of the leading sources of stress; focus on the future, and stop worrying about the past.

10.13. You can't change anything

One important question that will help you stop thinking so much about the past is: can you go back in time and change certain events? The answer is, definitely not. No matter how dissatisfied you are with your past, always remember that you can do absolutely nothing about it.

10.14. Learn how to take control and become happy

Another reason you need to stop thinking about the past and start living in the present is positivity. Positivity is an important part of life that helps make peace, adopt healthy habits, and bring positivity to life.

10.15. Release your fear

Fears are usually very difficult to deal with, and one of the reasons for their appearance is the lack of courage to deal with them. One way to stop living in fear is to indulge yourself and stop thinking about the past and certain events that caused you to live in fear.

10.16. What steals your inner peace?

Are you addicted to something? If you are currently experiencing addiction, try to stop it because it will make your life better. If you stop being addicted to something, then keep that attitude. Make sure you completely forget that you have ever been addicted to anything.

10.17. Love yourself

If you think about the past and some of the bad events that you have faced and what you resent about yourself, you will certainly not be happy. Live in the present and stop thinking about the past because it will bring you love for yourself.

10.18. Get happier

The health of the body is very important when it comes to being able to live a fulfilled life. Poor health will make it difficult to perform certain activities, and you certainly do not want to be that kind of person. Get rid of the past and focus on the present, because then you will become healthier and, ultimately, happier.

10.19. Make new friends

Friends are a necessary part of life; without them life would not make sense. Good friends make our days happier and more beautiful. If you live in the past, all you have to think about is problems and you will continue to believe that no one wants you. You need to think solely about the present because it will give you confidence and will attract new people into your life.

10.20. Yesterday is history

What has happened in the past is now unattainable. Given that the past cannot be changed, the future is the only point in focus.

10.21. The present is important

The past is important and it is something we can learn from. In the present, where you live and act, you need to stop worrying about the past and become interested solely in the present.

Freedom is a blessing that cannot be replaced by anything else. Freedom is about doing whatever you want whenever you want. Don't limit yourself and stop being a slave to the past. Always think only about the present and how you can learn from past mistakes.

10.22. The past affects your present abilities

Have you ever thought that the past can cause your present abilities to decline? The past can have such an impact on your abilities that you will start to feel like you have made a lot of mistakes and are still making them. This is why you need to forget the past to eliminate these thoughts.

10.23. Become successful

Who among us does not want to be successful, feel independent and do the things we have only dreamed of? Success doesn't just happen; you need to act, be patient and move forward. One way to achieve this is to leave the past behind and start living in the present.

10.24. Make your days happy

Happiness is something that needs to be strived for every day. Happiness is contagious and brings benefits not only to you but to the people around you. This way you build a healthy and positive living environment.

10.25. Avoid creating problems

Who wants extra problems? Do not create problems where there are none. It will affect you physically, morally and emotionally. If you continue to live in the past and stop hoping for a beautiful and bright future, you will create additional and unnecessary problems.

10.26. Stop being depressed

Depression is characterized by intense sadness caused by various events. Depression can cause many problems. You should do your best to avoid it and practice positive thinking and optimism. One of the leading causes of depression is thinking about the past.

10.27. Work on confidence

Self-confidence is the way we experience our abilities. Focusing on the past will never boost your confidence. Living in the moment while ignoring the past can help boost your confidence.

10.28. Set a goal

Setting goals is what will encourage you to achieve your dreams. Thinking about the past will discourage you from setting goals because you will think that you will never succeed.

10.29. Be a role model

It will have a positive effect on your life and be a pleasure for you. When you think about being someone's role model, you will instinctively start living the best you can, because only then will you be able to advise others to do the same.

10.30. Be positive

Positive thinking is a state of mind in which thoughts, images, and ideas with positive effects inhabit, grow and spread, cheering a man on and filling his glass forever so that it is not half empty. Negative thoughts are said to attract negative situations, and positive ones are good, joyful and blessed. Therefore, changing your attitude for the better will help you to create your life exactly the way you want it.

The power of positive thinking should be gradually built up and only then will you help reap its fruits.

If you decide to build your life on an ever-optimistic basis, read below about the benefits of positive thinking.

10.31. More energy

Sometimes fatigue is in the brain and mind, not in the body. If you are positive you will forever fly on the wings of good energy. You will find it easier to cope with day-to-day situations and to cross any obstacles that come your way.

10.32. Better health

The way of thinking greatly affects the functions of the body. When you replace negative thoughts with calmness and self-confidence, the anxiety and worry will just disappear. It also means that the muscles in your body will relax and any disturbance of sleep and fatigue will be absent. Positive people also suffer less from depression. So start being positive – now.

10.33. Start creating a new chapter in life

So far, your life has not even come close to being good. There is no doubt about that. You never received anything; you were not appreciated enough, as a child you suffered a lot. It's time to close that chapter in your life.

Teach yourself to live your life to the fullest. Turn your head to the other side. There is no need to wear a mask, no need to hide. Forgive your mother, let go of the past, and be positive.

Seek the help of an expert to guide you towards healing, but most importantly, have the will. Will is the key, will has led you to this book and you have already made the first steps.

This book ends, but your story is just beginning. You are closing the cover, but at the same time, you are opening the cover of a new, happy and beautiful story. And remember - you are the blacksmith of your fortune.

CONCLUSION

In this book, we have touched on a very sensitive topic. We talked about Borderline Personality Disorder and how this condition can affect life. It is important to know how dangerous Borderline Personality Disorder is, and hopefully we have been able to reach people. People need to become familiar with this topic. People need to learn about this topic because it has not been sufficiently studied. This book is even more important because it emphasizes a critical point in this condition. In this book, we have touched on the relationship between a mother suffering from Borderline Personality Disorder and a child who is in a victim position.

This book defines this condition and serves as a guide to identifying Borderline Personality Disorder, and through the chapters you will have found out everything you need to recognize the condition, to spot symptoms that can often be so masked that they are almost impossible to recognize. This book is will help you see these symptoms and respond appropriately. This is a serious problem and it is even more significant when you bear in mind that victims are the most sensitive social category – children. Through the book, you have learned what Borderline Personality Disorder is, what the different types of Borderline Personality Disorder are, and how a mother suffering from this condition behaves. We have also examined how it affects the child, how can the child be protected, what the main problems these children face are, how children may feel like victims and what the consequences of this toxic mother-child relationship are.

The most important part of this book is the healing process. We believe that if you have gone through everything in the book, you can protect yourself, act preventively, and keep yourself safe. You must know that you are not alone and that you can look at life with fresh eyes. You were a victim, but that doesn't mean you can't get your life back.

You need to understand that life has no reprise. You only have one life and you should not live as a victim. Help yourself and know that you will succeed. All you need is to be persistent, to let go of the past, and to move boldly forward.

Because of this, love yourself and know that you are the only driver in your life.

DIALECTICAL
BEHAVIOR THERAPY

DAVID LAWSON PHD

INTRODUCTION

DBT works as a continuous relationship between clients and therapists. In this type of therapy, patients are encouraged to sort out their life problems in collaboration with their therapists. This demands that people role-play new methods of interacting with others, finish homework assignments, and rehearse skills like calming themselves when upset.

These skills form a crucial part of DBT and are taught to patients in weekly lectures and homework groups. In this way, individual therapists help their clients master the skills of DBT and apply them to their lives.

Four Stages of DBT

Treatment with DBT is commonly broken down into four levels. Clients are assigned to these levels based on the intensity of their behaviors. Therapists are instructed to follow the framework defined in these levels to help their clients. No specific timeframe has been allotted to these stages. The therapist and clients are allowed to take as much time as required, depending upon the client's target.

Level One

In level one, the patient is usually miserable and has lost control over themselves: they may be attempting to harm themselves, using drugs, or involving themselves in other self-destructive activities. When such clients start DBT, they may liken their experience to "being in hell."

The main goal of this stage is to help move the client from a state of no control to one in which they learn how to get a better hold of themselves.

Level Two

In level two, clients often feel like their lives are filled with desperation. They have control over their harmful behaviors, but they are still suffering, mostly due to invalidation or past trauma. This often continues to the extent that it disturbs their emotional experience.

The main goal of level two is to assist such people to get out of their state of desperation and to reinstate the emotional experience. The treatment for people suffering from post-traumatic stress disorder (PTSD) falls into this level.

Level Three

In this level, the aim is to motivate the patients to live, find happiness and peace, and build self-respect. The therapist enables the client to live a normal life with moments of both happiness and sadness.

Level Four

For some clients, an additional fourth level is required to familiarize them with the concept of spiritual existence. This stage has been created for clients whose life of happiness and sadness does not help them find peace or feel connected to the world.

The main goal of this stage is to assist the client in moving on from a feeling of incompleteness to a life which grants them the ability to enjoy the feeling of freedom and joy.

What Makes DBT Different?

The world is convinced that DBT can do wonders, but why is it that it continues to work even when gold-standard treatments like CBT have failed?

In simple words, DBT tends to fill in the gaps left behind by most other therapies, including CBT. For example, CBT emphasizes changing behaviors and thoughts to the extent that the clients can be appalled. Most therapies targeting problems like stress, anxiety, PTSD, etc. do not encourage or support their clients to accept where they are right now. They invalidate people by using cognitive distortions as justification that their feelings are wrong. That's where DBT differs.

DBT Promotes Acceptance-Based Behaviors

Dialectical Behavior Therapy is a form of CBT, but what makes it more successful and unique is its emphasis on dialectical thinking and mindfulness. Instead of treating the symptoms as problems to be solved, this therapy puts equal focus on the acceptance of experiences by incorporating acceptance-based behaviors.

Dialectical thinking is a philosophical stance in which two truths or ideas, which seemingly oppose each other, exist at the same time. For example, a person coming for help may need to accept where they are right now as well as requiring motivation to change.

In simpler words, while DBT helps people promote feelings of acceptance, it makes them acknowledge that they have the capacity to create more positivity and do much better. This is something that can exclusively be achieved through DBT.

DBT Works with Emotions

DBT is a form of in-depth therapy that involves the process of learning cognitive and emotional skills and applying these skills to your life. It helps tackle distressing and difficult emotions and helps you improve your capacity for emotional regulation. By improving your emotional regulation, you are able to control and express your emotions in a much better way.

DBT Enhances Capabilities with Skills Training

What makes DBT different to other approaches is that it focuses on improving the capabilities of clients by teaching them different behavioral skills. Skills training is taught in a classroom setup. A group leader is assigned to every class, and their primary responsibility is to teach different skills through classroom activities, lectures, and take-home assignments.

This homework helps the client apply the skills they learn in class to their daily experiences. The groups meet every week for about 2.5 hours to discuss the happenings in their daily lives. To grasp the full curriculum, an average person requires 24 weeks. Sometimes, the program may be repeated to form a 1-year program.

Skills Training in DBT revolves around four different modules, each of which helps the client become stable in their lives. These modules include:

Mindfulness: This is the skill which helps you become aware and present in the current moment.

Distress Tolerance: This refers to the skill which helps you tolerate pain in tough conditions, instead of changing the situation.

Interpersonal Effectiveness: This refers to the skill of asking for whatever you need and learning to say no without compromising your self-respect and in your relationships.

Emotional Regulation: This refers to the skill of changing the emotions you wish to change.

But how does acquiring these skills help people?

Problematic behaviors occur as a way to manage a situation or resolve a difficult problem. While such behaviors provide a temporary solution or relief in the short term, they are rarely effective in the long run. DBT acknowledges this and assumes that patients are doing everything in their capacity, but at the same time, they need to acquire new behavioral patterns in relevant contexts.

DBT helps such clients develop behavioral skills in the following four areas: emotional regulation, distress tolerance, mindfulness, and interpersonal effectiveness. These skills help clients acquire useful ways to navigate situations occurring in everyday life, and help them tackle challenges.

DBT Enhances Motivation Through Individual Therapy

DBT is an individual form of therapy that is focused on improving the client's motivation and helping them apply learned skills to tackle specific events in their lives. It is a unique approach that helps them accept their flaws, yet motivates them to get up and do better instead of treating them like victims who need sympathy.

DBT Ensures Generalization

DBT includes telephone coaching and other types of coaching to provide clients with in-the-moment support. The goal is to coach them on how to use DBT skills to cope with hard situations as they arise.

Therapists are available all the time to guide clients through difficult situations, which is something that seldom occurs in other therapy sessions.

DBT Structures the Environment via Case Management

DBT incorporates case management strategies that help the client manage their own life, including their social and physical environments. Therapists apply the same validation, problem-solving, and dialectical strategies to enable the client to analyze their problems without any external help. This empowers them to manage their problems on their own with minimal interference from a therapist unless absolutely necessary.

Thanks for downloading this book. It's my firm belief that it will provide you with all the answers to your questions.

CHAPTER 1

WHAT IS DIALECTICAL BEHAVIOR THERAPY?

Dialectical Behavior Therapy, or DBT, is a form of Cognitive Behavioral Therapy that focuses on solving behavioral problems by incorporating dialectical processes and acceptance-based strategies. It is best suited to the needs of patients suffering from intense emotional distress that prevents them from experiencing a good quality of life.

DBT was developed by American psychology researcher and author, Marsha Linehan. She created the therapy as a result of her struggles with schizophrenia and suicidal thoughts at a young age. She was institutionalized for her mental illness until the age of 18.

Convinced that CBT left a gap that needed to be filled, Linehan developed DBT at the University of Washington years later. DBT consists of four key skill areas and main components: interpersonal skills training, distress tolerance, emotional regulation, and mindfulness training.

DBT treatment can be delivered in many ways, typically consisting of individual therapy sessions and/or DBT skills groups. For example, while some patients may complete individual therapy sessions without attending any skills group, others might opt for group sessions without individual therapy.

An individual therapy session consists of a one-on-one session with a DBT therapist. This ensures that the patient's therapeutic needs are attended to. Over the course of the treatment, the therapist will also help the patient apply DBT skills on a daily basis, appropriately address daily struggles that occur, and stay motivated.

DBT skills groups, on the other hand, encourage members to learn and practice skills with each other while they are led by a DBT therapist. Members provide mutual support and listen as others share their experiences.

Therapists in a group session teach skills and lead members in group exercises. Each member is assigned homework, which often involves practicing mindfulness exercises.

Group sessions are typically completed within six months. Weekly sessions are conducted with each one lasting around two hours. The exact length of each session depends on the needs of each member.

How DBT Works

To build a life worth living, which is the main goal of DBT, client and therapist first sit down and make plans. They then set their goals and expectations.

There are five components in a standard DBT treatment program: a) a skills group, b) individual therapy, c) skills coaching, d) case management, and e) a consultation team. This section will provide an overview of the standard program.

Led by a therapist group leader, group sessions for teaching and learning behavioral skills happen every week and last about 2.5 hours. They are run like a class, and homework assignments are given so that patients can practice their newfound skills.

Twenty-four weeks are required for the entire skills curriculum, and this can be repeated to create a 1-year program. Depending on the situation and the needs of the patients, a shorter subset of this curriculum can also be taught.

The Four Skills Modules in DBT

The purpose of this skills group training is to improve clients' capabilities so they can effectively deal with the problems and challenges that arise in their daily lives. They learn from these four skills modules:

1. Mindfulness (being aware of ourselves and the situation we're in),

2. Distress tolerance (learning how to tolerate our pain in tough situations),
3. Interpersonal effectiveness (learning both assertiveness and respect of other people), and
4. Emotion regulation (learning how to change our negative emotions).

Of these four skills modules, mindfulness and distress tolerance belong to the acceptance strategy of DBT; interpersonal effectiveness and emotion regulation belong to the change strategy.

Individual Therapy

The purpose of an individual psychotherapy session is to improve the motivation of each patient. Personal issues and struggles are talked about, with the therapist encouraging the patient in the light of DBT's focus on acceptance and change. Skills learned in group sessions are also reinforced. Furthermore, a real relationship of mutual help between therapist and patient is formed; the therapist becomes a true partner in the process, not just a teacher or observer.

Like with the skills group training, an individual therapy session happens every week and runs concurrently with it.

Skills Coaching

DBT patients can call their therapists at any time of the day, to ask for advice whenever problems arise. The goal of skills coaching is to train patients to practice and apply the skills they are learning in their lives.

Case Management

This is about helping patients manage their own lives. The therapist advises on the things to be done but intervenes only when necessary.

The Consultation Team

The therapists themselves are part of a consultation team, in which they are given support for the work they are doing. This way, they will stay motivated and competent. This kind of emotional support is especially needed for difficult cases.

Clients who choose to undergo Dialectical Behavior Therapy often have several behavioral problems to be treated, not just one. The therapist will then have to prioritize problems according to the following hierarchy: (1) threat to life, (2) interference to therapy, (3) interference to quality of life, and (4) the need to learn new skills. For example, suicidal thoughts of a patient will be dealt with first, before alcohol abuse.

Lastly, there are 3 to 4 stages of treatment for DBT. Stage 1 corresponds to the initial life of the patient being out of control. Stage 2 corresponds to continued silent suffering after some control has already been achieved. Stage 3 corresponds to the challenge of living life: setting goals, gaining self-respect, finding happiness. And Stage 4, which is needed only by some, corresponds to finding a deeper fulfillment and completeness through spirituality of some kind.

Is Dialectical Behavior Therapy really effective?

So, does it really work? The answer is a resounding yes. DBT is a treatment based on evidence, and research has shown that it is indeed effective against the mental health illnesses it is used on, which are many. It is also found to be effective on people of diverse backgrounds (in terms of age, gender, sexual orientation, and race), and it's already been implemented in more than 25 countries.

DBT has also received recognition from official authorities, like the American Psychological Association.

CHAPTER 2

DBT APPLICATIONS

DBT is most effective for people who experience emotions very intensely. They tend to be easily overwhelmed by life and relational stressors to the point that they feel that their emotional responses are out of control. Consequently, they often act in an impulsive manner in an attempt to temporarily relieve some of their distress. However, their reactions over the long term tend to create additional problems.

DBT was initially used to help individuals who were diagnosed with Borderline Personality Disorder (BPD). This was and continues to be a very effective form of therapy to use with these individuals. However, in more recent years, DBT has also been very successfully used with other individuals who demonstrate severe mood swings and are unable to apply coping strategies to successfully deal with these intense and sudden emotional urges. Many of these people struggle with severe depression, PTSD, eating disorders, severe compulsory disorders, Bipolar Disorder, ADHD, anger management, and/or substance abuse. Many people who seek out DBT also engage in self-harm, as this therapy has been shown to be very effective in helping individuals with this level of emotional trouble.

In order to really understand more about the person who generally does well in DBT, let's take a look at the specific characteristics that many of these people share. People who do well with DBT usually have a high level of emotional vulnerability. What this means is that they are prone to experiencing emotions in a very reactive and intense way. Sometimes, they are just hardwired to feel emotions more intensely than the average person. In fact, DBT theory asserts that the automatic nervous system of an emotionally vulnerable person is predisposed to be reactive to relatively low levels of stress. Their nervous system also takes much longer to return to baseline levels when the stressor is removed. Additionally, some people have mood disorders such as major depression or generalized anxiety that is not being effectively controlled by medication, and that influence how intensely they experience their emotions. Consequently, emotionally vulnerable people tend to have quick, intense, emotional reactions that are difficult to control. This keeps them on a roller coaster ride throughout their lives.

However, clinicians have found that most emotionally vulnerable people who seek DBT treatment are not JUST hardwired to have more intense emotions or have mood disorders. Typically, they have also been exposed to invalidating environments for extensive periods of time. Such environments generally stem from early childhood, but could have occurred at any point. These environments did not provide them with the support, attention, respect, or understanding that they needed to properly work through their emotions. Invalidating environments can range from ones involving severe emotional or physical abuse to mismatched parent and child personalities. Consider the shy child who is born or adopted into a family full of extroverts, and who is constantly teased about his or her introverted personality. Or perhaps it's the child with ADHD who has a mother and stepfather who are inflexible and constantly yelling at them. These are both examples of environments that are invalidating. When the person who already has a predisposition to experience more extreme emotions is placed in an environment that does not support or validate their feelings, they can become even more emotionally vulnerable. They may then begin to demonstrate even greater emotional reactivity because they inadvertently learned that the only time they were taken seriously was when they demonstrated extremely emotional behavior.

Let's take the introverted child as an example, and let's say it's a boy. Say he was constantly told by his father that he had to "man up" and become more aggressive in his approach to life. He felt ridiculed and began to think that there was something wrong with him. So, one day when his father was addressing him, the boy began to cry uncontrollably. His father immediately lightened up, and his mother came rushing to his aid, showering him with tons of attention. Then it happened again. And then again. An interesting thing began to happen. The young boy's unconscious mind began to see a pattern that looked like this: 'My dad harasses me, I cry uncontrollably, the hassling stops, I get lots of attention.' He began to do it more and more because it worked and each successful demonstration inadvertently reinforced the behavior. His emotional outbursts became validated, and then it ultimately becomes an ingrained coping skill.

The process described above unconsciously reinforced the child's emotional vulnerability, and you guessed it – made it worse. This is typically the pattern you see with people with Borderline Personality Disorder, Bipolar Disorder, eating disorders, and other disorders that DBT treats. The next section will give an overview of several of the disorders that are successfully treated with DBT.

Borderline Personality Disorder

People with Borderline Personality Disorder (BPD) experience emotions more intensely and for longer periods of time than other people. They are prone to frequent and chronic outbursts to the point that many mental health professionals have described this population as one that is experiencing an unrelenting crisis. They are nearly always in crisis mode as they have generally not learned the coping skills they need to better regulate their intense emotions.

Individuals with BPD are emotionally vulnerable, and it takes them much longer to return to baseline following an event. In addition, one of the patterns that therapists have described regarding people with BPD is their tendency to take on the same belief system as the invalidating environment that they are subjected to. This results in their own "self-invalidation," where they reject their own emotions and ability to solve problems. They also tend to develop unrealistic expectations for themselves and experience intense shame and anger when they fail to meet their goals or when difficulties arise.

Another defining characteristic of individuals with BPD is their tendency to make rigid and unrealistic demands of themselves and others. When things don't go as they planned or desire, they often resort to "blaming." Blaming is a thinking error that many people with BPD have. They blame everyone and everything for their problems and have trouble acknowledging the personal behavioral changes that need to be made in order to see different outcomes in their lifestyle.

Individuals with BPD have a poor sense of self and tend to struggle with interpersonal relationships. They tend to seek out individuals who will take control and solve their problems for them so that they can shrink back and not have to do so. However, they tend to wear the mask of competence so that others think that they are capable of solving their own problems and dealing with their intense emotions. Although they may have mastered certain areas of their life, they have not been successful at generalizing their competence in other areas.

Due to the lifestyle that most people with BDP have created, in combination with their difficulties in returning to baseline following an emotional event, they end up experiencing significant traumatic experiences on an ongoing basis. They also tend to avoid experiencing negative emotions altogether because they do not know how to regulate even healthy negative emotions. As a result, they do not know what to do when an emotional situation arises that they are unable to tolerate, which throws them into an intense and prolonged emotional state.

People with Borderline Personality Disorder sometimes engage in cutting or other self-harm and suicidal behavior to deal with the intense emotional pain. Emotional vulnerability is often seen in individuals who are suicidal or engage in chronic self-injury. The individual is highly emotionally reactive, and when exposed to very severe trauma such as physical or emotional abuse, they begin to think about suicide. Eventually, in an attempt to be relieved of the ongoing pain, they try to kill themselves and are taken to hospital. Here, they are given loads of attention, and for the first time, they begin to feel like they are being validated and taken seriously.

Consider the boy who engages in some type of self-injury, such as cutting or burning himself because he finds that it provides temporary relief. When someone else finds out that this is happening, people are suddenly taking him seriously. Similar to the experience of the first example, he is finally feeling validated.

What do you think happens in these two situations? Over time, the boys both continue to engage in these behaviors, because it is the only time they feel validated and supported. It becomes an ingrained coping skill.

Eating Disorders

An eating disorder is an illness whereby a person has eating habits that are considered irregular. However, the illness goes beyond simple disruption of food intake, as the person experiencing the eating disorder generally feels severe distress regarding their body weight and/or shape. In an attempt to regulate their appearance and feel better about themselves, people with eating disorders may begin to eat significantly less and become obsessed with exercise. This emotional and behavioral disturbance can occur in both sexes and generally has an extreme impact on the physical and emotional well-being of the person.

Although eating disorders can occur at any developmental stage, they typically emerge during adolescence or early adulthood and often coexist with other psychological and behavioral conditions such as substance abuse, mood disorders, and anxiety disorders. The three most common types of eating disorders are discussed below.

Anorexia Nervosa

An individual who experiences anorexia nervosa usually demonstrates a strong obsession with their weight. Due to their poor and unrealistic perceptions of body image, they are fearful of gaining weight and often refuse to maintain a weight that is healthy. Many people who struggle with this disorder limit the amount of food they eat to the point that their caloric intake cannot sustain their health. Even when they are visibly underweight and their appearance begins to generate concern in others, they continue to view themselves as overweight. Anorexia can lead to major health issues such as infertility, heart problems, organ failure, brain damage, and bone loss. People with this disease have a high risk of death.

Bulimia Nervosa

Individuals who struggle with bulimia generally fear being overweight and are very unhappy with the appearance of their body. This disorder is characterized by the cycle of binge eating followed by overcompensation for the binge eating. For example, a person may sit and eat excessive amounts of food in one sitting and then follow the eating with forced vomiting, excessive exercise, extreme use of laxatives and diuretics, or any combination of these compensatory behaviors. The cycle is done in secret as they generally harbor a lot of shame, guilt, and lack of self-control. Bulimia can also lead to health problems such as gastrointestinal problems, dehydration, and heart issues that result from an imbalance of electrolytes caused by the eating-purging cycle.

Binge Eating Disorder

Individuals who struggle with binge eating often lose control of their eating but do not engage in the purging process as with bulimia. Consequently, many people who experience binge eating may also have the corresponding disorder of obesity, which increases health-related problems such as heart disease. As with individuals with other eating disorders, individuals who battle this disorder often have feelings of intense shame, guilt, embarrassment, and feelings of loss of control.

It is believed that the development of eating disorders is multifaceted, as the disorders are generally quite complex. Some of the things that contribute to the emergence of an eating disorder include biological, psychological, and of course, environmental factors. These factors include:

- Biological factors such as irregular hormone functions and a genetic predisposition
- Nutritional deficiencies
- Psychological factors such as a negative body image and poor self-esteem
- Environmental factors such as a dysfunctional family unit
- Professions and careers that promote excessive thinness – like modeling
- Sports that promote thinness for performance such as gymnastics, wrestling, long-distance running, and others
- Sexual abuse in childhood
- Family, peer, and media pressure to be thin
- Transitions and life changes

Here are some of the signs and symptoms that someone may exhibit when struggling with an eating disorder:

- Chronic and excessive dieting even when underweight

- Obsession with caloric intake and the fat content of food

- Demonstrating eating patterns that are ritualistic. These rituals might include behaviors like eating alone, breaking food into small pieces, and hiding food for later consumption

- A fixation on food. Some individuals with eating disorders may prepare delicious complex meals for other people but refuse to eat the meal.

- People with eating disorders may also suffer from depression or lethargy

Although DBT has been shown to be very successful in treating individuals with eating disorders, they may need additional support in the early stages of treatment. Additional support may include being monitored by a physician to address any health issues that may have developed as well as working with a nutritionist until weight is stabilized. Often, the nutritionist will develop an individualized meal plan to help individuals return to a healthy weight.

Bipolar Disorder

This is also often referred to as Manic Depressive Disorder because of the individual's tendency to vacillate between manic episodes and more depressive states. This disorder is characterized by unusual and extreme changes in activity levels, energy levels, mood, and the ability to perform daily tasks. The symptoms are not the same as normal mood fluctuations, as they are severe and generally quite extreme to the point that individuals may damage relationships, jeopardize performance at work and school, and even contemplate suicide.

Like most psychological disorders, there is generally no single cause for Bipolar Disorder. It is often an illness that develops from a combination of biological and environmental factors. Many factors act together to produce the illness or increase the risk of the illness manifesting.

Genetics seems to play a role in the emergence of Bipolar Disorder as research has identified some genes that are more likely to influence the development of the disorder. Other research has shown that children from particular families or those who have a sibling with the disorder are more likely to develop the disorder themselves.

However, research has also shown that environmental factors play a strong role in its emergence. In identical twin studies where siblings share the same exact genetic makeup, when one twin develops the disorder, the other twin does not always. This indicates that something other than genetics is at work, which points to environmental triggers.

Individuals with this condition experience strong emotional states known as "mood episodes." Each episode can last for days or months. Each episode reflects an extreme change in presentation from the person's normal behavior. An exceedingly joyful, ecstatic state that is full of increased activity is typically the "manic" episode. The sad, dysphoric, hopeless, and sometimes irritable and explosive state is the "depressive" episode. A "mixed state" is when behavior characteristics of both a manic and depressive episode are present at the same time.

Here are some symptoms that are characteristic of Bipolar Disorder:

The manic episode includes symptoms such as:

- Feeling "high" for a long period, demonstrated by an excessively happy mood
- Fast-talking and hopping from one idea to another. This is reflective of running thoughts.
- Being easily distracted
- Excessive activity level and taking on many new projects
- Restlessness
- Limited sleep
- Unrealistic thoughts about what one can do
- Impulsiveness and preoccupation with pleasurable and risky activities

The characteristics of a depressive episode include:

- Long periods of extreme irritability

- Long periods of sadness or hopelessness

- Losing interest in events that a person once loved

- Tiredness and feeling sluggish

- Difficulties remembering, concentrating, and decision making

- Change in eating, sleeping, and other habits

- Suicidal ideation, gestures, and/or suicidal attempts may also be present

Bipolar Disorder can occur even when a person's mood swings are low. For example, hypomania, which is not severe, is experienced by some individuals with Bipolar Disorder. The individual may feel good during a hypomanic episode and is even highly productive. However, though they are functioning well, their friends and family note the significant difference in mood. The mood change is so remarkable that family and friends may wonder if symptoms of Bipolar Disorder are present. Hypomania may easily become full mania or symptoms of Bipolar Disorder may occur if a person does not get proper treatment.

As previously mentioned, Bipolar Disorder can be present in a mixed state. This is when a person experiences both depression and mania simultaneously. In a mixed state, one may feel very disturbed, experience sleep disruption, lose their appetite, and may even think of committing suicide. Individuals in this state may have a feeling of being hopeless or sad while still feeling extremely energized.

When experiencing a severe episode of depression or mania, an individual can experience psychotic symptoms such as delusions or hallucinations, as well. The psychotic signs tend to show and strengthen the extreme mood of an individual. For instance, if a person has psychotic signs in a manic episode, he may believe that he is the president of a country, has vast wealth, or has some kind of special power. Psychotic signs in a depressive episode might include believing that she is homeless, ruined, penniless, or a criminal on the run. Unfortunately, sometimes individuals with this condition are misdiagnosed with schizophrenia or another reality testing disorder because of their mood-induced hallucinations.

Individuals with Bipolar Disorder also often have the co-occurring disorder of polysubstance abuse or dependence. Anxiety disorders, such as Post-Traumatic Stress Disorder (PTSD) and phobias, also co-occur quite often. Bipolar Disorder also sometimes co-occurs with Attention Deficit Hyperactivity Disorder (ADHD). People with Bipolar Disorder also have a higher likelihood of diabetes, headaches, thyroid disease, heart disease, migraine obesity, and other physical sicknesses.

Bipolar Disorder usually begins to develop in the late teenage years or during early adulthood. However, some people have their first symptoms during childhood, while others may develop symptoms later on in life. At least half of all cases start before the age of 25.

Types of Bipolar Disorder are as follows:

- Bipolar I Disorder
- Bipolar II Disorder
- Bipolar Disorder Not Otherwise Specified (BP-NOS)
- Cyclothymic Disorder or Cyclothymia

If not diagnosed and treated, the bipolar condition can become worse. It becomes severe as episodes become frequent. This delay can result in the person demonstrating behavior that significantly impacts relationships, personal goals, finances, housing, work, school, and many other areas. DBT has been known to help individuals with this condition lead healthier and more productive lives. Many times, DBT has helped individuals decrease the episodes' severity and frequency.

Post-Traumatic Stress Disorder (PTSD)

The body has a built-in and naturally occurring mechanism that makes individuals seek to escape danger. This mechanism is known as the fight-or-flight response. When your brain receives the signal that there is imminent danger, your body goes into an automatic response mode. You naturally begin to feel afraid and your body gears up to either flee the situation to get to safety or to fight to ensure your self-preservation and survival. Your fear of dangerous situations triggers many split-second and unconscious changes in the body that prepares you to either flee or fight in a particular situation. This is a natural process that is biologically incorporated to help people protect themselves from harm. However, in certain individuals, repeated exposure to trauma, or exposure to one extremely high-level traumatic experience causes this normal "fight-or-flight" response to go haywire. When this process is damaged, and individuals become stressed or frightened even when they are no longer in danger, this is called Post-Traumatic Stress Disorder (PTSD).

PTSD generally occurs after someone experiences a terrifying and/or life-threatening ordeal. The ordeal usually involves some type of actual physical harm or threat of physical harm. The harm or threat to harm may have involved the person themselves, a loved one, or the person may have witnessed a harmful event that happened to someone else or a group of other people. Some examples of situations that can cause PTSD are:

- War
- Rape or sexual abuse
- Terrorism
- Robbery
- Train wrecks
- Car accidents
- Plane crashes
- Natural disasters such as floods, earthquakes, and tornadoes
- Childhood physical abuse
- Domestic violence
- Hostage situations
- Torture
- Bombings
- Any other very traumatic event

PTSD is caused by a combination of genetic and environmental features. The way that a specific individual is biologically wired to deal with fear sensations and memories has a lot to do with the development of PTSD. People who are more emotionally vulnerable to fear due to their brain chemistry are more likely to develop PTSD.

Environmental factors also play a significant role in the emergence of PTSD. Environmental factors such as trauma that occurred in childhood, head injuries, or a personal history of mental illness may also increase a person's risk of developing the disorder. Also, personality and cognitive factors such as thinking errors, ability to tolerate distress, pessimism, and other cognitive-related factors increase risk. Similarly, social factors such as the availability of a support system help people adjust to trauma and may help them avoid the experience of PTSD.

PTSD Symptoms

PTSD symptoms are categorized into three groups:

1. *Re-experiencing symptoms*
- Flashbacks.
- Nightmares about the event.
- Frightening thoughts that are intrusive and persistent. They pop up out of seemingly nowhere, and they are hard to get rid of.

Obviously, re-experiencing symptoms can be very disruptive to day to day functioning. They may cause problems in a person's everyday routine and interpersonal relationships.

2. *Avoidance symptoms*
- These symptoms are demonstrated when a person avoids anything that reminds them of the traumatic incident. They stay away because going near them triggers an out of control emotional response.

- Feeling emotionally numb is also an avoidant type of symptom. Rather than risk feeling an intense negative emotion, they feel emotionally numb. They avoid any emotional experience at all in an attempt to avoid negative feelings.

- Victims feeling strong worry, depression, or guilt without really knowing why is another example of an avoidant symptom. Rather than deal with the response to the incident directly, people with PTSD may have more generalized negative feelings.

- Victims may experience a loss of interest in activities they previously loved. Avoidance of all pleasurable activity is characteristic of PTSD.

- Difficulties in remembering the dangerous incident are also common. Rather than deal with what happened, sometimes it's easier to just stuff the whole experience into the subconscious. This is an example of avoidance.

- Change in routine is also avoidant in nature. Sometimes, people with PTSD will purposefully change their routines so they don't have to worry about dealing with a trigger. An example of this would be if a person avoids driving a car after a life-threatening car accident. This was very common after 9-11 when many people refused to get on airplanes after the terrorist attack.

3. *Hyperarousal symptoms*

- People recovering from PTSD are often easily startled, and they may feel tense more frequently than before the traumatic event.

- Their automatic nervous system is more active, so they experience troubles in sleeping and managing their anger. Angry outbursts may occur frequently.

- It should be noted that hyperarousal symptoms are usually constant and are present even without a specific trigger.

- It's completely natural for someone to experience one or even several of these symptoms after being involved in an event that is traumatic.

Keep in mind that children and teenagers may present differently when they are experiencing PTSD. In young kids, you may see:

- Reverting back to bedwetting after they have been potty trained
- Not talking after reaching a verbal developmental stage
- Reenactment of the traumatizing event when playing

In older children or adolescents, you may see symptoms that are more consistent with adult symptoms. However, you may also see an increase in disrespectful and explosive behavior. They can also become preoccupied with getting revenge or feel guilty for not doing more to prevent the event or the injuries that occurred in response to the event.

PTSD can happen at any age. Females have a higher risk of developing PTSD, and there seems to be a significant genetic link. Not all people who live through a risky event develop this condition.

There are several factors that determine if an individual will develop PTSD. Factors that increase the probability an individual getting PTSD are called risk factors. Factors that lower a person's chances of getting PTSD are called resilience factors. Some of these risk and resilience factors are present before the trauma, while others develop during or after a traumatic event.

Resilience factors for PTSD include:

- Access to an adequate support system following a trauma
- Having an effective coping strategy
- Feeling good about individual actions when there's trouble
- Therapy or counseling that addresses adjustment post-trauma

Risk factors for PTSD include:

- Experiencing a trauma
- Personal history of mental illness

- Physical injury

- Witnessing people getting killed or hurt

- Inadequate or lack of social support after an incident

- Loss of a home, job or a loved one

Obsessive Compulsive Disorder (OCD)

This is a psychological disorder that has the potential to be quite disabling if left untreated. It traps people into a relentless and never-ending series of behaviors and thoughts that are repetitive. They become overwhelmed with thoughts, fears, and images that they cannot control. So, they instead obsess about them continuously. These endless and negative thoughts produce anxiety that causes these individuals to feel an urgent and immediate need to engage in certain rituals, routines, or safety-seeking behavior. These compulsive behaviors are the person's way of trying to eliminate the anxiety that comes with obsessive and ruminating thoughts.

Although the ritualistic behavior generally does temporarily alleviate the anxiety, it becomes a chronic problem because the person must carry out the ritual again when the obsessive thoughts come back. This OCD cycle can really begin to impact the person's relationships and even personal health. It is not uncommon for a person with OCD to take up hours of their time that they would normally be using to engage in normal activities to complete the ritualistic tasks. People with OCD are often aware of their behavior, and they know that their rituals are unrealistic and problematic, but they cannot stop them.

Common obsessions include:

- Fear of dirt

- Fear of causing harm to others

- Fear of making a mistake

- Fear of being embarrassed

- Fear of behaving in a socially unacceptable manner

- Fear of thinking thoughts that are sinful or evil

- Excessive doubt and the need for constant reassurance

Common compulsions include:

- Repeating specific prayers, phrases, or words

- Washing hands, showering or bathing repeatedly

- Eating in a certain order

- Having to do errands a certain number of times

- Declining to touch doorknobs or shake hands

- Hoarding

While it is not entirely known what causes OCD, research has indicated that a mixture of environmental and biological factors is involved, consistent with most other mental and behavioral health disorders.

Biological Factors

It is thought by researchers that OCD comes from problems in the pathways that link the parts of the brain that deal with planning and judgment with the part responsible for filtering body movement messages. Moreover, some evidence shows that OCD is passed to children from their parents.

Environmental Factors

Environmental stressors can cause OCD in some individuals. Other factors may make the symptoms worse. Some of these are:

- Abuse
- Moving house
- Sickness
- Work changes
- Death of someone close
- School problems
- Relationship concerns

A recent statistic indicated that 1 million children and adolescents, and 3.3 million adults, are affected by OCD in the United States. This disorder responds well to therapies such as CBT and DBT.

Severe Major Depression

Almost everyone has experienced some level of sadness in their life. Sadness is a normal emotional response to bad situations. However, when sadness becomes so pronounced that it interferes with daily performance and activities, help may be needed.

Major depression or clinical depression is characterized by a depressed mood that is prevalent throughout the day and can be particularly prevalent in the morning. The disorder is characterized by a lack of interest in relationships and normal chores and symptoms are present every day for at least 2 weeks.

Here are the typical symptoms of major depression:

- Fatigue
- Indecisiveness
- Feeling guilty

- Reduced concentration
- Insomnia or hypersomnia
- Sluggishness or restlessness
- Recurring thoughts of death or suicide
- Weight gain or loss

Major depression affects almost 10% of the US population over the age of 18. Some statistics indicate that between 20% and 25% of all US adults suffer an episode of major depression at some point during their lifetime. Major depression also affects elderly adults, teenagers, and children, but unfortunately, the disorder often goes undiagnosed and untreated in these populations.

Almost twice as many women as men have been diagnosed with major or clinical depression, which means that more women than men will likely be in treatment. Hormonal changes, pregnancy, miscarriage, and menopause may also increase the risk. Other factors that boost the risk of clinical depression in women who are biologically vulnerable include environmental stressors such as increased stress at home or work, balancing family life with career, and caring for an aging parent. Being a single parent has also been shown to increase the risk of depression.

It is believed that one of the reasons that women outnumber men diagnosed with major depression is because men are less likely to report symptoms. In fact, major depression in men is extremely underreported. Unfortunately, men who suffer from clinical depression are less likely to seek help or even talk about their experience.

Signs of depression in men may be a little different than in women. Here's what you can expect to see:

- Increased irritability and anger
- Substance abuse
- Violent behavior directed both inwardly and outwardly (due to repressed feelings)

- Reckless behavior

- Deterioration of health

- Increase risk of suicide and homicide

Here are triggers that are common:

- Grief from losing a loved one through separation, divorce, or death

- Major life changes such as moving, graduating, job change, promotion, retirement, and having children

- Being isolated socially

- Relationship conflict with a partner or supervisor

- Divorce

- Emotional, sexual, or physical abuse

Individuals who experience the various disorders described in this section experience extreme difficulty regulating their emotions. In addition, there is generally a social component that contributes to the manifestation of the disorder. DBT takes the psychosocial components that traditional CBT therapies take into consideration with the intention of helping individuals learn how to manage their out-of-control emotions and behaviors. As you will see in the following chapters, two of the models of DBT emphasize acceptance while two of them emphasize change so that the individual feels both validated and motivated to make the necessary behavioral changes.

CHAPTER 3

WHY MINDFULNESS IS A SUPERPOWER

Mindfulness is having a wise mind and being present in the moment. There are many facets to being mindful. It consists of observing, describing, and participating in the present moment. What does it mean to do these things? It means not to let your mind wander. Bring it back to the present moment.

Even if you don't have BPD, or any diagnosed mental illness, learning mindfulness and learning how to live in the present without worrying about the future or the past is a useful skill for anyone.

Mindfulness is a basic psychotherapy technique used to treat anxiety, anger, depression, and other psychological problems. While it has its roots in the mysticism of eastern cultures, western science has studied the subject a great deal. Psychotherapists even recommend mindfulness meditation for individuals who are suffering from certain mental health problems. Developing mindfulness is a crucial part of CBT, as well as DBT and ACT (Acceptance and Commitment Therapy). In fact, it is one of the four skills modules in DBT.

Basically, mindfulness is the state of mind that can be achieved by focusing our awareness on what is happening in the present. It also involves the calm acceptance of our feelings, sensations, and thoughts.

The challenge of focusing on the present may seem trivial for some, but this is actually easier said than done. Our mind may wander away, we lose touch with the present moment, and we may even be absorbed into obsessive thoughts about the things that have happened in the past or worry about the future. But regardless of how far our mind drifts from the present, we can use mindfulness to immediately get us back to what we are presently doing or feeling.

Even though it is natural for us to be mindful anytime we want, we can further cultivate mindfulness through effective ACT techniques that you will learn later on.

Mindfulness is usually linked with meditation. While meditation is an effective way to achieve mindfulness, there's more to it. Mindfulness is a form of being present which you can use any time. It is a form of consciousness that you can achieve if you intentionally focus on the present moment without any judgment.

Elements of mindfulness

Attention and attitude are the two primary elements of mindfulness.

Attention

Many of us suffer from what is known as "monkey mind," whereby the mind behaves like a monkey swinging from one branch to another. Our mind may swing away and back again, and we usually don't have any idea how we ended up thinking about something.

The monkey mind usually dwells in the past, ruminating on what has happened or what you think would have happened if you had acted differently. It also swings away to the future, being anxious about what could happen. Nourishing the monkey mind will steal away the experience of the present moment.

Remember, mindfulness is focusing your attention on what is happening now.

Attitude

Suspending judgment and kindness are the basic tenets of mindfulness. Hence, a genuinely mindful person knows how to accept reality and doesn't engage in arguing with it. This may seem an easy task, but once you begin practicing mindfulness, you will become aware of how frequently we judge ourselves and our thoughts.

Here are some examples of sentences used in the judgment of ourselves and others:

- I'm not good at this task.

- My shirt looks lame.

- I don't like my home.

- I really don't like my neighbor.

- What a grumpy waitress.

Mindfulness is also the art of calming our inner judge. It allows us to erase our internal expectations and become more embracing of how things are in the present moment. But take note that this doesn't mean you don't need to make necessary changes.

Remember, you are only suspending your judgment so you can have more time to think about the situation and do something about it. The main difference is that you can make changes from an ideal state of mind for change and not during times that you are influenced by tension or stress.

Moreover, mindfulness will allow you to be more compassionate with yourself, more embracing of your experience, and more caring of the people around you. It will also allow you to be more patient and non-judgmental if you have some lapses. As you practice mindfulness, you can reshape your brain to become kinder and more compassionate.

How Mindfulness Can Reshape Your Brain

In the past, people believed that the human brain could only develop to a certain level, usually from early childhood to adolescence. But various studies have revealed that our brain has the capacity to reorganize itself through forming neural connections. This is known as neuroplasticity, and it has no virtually no limits.

Neuroscientists shattered the old belief that the human brain is an unchanging, static organ. They discovered that despite age, disease, or injury, the human brain can compensate for any damage by restructuring itself. To put it simply, our brain is capable of repairing itself.

Studies also support the idea that mindfulness can significantly help in the brain's development. It specifically helps in the process of neuroplasticity. It is really amazing to know that we can change our emotions, feelings, and thought processes through neuroplasticity and mindfulness.

There are three major studies that show how mindfulness can rewire the human brain through neuroplasticity.

Mindfulness Can Improve Memory, Learning, and Other Cognitive Functions

Even though mindfulness meditation is linked with a sense of physical relaxation and calmness, practitioners claim the practice can also help in learning and memory.

Sara Lazar, a professor at Harvard University Medical School, pioneered an 8-week meditation program that primarily uses mindfulness. With her team of researchers from Massachusetts General Hospital, she conducted the program to explore the connection between mindfulness and the improvement of cognitive functions.

The program was composed of weekly meditation sessions as well as audio recordings for the 16 volunteers who practiced meditation alone. On average, the participants practiced meditation for around 27 minutes. The underlying concept of mindfulness meditation for research was on achieving a state of mind in which the participants suspend their judgment and just focus on feeling sensations.

Later, the team used Magnetic Resonance Imaging (MRI) to capture images of the brain structure of the participants. A group of individuals who were not meditating (the control group) were also asked for an MRI scan.

The researchers were amazed by the result. Primarily, the study participants revealed that they experienced significant cognitive advantages that were proven in their responses in the mindfulness survey. On top of that, researchers also noted measurable physical differences in the density of the gray matter as supported by MRI scan.

- The gray-matter density in the amygdala, the area of the brain responsible for stress and anxiety, was decreased.

- There were significant changes in the brain areas responsible for self-awareness, introspection, and compassion.
- The gray-matter density in the hippocampus, the part of the brain responsible for memory and learning, was increased.

This Harvard study reveals that neuroplasticity, through practicing meditation, can play an active role in the development of our brain. It is exciting to know that we can do something every day to improve our quality of life and general well-being.

Mindfulness Can Help Combat Depression

Millions of people around the world suffer from depression. For example, in the US, there are about 19 million people who are seeking medication to combat depression. This is around 10% of the whole US population.

Dr. Zindel Segal, a Psychiatry Professor at the University of Toronto, used a research grant from the MacArthur Foundation to explore the advantages of mindfulness towards alleviating depression. The research, that was mainly focused on the administration of mindfulness-based stress reduction sessions, was considered a success, and he conducted follow-up research to study the effectiveness of mindfulness meditation in patients afflicted by depression. This has resulted in the establishment of Mindfulness-Based Cognitive Therapy or MBCT.

The study involved patients suffering from depression, with 8 out of 10 having experienced at least three episodes of depression. Following the stress reduction sessions, around 30% of participants who experienced at least three episodes of depression did not relapse for more than a year, in comparison to those who followed prescribed other therapies such as antidepressants.

Segal's study has become a precursor to studies sponsored by Oxford and Cambridge Universities in the United Kingdom, with both studies generating similar outcomes. The research has proved significantly valuable in using mindfulness meditation as an effective and healthier alternative to medication in the UK, and has convinced mental health practitioners to prescribe mindfulness meditation to their patients.

Mindfulness meditation and research studies on MBCT are gradually gaining a foothold within medical and scientific circles in the US and other parts of the globe.

Mindfulness Can Help in Stress Relief

A study conducted at Carnegie Mellon University has revealed that the practice of mindfulness, even for 25 minutes a day, can alleviate stress. The study, led by Prof. David Creswell, involved 66 participants aged between 18 and 30 years.

One group of study subjects was asked to undergo a short meditation session composed of 25 minutes of mindfulness for three days. This group was asked to do some exercises designed to get them to concentrate on their breathing while turning their focus to the present moment. The second group used the same time to assess poetry readings to improve their problem-solving skills.

During the evaluation phase, all the participants were asked to complete math and speech tasks in front of evaluators who were asked to look stern. All participants reported their stress levels increased and were asked for saliva samples to measure the levels of the stress hormone cortisol.

The group who was asked to practice mindfulness meditation for at least 25 minutes for three days reported less stress during the task, showing that practicing mindfulness even in the short term can increase the body's ability to handle stress.

It is interesting to note that the same group showed higher levels of the stress hormone, which was not expected by the researchers.

The research concluded that when participants learn mindfulness meditation, they have to actively work on the process – particularly in a stressful situation. The cognitive task may feel less stressful for the individual, despite an elevated cortisol level.

The team is now focusing on automating the mindfulness sessions to make it less stressful while reducing cortisol levels. But it is clear that even in the initial phases, short-term meditation can do a great deal in relieving stress.

Other Benefits of Mindfulness

Aside from the benefits described above, mindfulness meditation provides great benefits for our emotional, mental, and physical health.

Emotional Benefits

Mindfulness allows us to be more compassionate. Those who practice mindfulness meditation show changes in specific areas of the brain that are associated with empathy.

Mindfulness meditation decreases our reactivity to our emotions. A study conducted in the Massachusetts General Hospital revealed that mindfulness reduces the size of the amygdala, which is responsible for fear, anxiety, and aggression.

Mindfulness meditation can help us avoid negative thoughts, which our brain usually resorts to once left on its own.

In 2007, a study was conducted among students who were taught meditation strategies. It revealed that mindfulness helped the students increase their focus and decrease self-doubt, anxiety, and depression. There was also a notable decrease in suspensions and absenteeism in schools where mindfulness sessions were encouraged.

Mindfulness is also now used to ease symptoms of anxiety and depression. Many psychotherapists now prescribe mindfulness meditation for patients who are suffering from depressive episodes.

Mental Health Benefits

A study published in the *Journal of Psychological Science* revealed that students who practiced meditation before taking an exam got better results compared to students who did not. The study discovered a link between mindfulness and better cognitive function.

Mindfulness increases the activity in the anterior cingulate, which is the part of the brain responsible for memory, learning, and emotional regulation. It also increases activity in the prefrontal cortex that is responsible for judgment and planning.

Mindfulness is linked to improved concentration and longer attention span.

Mindfulness meditation also increases the brain's neural connections and has been proven to fortify myelin, which is the protective tissue that surrounds the neurons responsible for transmitting signals in the brain.

Physical Benefits

Deep breathing can deactivate our sympathetic nervous system, which is responsible for our fight or flight response. It also activates the parasympathetic nervous system that is responsible for our rest and digest mode.

Mindfulness decreases the level of cortisol in the body. This stress hormone increases levels of stress and encourages hypertension.

In one study, participants who practiced mindfulness meditation reduced their risk of heart attack by more than five years and also reduced their blood pressure.

Mindfulness allows our mind to become aware of what we eat and has been used for weight loss programs.

Mindfulness is also responsible for increasing telomerase, which is believed to help in the decrease of cell damage.

Mindfulness meditation has been shown to increase the production of antibodies that combat the flu virus. This shows that meditation can help boost our immune system.

What Mindfulness Truly Means

Mindfulness means being aware of the things happening right this very moment in both our immediate surroundings and in ourselves — our thoughts, our emotions, our physical sensations, and our behaviors. The purpose of this awareness is to prevent us from being controlled by these events. This awareness must be nonjudgmental and passing, that is, we focus only on the facts and accept them, avoiding our own evaluations or opinions, and then we let them go.

Suppose your boss has severely criticized you about the work you've done. You know that you do not deserve it – both the criticism and the way it was delivered, and so you become very angry.

However, instead of letting your emotions dictate your response, you take a step back and mindfully think about the situation. You say to yourself something like this, 'My boss is under a lot of pressure right now, cranky and easily angered. His criticism of me was unfair. I did not deserve it, and so I got furious.' And then you move on.

There are different psychotherapy skills associated with mindfulness, and the above example is only one application of them. Those who are learning these skills complete exercises, like meditation and mindful walking. But from this example alone, we can now easily understand and appreciate the benefits of mindfulness.

Three States of Mind

There is what is called the Wise Mind, which is one of the three states of our mind. This is the balance between our Reasonable Mind (when we act and behave based solely on facts and reason) and our Emotion Mind (when our thoughts and actions are dictated by our feelings). When we are using our Wise Mind — the wisdom in each one of us — we recognize and acknowledge our feelings, but we respond to them rationally.

The Wise Mind, or the practice of using our wisdom, is actually the first of the mindfulness skills. As illustrated in the example above, mindfulness helps us manage and control ourselves, especially in sudden and emotionally-intense situations, where we are more likely to react with our Emotion Mind. This benefit alone has many positive consequences in the long run — better relationships, more self-esteem and self-respect, better responses to unexpected crises, and lesser symptoms of anxiety and depression.

More importantly, when we are mindful, we also get to experience life more fully.

Mindfulness skills also train our minds, so we get the added benefits of improved memory, sharper focus, and faster mental processing. Our anxiety is also reduced, and we gain more control over our thoughts.

The Core Mindfulness Skills

And so, what exactly are these mindfulness skills? They are divided into three groups: Wise Mind, the "what" skills, and the "how" skills.

Wise Mind

As explained above, this is the middle state between our Reasonable Mind and Emotion Mind, where we recognize both our reason and emotions, and act accordingly.

The "What" Skills

These skills are in answer to the question, "What are the things you must do to practice mindfulness?" The answers are (1) observe, (2) describe, and (3) participate.

Observe

To observe is nothing more than to experience and be aware of our surroundings, our thoughts, our feelings, and the sensations we're receiving. This is stepping back and looking at ourselves, especially for reorientation when we are too preoccupied with our problems.

Describe

To describe is to put words to our present experiences — acknowledging what we feel, think, or do — and using only the facts to do it, without our own opinions. For example, we say to ourselves, "My stomach feels hungry," or "I'm thinking about my mother." Doing this lessens distraction and helps our focus.

Participate

To participate is to give ourselves fully to what we are doing at the moment (eating, talking, or feeling satisfied). We forget ourselves in it, and we act spontaneously.

The "How" Skills

These skills, on the other hand, answer the question, "How are you going to practice mindfulness?" The answers are: (1) non-judgmentally, (2) one-mindfully, and (3) effectively.

Non-judgmentally. A non-judgmental stance sees only the facts without evaluating, and without personal opinion. We accept each moment as it is, including our circumstances and what we see in ourselves: our thoughts, our feelings, our values, etc.

One-mindfully. Practicing mindfulness one-mindfully is doing only one thing at a time, and giving it all of our attention — whether that be dancing, walking, sitting, talking, thinking. This is about maintaining our focus and increasing our concentration.

Effectively. Practicing mindfulness effectively is keeping our goals in mind, and doing what is needed to accomplish them. We do our best, and we do not let our emotions get in the way.

These core mindfulness skills are central to Dialectical Behavior Therapy, and they support all the other skills. They are called "core" mindfulness skills because there are a few other skills or perspectives on mindfulness that are less commonly practiced. We will not talk about them in detail, but among these other perspectives is one taken from a spiritual point of view, designed for those who need further help in mindfulness in light of their spirituality.

Mindfulness Exercises

Now that we know the skills, it is time to apply them to exercises so that we can see them in action. The following is a small sample from the wealth of mindfulness exercises that have already been developed for DBT.

Meditation

To observe the present moment — in a nonjudgmental way — is the purpose of meditation.

To practice meditation, find a quiet place where you won't be disturbed. The goal is daily meditation of at least 30 minutes. For beginners, 10 minutes is advised.

Sit on a chair or a cushion on the floor. Sit with your back comfortably straight, with your arms at your side, and your palms on top of your thighs.

Then bring your attention to your breathing — pay close attention to your inhalation, exhalation, and the sounds they make. Try to do this for the entire duration. Your breathing is what you are using to ground yourself in the present moment.

However, your mind will soon wander, and that is all right. Simply acknowledge your thoughts without judgment, and then return your attention to your breathing.

You may also experience some uneasy feelings while meditating, and that is all right too. Again, simply acknowledge your feelings without judgment, and then return your attention to your breathing.

Do this again and again, always returning to your breathing whenever you are distracted, until the time is up.

Mindful Walking

Mindful walking is simply practicing mindfulness while walking, to observe one's own physical body and surroundings.

First, take note of how your body moves and how it feels as you take your steps. Notice the pressure on your feet, and the aches in your joints if there are any. Notice the increased rate of your heartbeat.

Then, expand your awareness to what is around you. What do you see? What do you hear? What do you smell? Do you feel the wind or the heat of the sun on your skin?

Five Senses

This is about using your five senses to observe your present moment. Notice at least one thing that you see, feel, hear, smell, or taste.

Mindful Breathing

You can do this mindfulness exercise sitting down or standing. If the time and place allow you to sit in a lotus position, do it, if not, no problem. You just need to ensure that you are focused on your breathing for at least 60 seconds.

Begin by slowly breathing in and breathing out. One cycle of breathing must last for about six seconds.

Remember to inhale through your nose and exhale through your mouth. Allow your breathing to flow without any struggle.

While doing this exercise, make sure that you can let go of your thoughts. Also, learn to let go of the things that you have to complete today or pending projects that require your attention. Let your thoughts flow their own way and focus on your breathing.

Be aware of your breathing, concentrating on your consciousness as air enters your body and gives you life.

Mindful Listening

This mindfulness exercise is intended to develop our hearing in a non-judgmental manner. This is also effective in training our brain to be less distracted by preconceptions and previous experiences.

The majority of what we feel is affected by our previous experiences. For instance, we may hate a specific song because it triggers bad memories of a moment in your life when you felt really bad.

Mindful listening is designed to allow you to listen to neutral sounds and music, with a present consciousness that is not blocked by any preconceptions.

Choose music or a soundtrack that you are not really familiar with. Perhaps you have something in your playlist that you have never listened to, or you may choose to turn on the radio to find music that you can listen to.

Close your eyes and plug in your earphones.

The objective is to suspend your judgment of any music you hear – its genre, artist, and title. Don't prejudge the label and try to go with the flow of the music.

Let yourself discover the music, despite the fact that you may not like it at first. Let go of your judgment and allow your consciousness to be with the sound.

Navigate the sound waves by discerning the vibe of every instrument used in the music. Try to separate every sound in your mind and assess each.

Also, be aware of the vocals – their tone and range. If the music has several voices, try to separate them as you did with the musical instruments.

The goal here is to listen mindfully, to become completely entwined with the music without any judgment or preconception of the music, genre, or artist. This exercise requires you to listen and not to think.

Mindful Observation

This mindfulness exercise is one of the easiest to do but is also among the most powerful because it allows you to appreciate the simpler aspects of your surroundings.

This exercise is intended to reconnect us with the beauty of our environment; something we often ignore when we are driving to work or even walking in the park.

- Select a natural object that you can easily focus on for a couple of minutes. This could be the moon, the clouds, an insect, or a tree.
- Try not to do anything except observe the thing you have chosen to focus on. Just relax and try to focus on the object as much as your mind allows.
- Look at the object and try to observe its visual aspects. Let your consciousness be consumed by the presence of the object.
- Let yourself be connected with the object's purpose and energy within the natural environment.

Mindful Awareness

This mindfulness exercise is intended to develop our elevated consciousness and appreciation of simple everyday tasks, as well as the outcomes they achieve. Consider something that you do every day that you usually take for granted, such as brushing your teeth.

When you grab your toothbrush, stop for a few moments and be mindful of your presence, your feelings in that moment, and what that action is doing for you.

Likewise, when you open the door before you go out and face the world, take a few moments to be still, and appreciate the design of your gateway to the rest of the world.

These things don't necessarily have to be physical. For instance, every time you feel sadness, you may opt to take a few moments to stop, identify the thought as harmful, accept the fact that human beings get sad, and then move forward, letting go of the negativity.

It can even be something very little, like every time you see a flower on your way to work, take a moment to stop and appreciate how fortunate you are to behold such a visual delight.

Select a touchpoint that really resonates with you today and rather than going through your everyday tasks like a robot, take a few moments to step back and develop purposeful consciousness of what you are currently doing, as well as the gifts these actions will generate in your life.

Mindful Appreciation

In this mindfulness exercise, you will be observing five things in your day that you often ignore. These things could be people, events, or objects. This is really your call. At the end of the day, write down a list of five things that you noticed throughout the day.

The goal of this exercise is to basically show your gratitude and appreciation of the things that may seem insignificant in life. That is, the things that also play their role in our human existence, but we often ignore because we focus way too much on the "bigger and more important" things in life.

There are so many of these little things that we barely notice. There's the clean water that nourishes your body, the cab driver who takes you to your workplace, your computer that allows you to be productive, your tongue that allows you to savor that delicious lunch you had.

However, have you ever taken just a few moments to pause and think about your connection to these things and how they play a role in your life?

- Have you ever stepped back and observed their more intricate, finer details?

- Have you ever wondered what your life would be like if these things were not present?

- Have you ever properly appreciated how these things give you advantages in your life and help the people you care about?

- Do you really know how these things really work or how they came into existence?

After identifying these five things, try to understand everything you can about their purpose and creation. That's how you can genuinely appreciate the way that they are supporting your life.

Mindful Immersion

Mindful immersion is an exercise that will help you develop satisfaction in the present moment and let go of persistent worry about what the future may bring.

Instead of anxiously wanting to complete our daily work so we can get on to the next item on the list, we can take the task and completely experience it. For instance, if you need to wash the dishes, focus on the specific details of the activity. Instead of treating this as a common household chore, you can choose to develop a completely new experience by taking a closer look at each aspect of your action.

Feel the rush of water when washing the plates. Is it cold water? Is it warm water? How does the running water feel on your hands as you do the dishes? Be aware of the movement you use in scrubbing off grease.

The concept is to be creative and find new experiences for a task that is quite monotonous and very common. Rather than struggling through and persistently thinking about completing the task, be conscious of each step, and completely immerse yourself in the process. Choose to take the task beyond a routine by aligning yourself with it mentally and physically – and even spiritually, if you're the spiritual kind.

Mindfulness Is for Anyone

You have now learned what mindfulness is, its benefits, the skills associated with it, and the exercises to boost yours. You will need it not just in CBT but also in DBT and ACT, as you'll see in the following chapters.

Without a doubt, becoming more mindful and learning these skills are very useful and rewarding. It is not just a treatment option for those who are afflicted with a mental disorder. Learning to act wisely, despite our irrational feelings, and being more observant of ourselves and the things around us, is sure to bring us more happiness and contentment. Nurturing our ability to be aware of every moment in our life is a beneficial practice that can help us better manage the negative feelings and thoughts that may cause us anxiety and stress.

Through regular practice of mindfulness exercises, you will be far less likely to succumb to bad habits and become influenced by fear of the future and the negative experiences of your past. You can finally develop your ability to set your mind in the present and manage the challenges of life in an assertive yet calm manner.

You can, in turn, reshape your brain to harness a completely conscious mindset that is free from the bondage of self-limiting thinking patterns. This will allow you to be totally present to focus on positive emotions that could enhance your compassion, and finally understand yourself and the people around you.

CHAPTER 4

FUNDAMENTAL DBT SKILLS

DBT Distress Tolerance Skills

The distress tolerance skills module of DBT acknowledges the higher tendencies in certain individuals to exhibit negative behaviors. It recognizes that, for such people, these behaviors may be overwhelming; therefore, they need to be addressed at once. It is common for such people to become overwhelmed even when the slightest amount of stress arises, and they often end up developing negative behaviors. To help these people, most conventional treatment approaches emphasize avoiding painful situations. However, in the distress intolerance module, the aim is to make the clients acknowledge that sometimes it is impossible to avoid pain, and the best way to tackle such situations is to accept the things as they are and practice tolerating the pain associated with them.

The concept of radical acceptance forms the foundation of the distress tolerance module. This means succumbing to the reality of a stressful moment and acknowledging that there is nothing you can do to change it. By practicing the concept of radical acceptance without fighting reality or being judgmental, patients become less vulnerable to developing prolonged and intense negative feelings.

The distress tolerance module in DBT comprises four different skills. These skills are meant to help individuals cope with difficult situations and experience distress without making it worse.

- Distracting
- Self-soothing
- Improving the moment

- Focusing on the pros and cons

Distracting

Distraction helps the patient shift their focus from upsetting emotions and thoughts to neutral or more enjoyable activities. It basically deals in anything to help distract you from the distress, for example, a hobby, a quick walk in the garden, helping others, or watching a movie. These activities help clients separate themselves from a distressing situation or a troubled state of mind.

The acronym "ACCEPTS" is used to help individuals practice the skill of distraction.

- Activities – Using positive activities to get over a distressing situation.
- Contribute – Helping out people around you or your community.
- Comparisons – Comparing yourself to people who have more difficult lives than you or to yourself at your worst.
- Emotions – Making yourself feel different by provoking a sense of happiness or humor with corresponding activities.
- Push away – Pushing your situation to the back of your mind for some time and replacing it with something less stressful on a temporary basis.
- Thoughts – Trying to forget what's distressing you and diverting your mind to think about other stuff.
- Sensations – Doing something intense to give yourself a feeling, which is different from the one that you are already going through, for example, eating a spicy meal or hopping into a cold bath.

Self-Soothing

The self-soothing module is all about teaching you to respect yourself and treat yourself kindly. It includes doing anything that helps you develop a positive image of yourself with the help of your 5 senses. For example, observing a beautiful view from the window (vision), enjoying the sounds of nature like birds chirping (hearing), lighting a scented candle (smell), enjoying a hearty meal (taste), and petting an animal (touch).

This skill entails using self-managed tools to calm clients when they are irritable and stressed. Learning to self-soothe is a significant milestone in the distress tolerance module of DBT. When you self-soothe, you treat yourself with care, kindness, and compassion. This helps you build resilience and makes it easier to bounce back from difficult situations.

Improving the Moment

In this skill, the basic aim is to utilize positive mental forces to improve your current image in your own eyes. This skill can be practiced by keeping in mind the acronym IMPROVE.

- Imagery – This includes visualizing anything that relaxes you in order to melt away the negative thoughts.

- Meaning – This includes deriving meaning or purpose from pain or a difficult situation. In simple words, it is all about finding a silver lining in everything you do. This helps the client find positivity in every situation and helps them learn something.

- Prayer – This includes praying to God to gain strength and confidence. Prayer tends to strengthen the spiritual side of many clients and helps them pacify themselves.

- Relaxation – This includes calming down your physical body and tensed muscles by doing relaxing activities such as listening to music, drinking warm milk, or getting a massage.

- One thing in the moment – This encourages the individual to be mindful and focus on a neutral activity going on in the present.

- Vacation – This includes encouraging clients to take a mental break from a difficult situation by imagining something pleasant or doing something that makes them happy. It can be anything, including taking a trip or simply ignoring all phone calls for some time.

- Encouragement – This involves making conversation with yourself in a supportive and positive manner to get through a tough moment.

The IMPROVE skill helps clients tolerate frustration or distress without making it worse, and in ideal conditions, aims to improve it. It is particularly for people who feel stuck in situations which are hopeless and out of their control. Such people are unable to do anything about these critical situations and hence, feel hopeless, hurt, and depressed. For many people, such a situation may feel like a constant crisis, so the use of the IMPROVE skill helps them get through this situation and regain confidence.

Focusing on Pros and Cons

With this particular skill, you are usually asked to make a list of all the pros of tolerating a stressful event and compare it with the cons not tolerating it (i.e. coping with it through self-destructive behaviors). The main idea of this is to help them remember how avoiding confrontation in a difficult situation in the past affected them in a negative way and to make them realize how it will feel to be able to tolerate the current stress without acquiring negative behaviors. This helps patients reduce impulsive reactions.

Summary

The distress tolerance skills taught as a part of DBT mainly focus on dealing with the suffering and pain that is inevitable to the human condition. The distress tolerance module provides the clients with beneficial tools to help them maintain their sense of balance in critical conditions. It teaches them to accept distress and manage it in healthier ways instead of acquiring negative behaviors. Following it supports the clients to learn how to authentically connect with other people, be open to your emotions, and respond flexibly to the ups and downs of life.

By practicing how to distract themselves, improve their current moments, self-soothe their mind and body, and balance the pros and cons of a particular situation, the clients are able to weather any distressing moment and reduce the destructive impulses and painful feelings. It will help them take a break and return to life in a calmer, rejuvenated, and more focused state, like a full gas tank which can now go on for miles.

DBT Interpersonal Effectiveness and Emotion Regulation Skills

We all go through millions of emotions on a daily basis. These emotions not only affect our own state of mind but also govern our interpersonal relationships which, in turn, define our personal and social lives. Dialectical Behavior Therapy acknowledges the importance of emotional regulation and interpersonal relationships and comprises two separate modules to address the problems related to these aspects.

DBT Emotion Regulation Skills

Emotion regulation forms an important module of Dialectical Behavior Therapy, with the purpose of teaching clients the necessary skills to get a hold of themselves in negative situations and focus on increasing positive experiences. Emotional regulation refers to a complex combination of ways through which a person can relate to and act on his/her emotional experiences. This generally includes understanding and accepting emotional experiences, the ability to rely on healthy strategies to manage uncomfortable emotions whenever necessary, and the skill of observing appropriate behaviors in a stressful state of mind.

"Control your emotions or be controlled by them."

It is common for clients with high emotional sensitivity to get stuck in a vicious cycle of negativity, often initiated by negative circumstances. These thoughts prompt an individual to respond by developing adverse or heightened emotions, eventually leading to harsh choices and self-destructive behaviors. More negative emotions, such as self-loathing or shame, may follow this detrimental behavior. For such clients, emotion regulation in DBT may be of significant help.

People who have good control of their emotion regulation are better able to control the urges to engage in impulsive behaviors like self-harm, physical aggression, or recklessness during times of emotional stress.

The DBT emotion regulation module comprises 3 goals:

1. To develop a better understanding of your emotions
2. To decrease emotional vulnerability
3. To reduce emotional suffering

A significant feature of DBT emotion regulation is making yourself understand that it is not bad to suffer from negative emotions. They are not something that you must struggle to avoid at all costs. You must make yourself realize that negative emotions are part of your normal life and will occur, no matter how hard you try to avoid them. At the same time, there are different ways of accepting these emotions and allowing yourself to better manage them so that you do not remain under their control.

1. Understanding Emotions and Naming Them

This skill involves recognizing emotions and labeling them. Clients are familiarized with the concept of descriptive labeling. They are then taught to use labels such as "anxious" or "frustrated" instead of general terms like "feeling bad." This is because vaguely defined emotions are much harder to manage. Another important aim of this skill is to teach the client the difference between primary and secondary emotions.

A primary emotion refers to your first response to any moment or triggers in the environment surrounding you. On the other hand, a secondary emotion refers to a response directed towards your own thoughts, for example, feeling sad about letting your anger out. These emotions are usually destructive and increase your likelihood of developing destructive behaviors. So, it is important to not only label your primary and secondary emotions but also to accept your primary emotion without judging yourself for having to deal with it in the first place.

In a normal DBT skill session, group leaders tend to discuss the myths relating to emotions that have plagued our society, for example, the common misinterpretation that there are certain "right" or "wrong" ways to feel in particular situations. An additional topic is to explain the primary purpose of emotions – which is to alert you that something around you is either problematic or beneficial. These emotional responses get stored in your memory and help you prepare yourself to encounter similar situations in the future. In addition to this, your emotions help communicate messages to others via words, body language, and facial expressions.

2. Decreasing Emotional Vulnerability

To practice this skill, a suitable acronym is PLEASE MASTER.

PL – indicates taking good care of your physical health and treating any illness or pain.

E – represents eating a nutritious and balanced diet and shunning foods with excessive caffeine, fat, and sugar.

A – indicates avoiding drugs and alcohol, which aggravate emotional instability and are not good for your mental health.

S – signifies getting adequate sleep on a daily basis.

E – involves exercising every single day.

MASTER – involves performing any task that builds competence and confidence every day.

This component of emotion regulation focuses on decreasing the emotional vulnerability by building positive experiences and balancing negative feelings. For this purpose, clients are asked to plan more experiences that bring them happiness and provide them with positivity. This may include participation in a sport or hobby, going out for coffee with a childhood friend, reading a good book, or doing any activity that provides them with individual contentment.

While doing these activities, clients are asked to remain mindful, focusing on what they are currently doing. If a client is finding it difficult to focus their attention on the current activity, they have a choice to try out another activity. Planning the future and establishing goals brings positive experiences for most clients. So, it is a part of this activity to plan ahead for the future, for example, choosing a different career or moving to a different city.

3. Reducing Emotional Suffering

Reduction of emotional suffering is the last part of DBT emotion regulation, which encompasses the following skills:

- Letting go
- Taking the opposite action

Letting go means using mindfulness to have complete awareness of your current emotional state. It further involves labeling this emotional state and allowing it intentionally instead of avoiding it, fighting it, or dwelling on it. This may require you to take a deep breath and imagine yourself floating away from the problem. Compare your emotion with a wave of water that keeps on coming and going.

Taking the opposite action includes engaging in certain behaviors that are opposite to whatever a person is feeling in the moment. For instance, if a person is sad, they may try to be active, stand straight, and speak confidently, as a person would if they were happy. When an individual experiences anger, they may behave as if they are calm by adopting a soft tone or doing something good for someone. This skill does not aim to deny the current emotion; the client must still name the emotion and be able to let it go. However, acting the opposite is likely to lessen the duration and intensity of the negative feelings.

DBT leaders try to make the clients learn these skills in group therapies. Sometimes, clients are asked to get involved in role plays to help them use these newly learned skills in their everyday lives. Ultimately, these skills help empower people to regulate their emotions instead of being regulated by them.

DBT Interpersonal Effectiveness Skills

Interpersonal effectiveness means the ability to interact with other people. It encompasses all the skills you use to:

- Attend to your relationships
- Maintain a balance between priorities and demands
- Balance out your "wants" and "shoulds"
- Develop a sense of self-respect and mastery

The Importance of Interpersonal Effectiveness Skills

DBT considers interpersonal skills as important parts of the treatment because they teach us methods of communicating with other people. The way we communicate with others determines the quality of our social life which has a major influence on our overall well-being, self-confidence, and self-esteem. For this reason, interpersonal effectiveness is the main focus of DBT. In fact, it is taught as the second core skill module in DBT sessions, with lots of resources and materials dedicated to improving the interpersonal skills of the clients.

To enable the clients to establish communication with others, they are taught certain skills that help them get involved in everyday chats more thoughtfully and in a deliberate manner instead of speaking impulsively due to sheer stress or a distressing emotion. While there are a lot of skills associated with communication and interactions, DBT focuses on two components:

1. The skill of asking for things that you need or want
2. The skill to deny requests when suitable

DBT founder, Dr. Marsha Linehan, has identified three different forms of effectiveness that need to be addressed in this module:

- Objective effectiveness
- Relationship effectiveness
- Self-respect effectiveness

Under any circumstances, all the above-mentioned types must be taken into account. It is also important to prioritize them according to need, as this satisfies a person with their interactions as well as the outcomes.

'Objective effectiveness' refers to the goal or main motive behind a certain interaction that is directly linked to a tangible result. A typical example is a woman who wishes her husband would call her to inform her whenever he is working late. 'Relationship effectiveness' indicates the ultimate goal of a conflict-free relationship. In the previous example, the wife may rank harmony and emotional closeness as her first and highest priority. 'Self-respect effectiveness' can also be considered a priority in the case of this woman, if she starts feeling that her husband is being disrespectful by not calling her according to her wishes.

Dialectical Behavior Therapy utilizes different acronyms to help clients learn the skills tied to each type of effectiveness. In the case of objective effectiveness, DEAR MAN is the acronym of choice.

Describe: Describing the situation in solid terms, while avoiding any judgment.

Express: Expressing feelings and communicating them to the other party to let them know how the situation is making you feel.

Assert: Asserting your wishes and clearly stating what you want or do not want.

Reinforce: Reinforcing why you desire a particular outcome and rewarding people who respond positively to your request.

Mindful: Being mindful and investing your attention in the current moment, focusing on the task at hand.

Appear: Appearing confident, acquiring a confident tone and posture, and maintaining eye contact during conversations.

Negotiate: Being ready to get into negotiations, believing in "give and get," and acknowledging that everyone involved in the negotiations possesses valid feelings and needs.

For relationship effectiveness, the acronym used in DBT is GIVE:

Gentle: Approaching the other person in a non-threatening and gentle manner, avoiding judgmental comments and attacks.

Interested: Acting interested by giving others a chance to speak and listening to them wholeheartedly, and avoiding interrupting them just to give your own opinions or judgments.

Validate: Validating and acknowledging the wishes, opinions, and feelings of other people.

Easy: Assuming an easy manner by adopting a light-hearted tone and always having a smile on your face.

Lastly, the acronym used for self-respect effectiveness in DBT interpersonal effectiveness module is FAST:

Fair: Being fair to yourself and others to avoid the development of resentful emotions on both sides.

Apologize: Apologizing less and taking responsibility only when it is appropriate.

Stick: Sticking to your core values and not compromising your veracity in order to achieve a certain outcome.

Truthful: Being truthful while avoiding exaggeration or the portrayal of helplessness to manipulate others.

CHAPTER 5

LEARN NOT TO BE OVERWHELMED
BY PAINFUL SITUATIONS

Managing Stress Using DBT

The Distress Tolerance Skills taught as part of DBT can enable you to survive stressful situations without harming yourself. They may not provide you with strategies to help you in the long run but can help you learn skills to manage yourself successfully when times get tough. Strategies you can apply to get through intense stress include:

Distraction

Stress can cause you to get stuck in rumination and worry. Indulging your mind and body in a task that diverts your attention and prevents you from thinking about whatever is stressing you, at least for some time, can provide you with enough time to think about the stressor and ponder over how to get through it. Call a friend, work out, read your favorite book, or watch a funny movie to distract your mind from the stress.

Self-Soothe

Remember to be gentle and kind to yourself. It is common to be hard on yourself, especially during times of stress. You judge your abilities and feel like you are unable to handle your problems. Incorporating soothing activities in your everyday life can help you handle times of stress and tension. Listen to soothing music, bake cookies, watch a beautiful sunset, or eat your favorite food to soothe your body.

Try Relaxing

Following the distress tolerance module requires you to practice relaxation, for both the mind and the body. Try all the activities that will calm you. Take part in relaxation exercises or have a hot shower. Avoid performing multiple tasks at the same time, and try focusing on the current activity only. Form a soothing image in your mind.

Ponder the Pros and Cons

Take a paper and pen and make two lists stating the advantages as well as the disadvantages of a stressful situation. Pen down how stress can damage you if you do not care about it. Think of all the ways in which stress will help you evolve and grow as a person. Once you are done, go through the lists once again to motivate yourself.

Breathe

Observe your breathing pattern a little more closely. Try deep breathing or count your breaths to increase the focus of your mind. This can help you calm down and be more attentive.

Summary

These days, it is quite easy to fall into a rabbit hole and lose sight of the most important things in your life, all thanks to consistent stress. Keep in mind that in any moment of distress, you have control, even if this means letting go of things over which you have no influence. It may not be possible for you to solve every single problem in your life, but with DBT distress tolerance skills, you can definitely manage your frustrations much more confidently.

Do not let stress get the best of you!

Managing Worry Using DBT

There is no overnight solution to managing worry, but there is one that actually works: DBT. The troubling thoughts might linger for a very long time, but you can easily develop a Teflon mind. It only requires a bit of effort.

Look for the Canaries in the Coal Mine

Recognize that the thoughts that are worrying you are nothing but thoughts. It may take time to develop this skill, but it is possible to adopt it relatively quickly. It is the negative emotions that are trickier to handle. These two may gang up on you; thoughts that are negative leading to emotions that are negative and vice versa; trapping you in an awful loop.

When you lose yourself in worrying thoughts, you have a tendency to forget your body. Try to recognize the physical sensations that follow your emotions such as sweating, shallow breaths and muscle tightening.

Get a paper and a pen and start making a list. Recall every little thought that crosses your mind when you are worried. Note down any physical manifestation that comes by during a stressful event. This is what you call finding the canaries in the coal mine. Notice what actions you take when you are worried (such as procrastination, drinking alcohol, etc.). Familiarize yourself with these actions, so that the next time worry strikes, you know what you are dealing with.

Avoid Avoiding

Why should you avoid avoiding? Because you should prove your worries wrong. If you keep avoiding triggers, it is just going to keep the anxieties alive in you. Worrying and then realizing that your concern was silly produces a phenomenon called "extinction," and the worry eventually stops.

On the other hand, persistently avoiding what you feel makes you believe these things are real and that fearing them is the right thing to do. This is what you call "reinforcement" and it only strengthens the worry.

Whenever your mind signals you to avoid a certain situation, recall that this is wrong. Allow yourself to appreciate the moment by considering it a chance to fight your fear and get away from your worries. Move your focus from the disturbing thoughts to the real world.

Now you know about the most important thing to avoid, let's move on to the one that you should be doing.

Identify

Do you at times look back at a moment of worry and think, "wow that really freaked me out?"

This is because you failed to realize this at the moment it occurred. Worries tend to sneak up on a person, and as you undergo cognitive fusion, the worries overtake you. This urges you to go and make bad decisions. The best way to bypass this problem and all the fuss it creates is by identifying the increasing anxiety before it is too late.

By now, you will have made your own canaries list. Great. Now what you should do is begin identifying these things as soon as they happen. The sooner you identify these thoughts, the action impulses, and the accompanying physical manifestations, the quicker you will be able to quell them.

It is easy to identify your problem once you understand what you are looking for. This enables you to control it or handle it, at least.

Engage

Have you ever found yourself swamped by troubling thoughts about a certain problem and a bigger trouble strikes you? This newly emerged problem forces you to forget about your past tensions and use whatever energy you have left in worrying about it. Notice how you are able to shift your attention. Doing it on purpose is, however, the tricky part.

The aim of this skill is to help you develop a connection with your feelings and experiences. It will help you learn how to remain in the current moment and establish a better connection with your life instead of wasting your energy on troubling thoughts. So, whenever you get stuck in a stressful or worrying situation, remember to focus only on the problem at hand while avoiding any worrying thoughts which may distract you.

Channel all your attention to living the current experience. If the worry is making you distracted, remember this point, and think only about the actual problem and make efforts to deal with it only.

Tend to Your Emotions

The first thing to do to tend to your emotions is to learn how to identify worry. Once you have recognized that you are stuck in troubling circumstances, observe your body closely. Look for any signs related to your heightened emotions. You may notice your heart pounding, your muscles tensing up, or your stomach sinking. Whatever you feel, pay close attention to it.

It is possible for your mind to divert its attention to any other topic. You may also feel like drowning in the pool of worries, which diverts your attention far from the actual problem. As soon as you find yourself in this situation, get yourself together. Try diverting all of your attention back to the body and focusing on the actual problem. Do not get involved in thoughts which are troublesome. You only need to notice them and keep returning your mind back to the body over and over again. Label your emotions, whether they are fear, anxiety, irritation, sadness, or shame. Remind yourself it is normal to feel how you are feeling right now, and your emotions are not going to kill you.

In short, examine, admit, and mark. The worrisome feelings will eventually dissipate. It is a skill, and it takes some time. But it definitely works. When you get good at it, it will be your superpower against worry.

Use Opposite Action

This may seem like advanced Kung Fu, so take it slow. In the end, this skill is what's going to take you from being a chronically worried individual to being a person who seldom worries. It is a mild form of "exposure therapy" and revolves around the concept of "facing your fears."

Opposite action helps your brain figure out which people and places are not dangerous, hence, do not need to be avoided. Once your brain is able to establish this connection, your fears start diminishing. You stop avoiding people or things and gain the freedom in life to do whatever you want and go wherever you like.

Take a moment to answer the following questions:

- Do you worry about things that do not pose a real or immediate threat?
- Do you worry so much that it becomes difficult to enjoy things?
- Are you more likely to be unhappy than happy?
- Are you unwilling to take reasonable risks?
- Does worry interfere with your day-to-day activities?

If you answer no to the questions above, you are likely a healthy person. So, keep doing whatever you are doing because you are only sensitive to real threats. You will take every reasonable step to live a happy life.

However, if the answer to most of the above questions is no, you are suffering from worry. It is necessary to take the steps mentioned above to take the unnecessary burden off your shoulders and start living.

Unfortunately, there is no magic pill that is going to relieve you or your worries overnight. Following DBT in a stepwise approach, as mentioned above can, however, significantly impact your life and make it easier for you.

Dealing with Post-Traumatic Stress Symptoms using DBT

DBT is a powerful method of thought control, which teaches you the necessary skills to deal with unpleasant thoughts and situations that lead to suffering. Through acceptance and change strategies, people suffering from PTSD can learn how to:

- Keep themselves aware of the triggers that cause negative reactivity

- Practice self-soothing activities to calm their body and soul

- Learn intolerance skills to deal with uncomforting feelings, situations, and thoughts

The DBT distress tolerance acronym ACCEPTS can help you manage PTSD. This skill stands for Activities, Contributing, Comparisons, Emotions, Push away, Thoughts, and Sensations. These techniques have been specially designed to manage your emotions and get over your past.

Activities

Engage in an activity. This can be any activity as long as it is healthy. Read a book, go for a walk, make some jam, or do the dishes. Anything that keeps you busy and your mind off the negative emotions associated with the past will help. When you are done, pick up a new activity. In this way, you can have a highly productive day without bringing back any haunting memories of the past.

Contributing

Do something kind for another person. Offering help can relieve you of your emotional stress in a lot of ways. An act of service is also a type of activity which will keep you distracted and take your mind off the problem. In addition to this, contributing will help you feel good about yourself. You are not always required to do something big. Help someone cook dinner, bake cookies for a relative, or offer to mow your neighbor's lawn. Each of these activities will keep you from remembering your misery.

Comparisons

It is time to put your life in perspective. Was there ever a time when you faced more difficult challenges than you are facing now? Maybe not. Maybe this is actually the most intense situation and emotion that you have ever experienced. In this case, compare yourself to another person. Has that person suffered more than you? Are you at home, comfortably lying in your bed after having a delicious dinner while in another part of the world someone is searching for leftover food in the trash and a place to sleep after suffering a natural disaster?

The purpose of this exercise is not to increase distress or the emotional pain of your current condition. Instead, use it to add a new perspective to what you are currently experiencing.

Emotions

You have the ability to invoke the opposite emotion of what you are feeling right now. Meditating for 15 minutes can help your anxiousness too. If a past trauma is making you depressed, watch a comedy movie. Adding a bit of the opposite emotion can help reduce the intensity of PTSD.

Push Away

If you feel like you are unable to deal with your past just yet, it is okay to push it away. Throw the problem out of your mind for a short duration. But how is this possible? By distracting yourself with other thoughts, activities, or mindfulness. You can set a time to come back and address your problems. Assure yourself that it will be addressed and stay calm in the interim.

Thoughts

Replace your anxious, negative thoughts with activities that occupy most of your mind, for example, reciting the alphabet backward or enjoying a Sudoku puzzle. These distractions will help prevent self-destructive behaviors and reliving the traumatic events until you achieve emotional stability.

Sensations

Make use of your five senses to soothe yourself during times of stress. A self-soothing activity can be anything such as taking a warm bath with relaxing music and a lavender bath bomb, eating your favorite food, or tuning in to a good TV show. Anything appealing to your senses can help you cope with PTSD for the time being.

These Dialectical Behavior Therapy skills can help you tolerate PTSD until you are able to resolve the problem once and for all. They can control the symptoms of PTSD and allow you to focus more on the present with no fragments of your traumatic past. While the AC-CEPTS skills will enable you to focus on your current life, other modules of DBT, such as group therapy and interpersonal effectiveness, will motivate you to enjoy life at a basic level.

CHAPTER 6

EMOTIONAL CONTROL

Using the mastery skills in this section will help you achieve Wise Mind. If you practice Wise Mind when the seas of life are calm, it will be easier to bring to mind those skills during times of turbulence.

Doing something that makes you feel a little better every day helps relieve stress and inspire confidence. Attaining confidence helps reduce stress in stressful situations as well as in everyday situations.

Taking care of yourself helps you stay grounded so that when difficulties arise, and they will, you can keep your cool and maintain a consistent level of emotions.

Build Positive Experiences

Building positive experiences is necessary for emotion regulation in that we need a well of positives to draw from when we're running on empty. Many experiences are wonderful at the time, and then we later may not be friends with the people we had the experience with. Do not let that mar the memory. Remember who they were when you had the experience together. There are two important categories in which to build positive experiences: the short term and the long term.

Short Term

Short-term memories include talking to a good friend, taking a walk, noticing a beautiful area, going to the dog park, reading a good book, watching a show or movie you love, dining out, having a picnic, and laughing on a break with a coworker. Most of us already do something to create short-term positive experiences daily without thinking about it.

This exercise asks you to create more short-term positive experiences and do it deliberately. Call up an old friend. Stay off social media after work for a few days. Make a concerted effort to tell ridiculous, silly stories with your kids. Send your nieces and nephews presents from the clearance aisle. Do something that will create positive experiences deliberately.

When you deliberately practice making and noticing positive experiences, you'll begin to make and notice more as part of your daily life. When positivity is a part of your daily life, you feel better emotionally and physically.

Do at least one of these things, or choose something else that makes you happy, every day for a week. Go out of your way to do it for a week. After that, try to make it IN your way. Do something you've never tried before. There are probably a few things you've never thought of trying:

- reading a good book
- writing a good story
- going out for drinks midweek
- going to a movie midweek
- sex
- eating a good meal
- going out just for dessert
- going to a poetry jam
- going to a karaoke bar
- joining pub trivia with friends
- learning to make sushi or another exotic dish
- trying a new exotic dish
- jogging
- kickboxing

- swimming
- watching a children's movie in the theater and focusing on the laughter
- stopping on the dog's walking route to smell the flowers
- doing something nice for a stranger
- doing something nice for a friend
- playing a carnival game
- getting the expensive, full inside and out car wash
- completing your to-do list
- writing a ridiculously easy to-do list so you can complete it
- taking pictures with a real camera
- going down a waterslide
- playing board games with friends
- playing interactive games, like "How to Host a Murder"
- going to a movie or concert in the park
- going to a new hobby class like painting or writing or learning to skate
- organizing your bookshelf or closet
- buying a new article of clothing, jewelry or book for yourself
- visiting a nursing home to sing or play bingo with the residents
- letting your kids teach you how to play their favorite video game
- getting a massage
- going to the chiropractor
- going to a play or the opera
- going to a high school play
- going to a college football game

- driving to a different city for dinner with a friend
- going sightseeing
- joining Toastmasters
- volunteering at a homeless shelter during the months they really need it: January-October
- carrying "homeless packs" in your cars: gallon Ziploc bags with personal hygiene materials, feminine hygiene products, smokes, granola bars, bottles of water, socks, candy bars, stuffed animals, cash, gift cards to McDonald's, etc. Put them with blankets, coats, and clothes you would've given away. Drive around the areas where there are homeless people and give these out.
- gardening
- planning a party
- getting your hair done
- talking in a different accent for an evening
- dedicating a song on the radio to someone
- writing in your journal
- spending some time alone without the television, radio, or internet; just you and a cup of the beverage of your choice
- going out to lunch with a friend
- playing volleyball
- playing hide and seek with your coworkers (and trying not to go home when their eyes are closed)
- singing in the car
- driving to the mountains

- roasting marshmallows
- going to the sauna
- sitting in a hot tub
- sitting in a cold tub
- making a fort in the elevator at work with a sign that says, 'No bosses allowed!'
- silently challenging the driver in the car next to you at a stoplight to a dance-off in your cars
- keeping a box of fruit snacks in your desk for anyone having a bad day
- having a song fight with your spouse
- convincing a stranger you think you're a vampire
- calling a radio station and telling them a funny story
- doing a jigsaw puzzle
- riding a unicycle
- going to a museum or aquarium
- going to a psychic, just for giggles
- getting a Reiki session done
- taking a stuffed animal for a walk, pretending to cry when anyone points out it's not real
- calling a radio station and pretending to be psychic. Google the DJ while you're talking and tell them all about themselves so they'll believe you.
- going to a belly dancing class

Long Term

Long-term positive experiences are more goal-oriented, creating a life worth living. What are some goals that you would like to achieve? Write down a few specific goals. Break them down into subcategories.

Money

- Many people have goals that are money-oriented. Write down how much you'd like to save each month or put towards your debt. If you put it in a place you'll forget or an IRA (Individual Retirement Account) you can't touch, you're less likely to spend it.

- Learn how to budget. Keep track of how much you spend versus how much you make. Keep track of all your expenses. See where you can cut back. Itemize your spending as you go – keep it on your phone until you put it into a spreadsheet. When tax time comes, you will already know how much you have spent on medical supplies or work-related expenses. Use your debit card instead of your credit card. Then you're only spending what you have, and if you don't keep your receipts, everything is on your bank statement anyway.

- Get out of debt as much as possible. You may always have debt for education, health, and home, but you can pay off your credit cards and chip away at the others.

- Save as much as possible. Save by packing your own lunch instead of eating out. Put that in a jar. Use those coins when your kid needs shoelaces or something. After a while of paying with change, you forget you ever had any dignity; it's cool.

- If your job offers a 401(k), take it. Immediately. The 401(k) follows the person, not the job. If your job offers overtime, do it. Pick up shifts. Show up in your uniform and ask who wants to go home. When a couple complains that they don't know where their waitress is, promise to take care of them yourself because she clearly doesn't value her customers. Then pocket that $20 tip. Find little tricks to make your job, and your screw-ups work FOR you.

Relationships

1. Repair a relationship.

   If you have a relationship in your life that you feel must be repaired in order for you to move on with your life, you may have to take the initiative. You may have to make the first move, offer the first apology. Not a fake "I'm sorry you feel that way" apology, but a sincere "I'm sorry I treated you that way" apology. Not even a half-sincere apology – "I'm sorry I treated you that way, but you deserved it and here's why…" Let that second half come about if they accept your apology and you can open a discussion.

2. End a relationship.

   Not all relationships can be saved, and not all should be. If you have offered a sincere apology and have been rebuffed, it may be time to cut your losses and move on. It may be sad for both of you, but some relationships over time become toxic for one or both parties. If this is the case, you might try one last-ditch effort, and then you should actually ditch it. If they come back, you can see how you feel at that time, and whether it's something you want to renew. Some relationships are better off dead. Reviving those is the true zombie apocalypse.

3. Create new relationships.

   The older we get, the harder it is to create new relationships. We have to actually go out of our comfort zone to meet new people. Talk to people at your bowling league. Start a bowling league. Talk to new people at functions you attend regularly, like church or kayaking or suing people. Or even family reunions.

Go to weekly things. Join Toastmasters. You'll migrate towards the same people each week, but how much do you really talk to them? Get to know someone, more than at just surface level. Ask probing questions like, "If you invented a superpower, what would it be?" None of this already-invented superpower business. That's boring. "You can travel to the past, before a huge disaster, with the ability to warn people, but you might get stoned or burned as a witch, or you can travel twenty seconds into the future every day. Which do you choose?"

4. Work on current relationships.

Work on maintaining the relationships you have. Develop deeper bonds with people. Do you really know their hopes and fears, wishes, and dreams?
Go out of your way to stay in touch. Most friendships are built on convenience – when it's convenient for both or all parties to talk or hang out. Texting is a great way to let them know you're thinking about them, and they'll respond when they can. It's also a great way to miscommunicate, but that can be done in any medium.

Positive Mindfulness

1. Be mindful of positive experiences.

Practicing mindfulness while you're doing something you enjoy helps to savor the moment. Stay focused on the positive experience and refocus your mind as often as necessary. This will get you in the habit of mindfulness and focusing on the positive aspects of the day or the moment. The more we focus on something, the more we notice it. That's just how our brains work. That's not to say it is actually more prevalent, but it is certainly more prevalent in our minds, which is where we have to live, so we may as well learn to enjoy the company.

2. Be unmindful of worries.

Distract yourself from thinking you don't deserve this happiness, or wondering when the positive experience will end or thinking about what chores need to be done elsewhere. Distract yourself from thinking about what awaits you at the end of the positive experience, or worrying about how much money you're spending on it. If you're at the circus, for example, instead of thinking, 'I don't deserve to be enjoying this,' focus on your surroundings – children laughing, cotton candy, the rides, the clowns, unless you have a deep fear of clowns. You might not want to focus on them then. Damn you, Stephen King!

3. Practice.

There is a lot of material in this section, and no one expects you to conquer it overnight. You shouldn't either. Like any habit, it needs to be practiced before it becomes an actual habit. And then it still needs to be practiced.

Be Mindful of Positive Emotions

Get in the habit of noticing your emotions and recognizing whether they're negative or positive. When they're negative, get in the habit of not dwelling on them. When they're positive, get in the habit of being mindful of the actual emotion. "I'm happy right now. It feels warm. It feels calm." Describe how the emotion feels, instead of getting caught up in why you're happy or peaceful, or what have you.

Using the Opposite to Emotion Action

What actions do you do with negative emotions? They're probably the go-to actions, preprogrammed by your psyche. It takes time, but you can reprogram your psyche by using the opposite actions you normally use. When you're afraid, your brain kicks in to fight, flight, or freeze mode. In some instances, this is still a vital response mechanism developed for our own safety. In other instances, the response mode has been passed down from our hunter/gatherer ancestors and serves no real purpose today. For example, test anxiety. It's real.

A test doesn't present the need for a fight/flight/freeze response that imminent death, beating, rape, a car accident, or a full-grown saber-toothed tiger would pose. However, the reaction is still the same, and we don't get to choose our subconscious reactions. But we do choose our conscious actions. In the test anxiety example, try giving yourself many practice tests to lose your anxiety.

Perhaps your fear is roller coasters. Go more often, with someone you feel safe with to desensitize you. Try to desensitize yourself to the fear. If your fear is clowns, go to McDonald's more. No need to hang around real clowns. Those freaks will eat you in your sleep.

If your reaction to anger is to yell and throw things, step away from the situation that makes you angry and work on breathing exercises. Unless you're driving. Then just work on breathing exercises.

If a particular person or politician makes you angry, try to find the small amount of truth they may have said to gain sympathy or empathy, or at the very least, not hatred. Scratch that. Turn off the television. Work on that with a real person in your life rather than a politician.

If your go-to reaction to sadness is self-isolation, take the opposite approach. Get out in the community and volunteer. Go out with your friends. Go to an ice cream store by yourself, just to get out of the house. And have some ice cream.

If you're feeling shameful, the first question to ask yourself is, "Why am I feeling like this?" Is it because you did something you're ashamed of? Admit it to yourself and your haters, then move on. The longer you deny it, the longer it draws out the feeling and adds further negative emotions to it, like anger. If you've done nothing wrong, but are being dragged through the mud for pointing out something someone else did, welcome to the patriarchy. Even males can be oppressed by it. Just hold your head high and live your life. People will soon see who you really are. And those who don't see it often filter out. Let them.

Guilt works in many ways, as does shame. If you need to offer a sincere apology, do so. Your refusal to do so, whether it's accepted or not, whether they've offered one or not, whether they actually deserved whatever action you need to apologize for or not – that's all irrelevant. Your refusal to do so only drives the wedge in further.

The opposite reaction works best when the emotion does not fit the scenario. If you should be angry at something, it's still best to breathe deeply and assess the situation calmly. However, the other person is allowed to know you're angry. If your anger motivates you toward positive change, so much the better.

CHAPTER 7

INTERPERSONAL EFFECTIVENESS

Using Objectiveness Effectiveness (D.E.A.R. M.A.N.)

D – Describe

Describe the event using facts only. Do not use emotions. Let it speak like a police report if you do use emotions. "Patient seemed upset." It works better to sound like a police report if you talk in third person. However, don't take this habit into the real world. That's just confusing. Don't make a request or "dry beg." Dry begging is saying obnoxiously passive-aggressive things like, "I really need thirty bucks," or, "Wow, that cake looks good. I wish I had some." The best response to dry beggars is: "Yep. You do." Or it could be, "Yep. It is." If they really want it, they'll get around to asking like an adult. It might go like this – say you're from a religious family, and your teenager decides not to go to church. You might reply, "I've noticed you don't like church. Let's discuss the options of staying home."

This is important so that the other party understands clearly what the situation is before you ask anything, entreat, or make an executive decision.

E – Express

Express yourself with "I feel" or other "I" statements. These types of statements help the speaker take accountability and prevent the listener from immediately going into defense mode. Let's go back to the teenager staying home from church example. Now, you might say something like, "I feel like you should believe what I believe, but I know that you're your own person, separate from me, and I can't force my beliefs on you. I would like you to come to church with us because my worry is you won't be productive at home."

This is important so that the other party understands where you're coming from when you express how you feel about the situation you've just described.

A – Assert

Assert your position by either directly asking for what you need or stating your position clearly. Don't beat around the bush, don't use euphemisms, and don't hesitate to the point of losing the other party's interest. To continue with the example, let's assert our decision for our hypothetical teenager. "I understand that you don't want to come to church with us, and you are old enough to stay home alone. So, if you choose to stay home instead of attending church, you will prepare dinner and set the table and have everything prepared for us to be able to eat when we return, and you will make enough in case we invite people over unexpectedly. If you are unable to complete this chore, and thus, be productive for the whole family while we are at church, you will come back with us, even if you don't believe it."

This is important because ambiguity creates miscommunication in relationships, and that is the biggest source of contention. Be unambiguous. Set boundaries now. If you're making a request, it must also be unambiguous, maybe even a little lawyerly.

For example, you might say, "Can I please borrow your car from Sunday to Tuesday? I'll return it by 7:00 pm with a full tank of gas and a wash."

The other party might have other caveats. Such as, "Yeah, but it overheats, so don't go over 55 mph, or over 55 miles away. And my tags are expired, so avoid cops. Or renew it for me."

In which case, you might say, "You know what? I can take the bus. Thanks, though."

R – Reinforce

Make sure the other party knows why they should grant your request, or acquiesce to your conditions without a fight. "Because I said so" is not a valid reason. Most people reciprocate naturally.

You might say something like, "You get to stay home from church on the condition that you are productive at home. Since you don't like church and I don't like cooking after church, it's a win for both of us."

Or in the example with the car, it might sound like this, "I actually need to drive to a different city for a few days, but I can't rent a car because of (XYZ), so I'll get your car diagnosed for you, and if I can afford to fix the overheating problem, I will. If not, I'll see if anyone else can part with their car for a few days, or find another solution."

In both examples, the other party can clearly see that they have nothing to lose by accepting your request, and everything to gain.

This is important because relationships are built on reciprocity. When one party feels slighted occasionally, it's not a big deal. But if one party feels slighted more often than not, they will most likely end the relationship.

M – Mindful (stay)

Stay focused on the conversation. If you're answering a text, they have no reason to listen to you. If they're answering a text, that's out of your control, but you can keep your mind on the conversation instead of what they're doing. If they become defensive, notice what you may have said wrong, and apologize if necessary, even if it's just to get them back on track.

This is important because it's too easy to go off track and lose focus, especially in an uncomfortable situation, where the other party might be looking to pick a fight. If you go off on tangents, whether they be to sing and dance because someone said a song lyric, or to fight, or because one of you saw a squirrel, you have less of a chance of getting what you want. Especially if you're the one singing and dancing or chasing squirrels.

Your teen may interrupt you to tell you they've been cutting church every week with their friends from Sunday School anyway, so there's no point in going. You may have to repeat yourself a few times, especially if you're letting them stay home as long as they're productive, as they may not believe their ears.

Again, repeat yourself as often as necessary, and if you have a real kid, you've done that a few times already this morning. And bring the conversation back to the topic. Detour…focus. If we're using the example of asking an adult friend for something, you don't have the clout you do as a parent. You still may have to repeat yourself, but the interruptions might just be singing and dancing.

You might say something like, "I understand you don't like church, and you cut Sunday School anyway. But you will get something out of it every week if you continue going, and I would like that." Or, "If you're going to stay home, you'll need to cook for us, and I'll take the added precaution of changing the Wi-Fi password every Saturday to make sure you'll be productive. If you can prove that you are, that you don't have friends over, that you cook and clean as you go, I'll stop doing that."

A – Appear Confident

Appear confident no matter how you actually feel. If you have this look about you all the time, little old ladies will ask you for a napkin at a restaurant when you're on a date, and it might not even occur to you to tell them you don't work there, so you walk into the kitchen and get the napkins.

Your nonverbal cues indicate confidence more than your verbal cues. Sit with your back straight, and your head held high. Make eye contact. Orient your feet towards the other person. Where your feet are oriented is where your mind subconsciously goes. Appear confident and stand your ground.

This is important because confidence signifies that your request isn't too difficult to grant and that you're harder to turn down. There's no need to be overbearing. If they do refuse you, in an adult-to-adult conversation, you might just ask if they're sure, then thank them for their time and let it go.

If your teenager refuses you, this might be a good time to tell them what the other option is. "Okay, you don't have to learn to cook. And if you can read, you can cook, by the way. You can keep coming to church with us, and thank you for letting me know about cutting Sunday School. I'll be sure to tell your friends' parents you all do that because they'll want to know too. I'll let them know you told me. Thank you for caring about the salvation of your friends, who also should go back to church." This will most likely ensure you an excellent meal every Sunday.

N – Negotiate

Negotiate. Remember, "give to get," as selfish as that sounds. Everyone wonders, What's in it for me? You aren't demanding something. You're asking for something or setting down a rule. Even in setting down rules, you aren't demanding. If you think you can demand something of someone, even a child, expect defensiveness and confrontation. Give options.

You may need to alter your request to make it more pleasing. In the borrowing the car example, you offered to get the car diagnosed (AutoZone does it for free) and fix it if you could – and if you couldn't, you'd find another solution to your problem.

This is important because building relationships may or may not be the most important reason we spend a few decades on this planet, but it certainly takes up most of our time. Whether we spend that time in actual relationships with other human beings or wondering why we drive other human beings away, we spend an inordinate amount of time either with other people or thinking about them, whether we know them personally or not.

So, if we spend our energy browbeating others and expecting them to kowtow to us, that only works if you have money, and even then, not everyone likes you, even if you somehow win elections. Mere mortals, without insane amounts of money, can't behave like that. We have to negotiate and play nice.

Going back to the example of the teenager, this is pretty much already a negotiation. They still refuse to go to church or cook, and they tell you they don't care if you call their friends' parents. They really do. This is when you pull out your phone and look up the numbers of the kids' parents, who you probably know, at least by name already. Google White Pages are great. Some rules are not to be negotiated. If, however, you start the conversation with trying to force them to go to church, this idea is a perfect negotiation, and now it seems (to them) that you've given in some.

But for example's sake, you do try to negotiate. You might say, "Okay, if you don't come to church with us on Sunday, you still need to be productive at home. Would you rather have a list of chores to do? What is your suggestion for being productive, other than homework, because I don't want you deliberately putting it off until Sunday?"

This approach helps your child feel like they have a say – like their voice is heard and not invalidated. If you start off demanding they go, then negotiate to this, you can offer it as a suggestion, and ask which of your suggestions they like best.

You can both leave the conversation feeling like you've accomplished something, like you've got a win, like you're helping the other person out, with no ill will.

Interpersonal Effectiveness Exercises

Step 1 - Choose an area in your life that you want to work on.

This may include community, romance, education, career, personal growth, environment, family, parenting, health, finances, and many more.

Step 2 - Establish goals that are SMART - Specific, Meaningful, Adaptive, Realistic, and Time-Bound.

Specific - Try to be as specific as possible as to what actions you want to take. Be sure that you are aware of the involved steps in taking the necessary action. A specific goal is easier to achieve compared to a general goal. For example, just setting up the goal of spending more time with your child may not allow you to know if you have already achieved it. A more specific goal is to have at least a one-hour playtime every day. Being specific with your goal will allow you to assess whether you have already accomplished the goal or not and monitor your progress.

Meaningful - Assess if your goal is genuinely based on your values in comparison with a strict rule or a sense of what you must do. If you think that your goals don't have a deeper sense of purpose or meaning, try to assess if the goal is really influenced by the values you hold dear. Take note that your core values should be based on things that provide meaning to your life.

Adaptive - Make sure your goal will help you follow a direction that you think will greatly improve your life. Assess if your goal will move you closer or is steering you away from the real purpose of your life.

Realistic - There's a big chance that you will only feel disappointment, frustration, or failure if you set goals that are not really attainable. Try to find a balance between setting goals that are quite easy versus goals that are impossible to achieve. Be realistic and practical so you can really push yourself to achieve your goals.

Time-Bound - You can specify your goals even more by adding a time and date by which you want to accomplish them. If this is not possible, or not realistic, try setting up a time frame and doing everything you can to make certain that you work within this limit.

Step 3 - Define the Urgency of Your Goals

The last step is to define the urgency with which your goal should be accomplished. Your goals could be:

- Long-term - Create a plan of the necessary actions you need to take so you can be closer to your goals over the span of six months to one year.
- Medium-term - Think about the necessary actions you need to take so you can move towards your goals within two to three months.

- Short-term - Make a list of the things you need to do so you can achieve your goals within a month.

- Immediate - What are the goals that you need to achieve within a week or even within the day?

Starting to live in accordance with your personal core values will fan the flames of your committed action.

Our best plan and values will not be meaningful if they are not supported by action. Equipped with the knowledge of the core values you really want to pursue, you can start moving forward towards living a valuable life.

Tips for A Better Life

What to avoid when trying to improve your self-esteem:

Putting other people down. Sometimes, when a person doesn't feel so great about themselves, they may have to resist the urge to tear someone else down. A great way of being masterful at this is to avoid comparing yourself to others. When you feel a sense of inferiority, then you may try to pull others down so you feel better about yourself. However, if you are not in competition with others then it's less likely that you'll feel inferior to them. When you put other people down, the positive feeling only lasts temporarily, and you don't get a positive response from others; in fact, it often just makes things worse. Focus on your own uniqueness, and not comparing yourself with others.

Thinking you're better than others. You are not better than anyone else, and no one else is better than you. This is a universal truth that all should embrace. When you start to tell yourself that you're better than other people, then you're essentially trying to replace your feelings of unworthiness with the unhelpful belief that other people are not as good as you. This tendency will ultimately make your relationships worse. Again, you should focus on your inherent value and uniqueness instead of trying to make yourself believe that you are above other people. Truly masterful people are so convinced of their own self-worth that they actually want to encourage others to have a masterful life too.

People pleasing. Often, people who are chronic people-pleasers also have a chronic and deeply-felt dislike of themselves, to the point that they feel like they have to win the approval of others. Often this dislike is subconscious, so you may not be aware of it. However, you do not have to be desperate for others to like you and approve of you. Whether they do or not does not change your own inherent value and self-worth.

Refusing constructive criticism. Everyone, without exception, has some areas that could benefit from some improvements. This is part of what makes you human. The consistent development of a person is a part of their ultimate destiny. No one ever totally arrives at it, as self-actualization is in the process. When you refuse constructive criticism, it signals that you believe critique means that you're inadequate. Change your beliefs to include the more helpful alternate belief that everyone needs healthy constructive criticism to become unstuck and continue to evolve as a person. Don't be ashamed of your shortcomings or try to use perfectionism to cover up weaknesses. Instead try to recognize them, receive constructive criticism, and grow in the process.

Avoiding failure or rejection. If you're constantly living life in a manner that you think will help you avoid failure or rejection, then you will probably benefit from revising your thoughts and creating some healthier alternatives. Temporary failure is inevitable at times and rejection may rear its ugly head periodically. However, you must learn how to tolerate the distress and keep moving forward or else you'll end up being stagnant out of fear of failure and rejection.

Avoiding emotions. Trying to block emotions is not healthy, nor is it something that is sustainable long-term. Having a wide range of emotions is a part of the human experience, and being strong doesn't mean avoiding them. Allow yourself to fully experience negative emotions and then use strategies to change the situation or change your thoughts about the situation.

Trying to control others. That is not your job. You do not have to prove your significance by trying to make other people conform to what you want. Instead, focus on your own self-improvement.

Over-defending your self-worth. No one is saying you have to be a doormat for others to stomp all over, but if you find you are compelled to always defend yourself, then that's an indicator that you're struggling with self-confidence. If you are okay with your own inherent self-worth, you won't feel the need to constantly defend yourself. Don't allow yourself to become outraged every time a person says something about you that you don't like or offers an opinion that differs from your own. Instead agree to disagree, tolerate any negative emotion, change how you think about your own inherent self-worth and keep moving forward with your goals. Remember, you can show yourself respect even if other people don't respect you in the same way.

Blaming other people for your problems. Of course, you have had your share of difficulties. In fact, more than half the American population has had some traumatic experience, so you are in good company. What separates people who accomplish their goals from people who don't are their attitudes and behaviors. Do not blame nature or other people for your problems. Don't blame your past, genetics, hormones, or anything else for what you're currently experiencing. Focus on accomplishing your goals and don't get sidetracked by playing the blame game.

Don't take yourself or life so seriously

Understand that you will make mistakes. You are human, which means that without question, you will make mistakes at some point in your life. During some stages of your life, you will make more mistakes than others. The key is to course-correct by changing your thinking and behavioral patterns. Expect that sometimes you will make mistakes and that they are important, because the lessons you learn are key for your own personal development.

Try new things. Don't be so afraid to try something different. The more you try new things, the more things you'll find that you're good at. Also, you'll become more confident as you see that trying new things can actually turn into positive experiences. If you "fail," surely you will have learned something in the process.

Be silly on purpose. This is a great way to avoid being ashamed when you mess up. Purposely engage in a silly activity in public. For instance, wear a big crazy hat on the train or walk through the mall wearing a loud, colorful, mismatched outfit. Practice self-acceptance skills while you're doing these silly things and you'll discover that you're not as easily shamed anymore.

Laugh at yourself. It really is that simple. When you feel the urge to be overly critical, or you start to feel shame creep up, begin to laugh at yourself. Stop taking yourself so seriously. Things happen. Learn to laugh about it instead of ruminating about it.

When in social situations, focus on things other than your own performance. Take the focus off of yourself and move your attention to a more external focus. What are your friends doing and saying? What does the atmosphere look like? What are the smells you're experiencing? Try to identify them. Enjoy the flavors of any meal you're enjoying. Try to be mindful of your environment instead of focusing on internal thoughts and impulses. This is a great distraction technique. Be intentional about not having a requirement to feel absolutely safe in your environment and learn to enjoy yourself.

Creativity. Tap into your creative side. If you have natural creative talents, express them. Take some time to participate in activities that you truly enjoy. The more masterful you become with your creative endeavors, the better and more confident you will feel overall.

Be adventurous. Stop trying to avoid unpredictable outcomes. The chances of you being able to accurately predict the outcome of every situation are slim, and your tendency to be overly cautious only makes life more chaotic for you.

CHAPTER 8

FREQUENTLY ASKED QUESTIONS

How are CBT and DBT different?

DBT has its roots in CBT, but it uses a more dialectical approach than traditional CBT therapies. Although most people are able to get significant results from CBT, it was found that there was a specific group of patients who were not getting the results that the average person was receiving. Instead, this group got frustrated with the process and quickly dropped out because they did not feel validated. So, a revised CBT process that combines emotional validation with behavioral change was developed. This is known as DBT.

Are CBT and DBT more effective than other therapies?

These therapies have been scientifically proven to be very effective, and most clients make lasting changes quickly. All therapies have their positive points however, cognitive-based therapies are often favorites among clinicians because they are action-oriented, thus obtaining in quicker results. The results that most people get in a year of talk therapy can be easily obtained in 3-4 sessions of CBT or DBT.

How does the therapy work?

The amount of therapy you need varies based upon your own individual needs, however most people do well with one individual session per week. DBT also includes one additional skill-building group session per week. Your commitment to the therapy process really is the best determining factor as to how the therapy will work. Some people do more than one individual session per week, while others are comfortable with the one session. That is something that you should discuss with your therapist to determine a specific treatment regimen.

How long does it take to see progress?

Progress varies depending on the person, but most people start seeing results very early, typically within 3-4 sessions. Of course, this depends largely on how much effort you put into the program. Doing the homework consistently and attending the group skill-building sessions every week is critical to your success in DBT. This book provides many of the techniques that you will learn during treatment.

What if I'm skeptical?

Give it a try. You won't know whether it works or not until you try it. Just like almost anything else in life, you won't know how effective it really is until you try it. Commit to doing your first behavioral experiment and see how it goes. If it works, great, keep going. If it doesn't, you can always stop.

Can I discontinue medication?

Although both CBT and DBT have both been found to be quite effective treatment approaches, even without medication, the decision to discontinue your medication should be taken very seriously and supervised by a medical professional. You should discuss that decision with your psychiatrist or another physician.

How does DBT prioritize treatment goals?

- Target 1: Life-threatening behavior and behavior that interferes with treatment
- Target 2: Decrease emotional suffering
- Target 3: Daily living management
- Target 4: Sense of wholeness and connectedness

This is the priority of the goals for DBT treatment. Of course, life-threatening goals take priority and moving through suicidal ideation or self-harm behavior is addressed first. Also, behavior that interferes with treatment is high-priority as well because no progress can be made unless there is commitment to the therapy process. The ultimate goal is to get you to a place of complete wholeness. You are one out of a whole universe, and you are universally connected with every other person in the universe. Whatever your religious or spiritual beliefs are, the ultimate goal of DBT is to help you embrace yourself, your life, and other people so that you can fully experience and enjoy life.

Is Eastern philosophy an underpinning of DBT?

DBT's core mindfulness component emphasizes staying in the present, and it does have its foundation in Eastern traditions. The goal is to help you stay in the present with your thoughts and emotions because most disturbances result from things that have happened in the past or thoughts about the future. The tradition of concentrating on the here and now has been practiced in the Eastern world for centuries and the Western world has more recently adopted the mindfulness theory. It has been very helpful for people who truly want to get unstuck so that they are no longer overwhelmed by their emotions.

CONCLUSION

Dialectical Behavior Therapy has offered much in the realm of therapies. Dr. Linehan has saved thousands of lives with her innovative work. Borderline Personality Disorder is not being "crazy" or "unhinged." It's simply mental illness. It includes many other mental illnesses as facets of it. Because of that, it only makes sense that an effective therapy for this condition would include many types of therapy and self-reflection.

Mindfulness is probably the most important aspect of DBT because we have been trained not to be mindful. We're like ants, scurrying around – hurry, hurry, hurry, but going nowhere.

Mindfulness forces you to focus on the present. Ask yourself, "Am I treading water? Am I at the bottom of a ladder I want to be on or the middle of one I don't?" When you choose mindfulness, you look at your life for a moment.

Your questions aren't all going to be answered in one moment of mindfulness. It's something that must be practiced every day. DBT is an excellent medium for learning the skills of mindfulness and interpersonal relationships. When therapy is complete, you've acquired an outstanding toolkit of skills to reach for in any situation.

Our entire lives are our memories and our interpersonal relationships. Because DBT focuses on mindfulness and interpersonal relationships, it is one of the most effective types of therapies. When we're mindful, we're creating memories. We're technically creating memories when we're not mindful as well – but not memories of what's actually happening.

In summary, by practicing the skills of DBT, we create memories and interpersonal relationships. And having good memories and relationships is what makes life worth living.

Made in the USA
Monee, IL
27 July 2021